# Sport Skill Instruction for Coaches

D1332583

## Craig A. Wrisberg, PhD
University of Tennessee

Human Kinetics

**Library of Congress Cataloging-in-Publication Data**

Wrisberg, Craig A.
  Sport skill instruction for coaches / Craig A. Wrisberg.
    p. cm.
  Includes bibliographical references and index.
  ISBN-13: 978-0-7360-3987-1 (soft cover)
  ISBN-10: 0-7360-3987-2 (soft cover)
  1.  Coaching (Athletics)   2.  Physical fitness--Study and teaching.   I. Title.
  GV711.W75 2007
  796.077--dc22                                          2006027901

ISBN-10: 0-7360-3987-2
ISBN-13: 978-0-7360-3987-1

**Acquisitions Editor:** Amy Tocco; **Developmental Editor:** Christine M. Drews; **Assistant Editors:** Maureen Eckstein and Heather M. Tanner; **Copyeditor:** Patricia L. MacDonald; **Proofreader:** Joanna Hatzopoulos Portman; **Indexer:** Sharon Duffy; **Permission Manager:** Carly Breeding; **Graphic Designer:** Robert Reuther; **Graphic Artist:** Yvonne Griffith; **Photo Manager:** Laura Fitch; **Cover Designer:** Robert Reuther; **Photographer (cover):** Dan Wendt; **Photographer (interior):** © Human Kinetics unless otherwise noted; **Art Manager:** Kelly Hendren; **Illustrator:** Keri Evans; **Printer:** Total Printing Systems

Copies of this book are available at special discounts for bulk purchase for sales promotions, premiums, fund-raising, or educational use. Special editions or book excerpts can also be created to specifications. For details, contact the Special Sales Manager at Human Kinetics.

Printed in the United States of America.         10   9   8   7   6

The paper in this book is certified under a sustainable forestry program.

**Human Kinetics**
Web site: www.HumanKinetics.com

*United States:* Human Kinetics
P.O. Box 5076
Champaign, IL 61825-5076
800-747-4457
e-mail: humank@hkusa.com

*Canada:* Human Kinetics
475 Devonshire Road, Unit 100
Windsor, ON N8Y 2L5
800-465-7301 (in Canada only)
e-mail: info@hkcanada.com

*Europe:* Human Kinetics
107 Bradford Road
Stanningley
Leeds LS28 6AT, United Kingdom
+44 (0)113 255 5665
e-mail: hk@hkeurope.com

*Australia:* Human Kinetics
57A Price Avenue
Lower Mitcham, South Australia 5062
08 8372 0999
e-mail: info@hkaustralia.com

*New Zealand:* Human Kinetics
P.O. Box 80
Mitcham Shopping Centre, South Australia 5062
0800 222 062
e-mail: info@hknewzealand.com

E2528

In memory of my dad, Art Wrisberg,
who was the best role model a son could ever have.

# CONTENTS

**PART III     Designing Practice Sessions                              75**

# ASEP SILVER LEVEL SERIES PREFACE

The American Sport Education Program (ASEP) Silver Level curriculum is a series of practical texts that provide coaches and students with an applied approach to sport performance. The curriculum is designed for coaches and for college undergraduates pursuing professions as coaches, physical education teachers, and sport fitness practitioners.

For instructors of undergraduate courses, the ASEP Silver Level curriculum provides an excellent alternative to other formal texts. In most undergraduate programs today, students complete basic courses in exercise physiology, mechanics, motor learning, and sport psychology—courses that are focused on research and theory. Many undergraduate students are looking for ways to directly apply what they learn in the classroom to what they can teach or coach on the court or playing field. ASEP's Silver Level series addresses this need by making the fundamentals of sport science easy to understand and apply to enhance sport performance. The Silver Level series is specifically designed to introduce these sport science topics to students in an applied manner. Students will find the information and examples user friendly and easy to apply in the sport setting.

The ASEP Silver Level sport science curriculum includes the following:

*Sport Mechanics for Coaches*—an explanation of the mechanical concepts underlying performance techniques; designed to enable coaches and students to observe, analyze, develop, and correct the mechanics of sport technique for better athletic performance.

*Sport Physiology for Coaches*—an applied approach to exercise physiology; designed to enable coaches and students to assess, initiate, enhance, and refine human performance in sport participation and to improve sport performance.

*Sport Psychology for Coaches*—a practical discussion of motivation, communication, stress management, mental imagery, and other cutting-edge topics; this text is designed to enhance the coach–athlete relationship and to stimulate improved sport performance.

*Sport Skill Instruction for Coaches*—a practical approach for learning to teach sport skills, guided by an applied understanding of the stages of learning and performance, individual differences and their impact on skill acquisition, and the critical elements required to create a learning environment that enhances optimal sport skill development and performance.

A variety of educational elements make these texts student and instructor friendly:

- Learning objectives introduce each chapter.
- Sidebars illustrate sport-specific applications of key concepts and principles.
- Chapter summaries review the key points covered in the chapter and are linked to

the chapter objectives by content and sequence.

- Key terms at the end of most chapters list the terms introduced in that chapter and remind coaches and students, "These are words you should know." The first occurrence of the word in the chapter is bold-faced, and the words also appear in the glossary.

- Chapter review questions at the end of each chapter allow coaches and students to check their comprehension of the chapter's contents. Answers to questions appear in the back of the book.

- Real-world application scenarios called practical activities follow the review questions. These scenarios provide problem situations for readers to solve. The solutions require readers to describe how the concepts discussed in the chapter can be applied in real-world scenarios. Sample solutions appear in the back of the book.

- A glossary defines all of the key terms covered in the book.

- A bibliography section at the end of the book serves as a resource for additional reading and research.

- A general index lists subjects covered in the book.

These texts are also the basis for a series of Silver Level online courses to be developed by Human Kinetics. These courses will be offered through ASEP's Online Education Center for coaches and students who wish to increase their knowledge through practical and applied study of the sport sciences.

# PREFACE

One of the major responsibilities of coaches at all levels of competition is to teach athletes the skills they need in order to perform at their best on a consistent basis. This book is one in a series of volumes making up the American Sport Education Program's (ASEP's) Silver Level curriculum. It is designed to provide coaches with the latest information from the sport sciences that deals with the teaching of sport skills. The book is written for both aspiring coaches and those with previous coaching experience who want to learn more about the teaching process.

*Sport Skill Instruction for Coaches* is divided into three parts. Part I contains chapters 1 and 2 and lays the foundation for skill instruction by helping you learn how to focus your teaching on the process of athletes' performance rather than just the outcome. Chapter 1 provides an overview of the three basic ingredients of skill instruction: athletes, the skills athletes need to learn, and the learning environment. Chapter 2 addresses the first basic instructional ingredient—athletes—in more detail. Here you are introduced to the concept of individual differences as well as to some athlete characteristics that you need to keep in mind when teaching skills. Part II contains chapters 3, 4, and 5 and deals with the second basic ingredient of instruction: the skills athletes need to learn. Each chapter in this section focuses on one of the three categories of skills you might teach your athletes: technical skills, tactical skills, and mental skills. Chapter 3 deals with technical skills, which are the fundamental movements found in every sport. Specific discussion is devoted to the various ways technical skills can be classified and to one important principle of technical skill performance: the speed–accuracy trade-off. Chapter 4 discusses tactical skills, which are the skills athletes need in order to gain an advantage in competition. Here you will learn how to identify the tactical skills your athletes need and how to help them develop those skills. Chapter 5 addresses the final skill category, mental skills, which are the skills athletes use to deal with the psychological demands of competition. Once they learn these skills, athletes can use them to achieve the thoughts and feelings that accompany effective performance of technical and tactical skills (e.g., focusing attention, controlling emotions, and adjusting arousal level).

Part III contains chapters 6 to 9 and offers a variety of suggestions to help you maximize the effectiveness of your practices. Chapter 6 contains information you can use to determine the skills you should teach your athletes. Included here are discussions of goal setting, the process of technical skill analysis, and the concept of target behaviors, which are observable indicators of the quality of athletes' performance. The final three chapters deal with the third basic ingredient of skill instruction, the learning environment. Put simply, these chapters address the "how to" of skill instruction. Chapter 7 focuses on a variety of topics relating to the content and structure of skill practice, including coach–athlete communication, verbal instructions, visual demonstrations, physical guidance, part practice techniques, slow-motion practice, the need for repetition and variation during skill rehearsal, and the development of anticipation. Chapter 8 covers the important topic of feedback, including the various forms it might take and some things you need to keep in mind when deciding when and how often to provide feedback to your athletes, how much to provide, and how detailed it should be. Finally, chapter 9 provides some suggestions as to how you can combine all three skill categories in your practices to prepare your athletes for any challenge they might face in competition.

At the beginning of each chapter, you will find a list of learning objectives. A summary of key points is provided at the end of each chapter, followed by a list of key terms (introduced in the chapter in boldfaced type) that represent the "language" of sport skill instruction. Also included are a number of review questions you can use to check your comprehension of the chapter's content and your ability to apply it in a possible teaching situation. At the end of the book, you will find a glossary containing all the terms introduced in the chapters, a list of references used to support the material presented, and an index containing the subjects covered.

# ACKNOWLEDGMENTS

This book is the product of a variety of personal and professional influences, including my academic training in the sport sciences, several people who contributed to my experiences as a competitive athlete, the many athletes I have assisted in my work as a performance consultant, and the skilled publication professionals at Human Kinetics.

My undergraduate program in physical education at Greenville College exposed me to the fundamentals of effective sport skill instruction. Later, while pursuing a PhD at the University of Michigan, I had the privilege of being mentored by Richard Schmidt, one of the top scholars in the field of motor learning. Among other things, Dick taught me how to analyze problems and ask the kinds of research questions that had the potential to contribute something to the existing knowledge base in skill learning. Not surprisingly, much of my published research over the past 30 years has focused on the strategies people use to learn skills and perform them effectively in a variety of situations.

My competitive athletic experience was more beneficial than it might otherwise have been as a result of the influence of several people. My father, Arthur Wrisberg, was my first performance consultant and taught me many of the tactical and mental nuances of the various sports I played. My uncle, Howard Wilson (who played competitive fastpitch softball into his mid-60s and was a near-scratch golfer and competitive bowler into his 80s), modeled for me a process orientation by the way he prepared for and competed in the sports he played. And finally, my baseball coach at Greenville College, Bob Smith, convinced me that becoming a better person was at least as important as developing my talents as a utility infielder.

Over the past 25 years I have had the opportunity to provide mental training assistance for many athletes at the University of Tennessee and at the professional level. In the process, I have learned as much or more from them as they have from me. Specifically, they educated me about the characteristics of coaches they appreciated the most (and least), the kinds of practices that benefited them the most (and least), and the importance of developing tactical and mental skills (in addition to technical skills) in order to achieve competitive success on a consistent basis.

Finally, I offer my sincere thanks to the skilled publication professionals at Human Kinetics, who provided both the substantive and technical assistance I needed throughout the development of this book. I especially appreciate the wisdom and encouragement of Chris Drews, who convinced me to stick it out when I was tempted to quit. In addition, I thank Patricia MacDonald, whose copyediting made the final product more reader friendly, and Bob Reuther and Laura Fitch, whose decisions on interior design and excellent choices in photographs, respectively, provided the look and feel that distinguish the best books from the rest.

# PART I

# Foundations of Skill Instruction

Good coaches are good teachers. They know the kinds of skills their athletes need to learn, and they know how to teach them those skills. Realizing that athletes have different levels of abilities and experience, good coaches try to design practices that are challenging and beneficial for each person. Good coaches know the kinds of questions to ask in order to help athletes perform at their best, and they tend to focus more on the process of effective execution than on winning and losing. Good coaches know that the best indicator of the quality of their teaching is the quality of their athletes' performance in competition. In part I, you'll discover how to become a better teacher by learning what to look for in your athletes' performance, asking the right questions, and adopting a process-focused approach to skill instruction.

# 1

# *Basics of Good Teaching*

**When you finish reading this chapter, you should be able to explain**

1. the difference between learning and performing,
2. the three basic ingredients of skill instruction, and
3. the process-focused approach to skill instruction.

*S*port Skill Instruction for Coaches is designed to help you teach your athletes the skills they need in order to perform at their best in competition. The book explains in simple terms the key ingredients of skill instruction and offers a variety of principles and concepts you can use to help your athletes learn and perform the technical, tactical, and mental skills of your sport. This first chapter discusses the concepts of learning and performing, the three basic ingredients of skill instruction, and the process-focused instructional approach.

## Differences Between Learning and Performing

Although learning and performing are related processes, they are not identical. **Learning** is the relatively permanent change in performance that occurs with practice. It is an internal state that can be inferred only by repeatedly observing athletes' actions. **Performing** is the observable act of skill execution. When athletes try to learn a sport skill, they do so by performing it on a repeated basis (e.g., basketball players may practice layups repeatedly). On the other hand, every time athletes perform a skill, they are also learning something about it as a result of that experience (see figure 1.1). A basketball player performing layups may be *learning* something about the rhythm and coordination of her lead arm and same-side leg. To maximize the benefits of practices, you need to promote the consistent performance of effective behaviors. Everyone has heard the phrase "Practice makes perfect," but when it comes to planning practices and providing effective instruction, you need to take that phrase one step further and ask yourself, "*What* will my athletes be perfecting when practicing today?"

Sometimes athletes are aware that learning is taking place when they are performing, while at other times they may be unaware that any learning is occurring. Motor learning

researchers refer to these two types of learning as intentional learning and implicit learning, respectively.

## Intentional Learning and Implicit Learning

Performing (or practicing) skills leads to changes in behavior, or learning. **Intentional learning** involves the learning of skills or components of skills that athletes deliberately focus on when they practice. For example, baseball and softball batters focus on executing swings that are level, on making solid contact with the ball, and on following through. As athletes get better at doing the things they are intentionally trying to improve, they often experience noticeable changes in performance. Batters might notice that the swing feels "smoother," the batted ball goes farther, and the position of the bat at the end of the swing is somewhere behind their

Both intentional and implicit learning occur when athletes practice their skills.

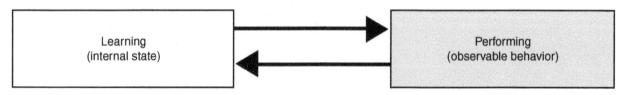

FIGURE 1.1   Learning and performing are related but not identical processes.

backs. Gymnasts might notice that they are remaining on the apparatus for longer periods of time. Swimmers might recognize that the speed of their strokes is increasing. Changes such as these are some of the observable signs of intentional learning.

## *Do You Know What to Look For?*

There is an important difference between learning and performing. Learning is an internal state that is strengthened as a result of repeated practice. Performing, on the other hand, involves observable behavior that takes place whenever an athlete attempts a skill. To assess improvements in your athletes' learning (i.e., internal state), you need to identify and measure observable behaviors that represent reliable (i.e., consistently accurate) estimates of performance. In chapter 6, you will find more detailed information about the assessment process. But here is a glimpse.

Figure 1.2 depicts some behavioral characteristics a basketball coach might observe when evaluating performance of the chest pass (from Wissel, 2004). As a quick test of your ability to identify the important observable behaviors in your sport, write down some behavioral characteristics you would look for in assessing the skill learning of athletes. If your sport involves a variety of different skills (e.g., spiking, passing, setting, and serving in volleyball), select one skill and list the characteristics you believe are most essential for successful performance of that skill. Remember that reliable assessments allow you to accurately observe these important behavioral characteristics each time you evaluate your athletes' performance. You might use a checklist like the one shown in figure 1.2 for periodically assessing improvements in your athletes' performance or for identifying characteristics they need to devote more attention to in practice.

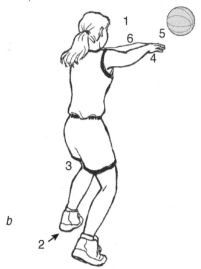

### Ball in Front of Chest

___1. Locate target without looking
___2. Maintain balanced stance
___3. Keep hands slightly behind ball in a relaxed handshake position
___4. Keep ball in front of chest
___5. Keep elbows in

### Chest Pass

___1. Look away or fake before passing
___2. Step in direction of pass
___3. Extend knees, back, and arms
___4. Force wrist and fingers through ball; force weak hand through ball
___5. Release ball off first and second fingers
___6. Follow through with arms extended, palms down, and fingers pointing to the target

FIGURE 1.2  Behavioral characteristics of *(a)* the preparation phase and *(b)* the execution phase of the basketball chest pass.

Reprinted, by permission, from H. Wissel, 2004, *Basketball: Steps to success*, 2nd ed. (Champaign, IL: Human Kinetics), 25.

However, in addition to these obvious improvements, other changes that athletes are not as aware of are occurring as they practice. Without realizing it, a defensive back may be getting better at anticipating a receiver's movements, a diver may be producing the components of a dive more consistently, or a golfer may be reading the lie of the ball more accurately. Changes such as these are examples of **implicit learning**.

Whenever athletes practice their skills, both intentional learning and implicit learning are taking place. The golfer may celebrate a round of 18 holes of par golf as a result of hours of deliberate practice (intentional learning) without being aware that the subtle mechanics of his chip shot are also becoming more consistent (implicit learning). Your challenge as a coach is to design the types of practice experiences that promote both types of learning.

### Specificity of Training

The best way to encourage both intentional and implicit learning is to have athletes practice their skills under conditions that are as similar as possible to the conditions they will experience in competition. A tried and true principle of skill learning is that of specificity. Put simply, the **principle of specificity of training** holds that the best way to practice skills is to include as many of the specific characteristics of the skills as possible in the practice setting. Soccer players should practice the skills of passing, shooting, and heading the way they need to perform them in games; swimmers should practice their turns the way they need to perform them in meets; and golfers should practice drives, chip shots, and putts the way they need to perform them on the golf course. By creating practices that simulate competitive conditions as closely as possible, you will promote the kind of skill learning (both intentional and implicit) that will prepare your athletes for effective performance during competition. You will learn more about the principle of specificity throughout this book.

## Three Basic Ingredients of Skill Instruction

There are three basic ingredients of skill instruction: the athlete, the task, and the performance environment (see figure 1.3). Whether you are coaching a beginner who is learning a skill for the first time or helping an accomplished athlete improve a particular aspect of her performance, you need to keep all three of these ingredients in mind.

### Athlete

Arguably the most important ingredient in any type of skill instruction is the person or athlete doing the learning or performing. Therefore, it is important to understand your athletes' personal characteristics if you want to create practice experiences that are fun and challenging rather than boring or overwhelming. The next chapter identifies some personal characteristics you'll need to keep in mind, such as age, sex, height and weight, physical assets, learning style, and previous movement experiences. If you are coaching youth soccer, your players will likely need considerably more technical instruction in the fundamentals of the game than if you

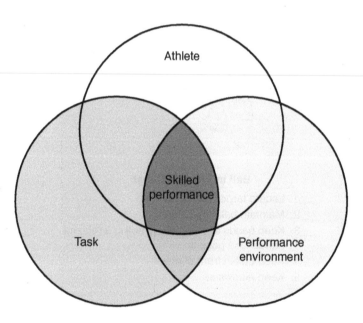

FIGURE 1.3   The basic ingredients of skill instruction.

are coaching college players. Advanced performers are more skilled, fitter, stronger, and more knowledgeable than young athletes, so they appreciate practices that challenge them to apply or strengthen their skills in a variety of competition-like scenarios.

In addition to knowing the more obvious personal characteristics of your athletes, it is also essential that you have some sense of what they are able to do and willing to do. Some athletes may have more background in the sport than others, some may be better conditioned, and some may have a more advanced level of skill or greater awareness of effective strategies. Some may have all those characteristics but may not be willing to do what it takes to get any better. As mentioned in the previous section, it is important to know what behavioral characteristics to look for when assessing your athletes' skills. In a similar vein, being sensitive to individual differences in the personal characteristics athletes bring with them to the sport setting and then tailoring instruction in ways that promote the greatest improvement possible for each participant are among the more challenging aspects of any coach's job. A more detailed discussion of the concept of individual differences is provided in chapter 2.

## Task

A second ingredient you need to consider when providing instruction is the sport task(s) athletes are trying to learn. Every task is made up of sensory-perceptual elements, decision-making elements, and motor control elements. **Sensory-perceptual elements** refer to the types of information athletes must be able to detect and interpret. Sensory-perceptual information may take the form of cues present in the performance environment (e.g., a moving ball) or sensations arising from the movement itself (e.g., balance). **Decision-making elements** refer to the choices athletes must make and the demands associated with those choices. A running back in football must decide how to use his blockers and when to cut back against the flow of the defense. **Motor control elements** represent the various components of the movement athletes are trying to produce in a coordinated fashion. A gymnast performing a balance beam routine must execute a variety of maneuvers within the confines of a narrow platform.

Different sport tasks place different types of demands on performers. A tennis player hitting a ground stroke must deal with a sensory-perceptual demand (e.g., visually tracking a moving ball) that is more difficult than that faced by golfer. The tennis player needs to detect the speed, trajectory, and spin of the approaching ball, while the golfer need only notice the position of a stationary ball.

Some sports require the performance of several tasks that place varying demands on athletes. A soccer goalie must deal with greater sensory-perceptual and decision-making demands when attempting to stop an opponent's shot

Good coaches are sensitive to individual differences in their athletes.

Different sport tasks place different types of demands on athletes. A soccer goalie must attend to many sensory-perceptual and decision-making demands.

than when attempting a free kick. In the first situation, the goalie must detect both the positions and movements of attacking players as well as the characteristics of the approaching ball. Once this is done, the goalie must quickly choose an appropriate response (e.g., no action if the shot is wide of the goal, hand save, kick save, hand or kick deflection to a teammate). In the free kick situation, the goalie need only identify the intended target and has ample time to produce the kick. In chapter 3, you will find more detailed discussion of the requirements of different sport tasks, or technical skills.

### Performance Environment

A third ingredient you need to consider when providing instruction is the performance environment. Different environments represent different types of demands. For example, a basketball player attempting a free throw alone in an empty gymnasium experiences a different environment than a player shooting a free throw in front of several teammates or with three seconds left and the score tied during a championship game. Effective practice involves the performance of tasks in the types of environments athletes must confront during competi-

tion. In chapters 7 and 9, you will find more detailed discussion of ways to create these types of environments in your practices.

## Process-Focused Approach to Providing Sport Skill Instruction

Another important feature of this book is its emphasis on a **process-focused instructional approach.** This approach emphasizes the correct execution of the technical, tactical, and mental skills (discussed in more detail in chapters 3, 4, and 5, respectively) of a sport rather than the end result. In other words, the focus is on the process of performing rather than on the final score. A basketball player who focuses on positioning his body effectively when rebounding (technical skill) should be praised regardless of the number of rebounds he ends up getting during a practice or game. In the same vein, the tennis player who makes good decisions during a point (tactical skill) should be complimented regardless of whether she wins the point or not. Finally, the baseball batter who maintains his composure after a bad call by the umpire (mental skill) should be complimented for that regardless of whether he ends up getting on base or not. Coaches who use a process-focused approach emphasize the things athletes are in control of and remind them that if they do those things correctly, they will be giving themselves the best opportunity to succeed. Therefore, regardless of the outcome of the competition (win or lose), success is measured in terms of the degree to which athletes consistently execute the technical, tactical, and mental skills necessary for successful performance.

The key to using a process-focused approach is your ability to ask the right questions when deciding how to instruct your athletes. Based on the preceding discussion, some examples of the kinds of questions you might ask when using a process-focused approach include the following:

- How does my instruction keep athletes focused on the process (i.e., the appropriate technical, tactical, and mental skills) rather than the outcome?

- What is the most important process cue I need to emphasize for this athlete (or team) at this moment?

- How can I keep this athlete (or team) focused on the process even in the heat of competition?

- What are some ways I can reinforce my athletes' focus on the process even when they don't get the outcomes they are hoping for?

- How can I assure my athletes that a focus on the process will give them the best chance of obtaining the outcome they desire?

- Which fundamental processes (i.e., technical, tactical, and mental skills) did this athlete (or team) execute well during today's practice or competition?

- Which processes did this athlete (or team) fail to execute well, and what are some ways I can help each athlete improve his or her technical, tactical, and mental skills during practices or in competition?

By asking (and then obtaining answers to) questions such as these, you will be able to provide your athletes with helpful assistance in just about any type of performance situation, whether it's in practice or in competition.

Another important aspect of the process-focused instructional approach is that it emphasizes the thoughts, feelings, and behaviors that accompany successful performance. When using this approach, you must first help athletes identify those thoughts, feelings, and behaviors and then provide them with opportunities to focus on those processes during practices. For example, with your help a pitcher might decide that the following thoughts, feelings, and behaviors are necessary for successful performance:

- An emphasis on one pitch at a time (thought)

- A primary visual focus on the intended target (position of the catcher's glove) (behavior)

- A relaxed but energized feeling in the body (feeling)

- A mechanically sound throwing motion (behavior)

During practices, you could encourage the pitcher to focus on these processes by developing a clear idea of the type of pitch he intends to throw each time; gripping the ball in an appropriate fashion; visually focusing on the center of the catcher's glove (which should always be positioned in the location of the intended target); taking a relaxation breath to prepare the body for action; and achieving a smooth, fluid execution of the desired throwing motion. By focusing on these processes on a consistent basis, the pitcher will not only make them more automatic but will also gain the confidence of knowing he is doing everything under his control to achieve success on each pitch.

A major assumption of this book is that athletes can successfully and consistently perform any sport task if they are taught to identify the essential thoughts, feelings, and behaviors associated with success and encouraged to focus on those processes during practices. A major purpose of the remainder of this book is to give you the tools you need to implement the process-focused instructional approach with your athletes.

Process-focused coaches know how and when to provide instructional assistance as well as what type of assistance to provide. Sometimes athletes need to be allowed to practice their skills on their own before they receive feedback. That way they can determine what is working and what isn't and can become more mindful of their strengths and weaknesses. If you attempt to provide assistance when athletes would prefer to practice on their own, you may be wasting a lot of time and breath. When athletes realize that their best efforts are producing unsatisfactory outcomes, they are usually more motivated to hear what you have to say. Athletes are also responsive to assistance when they mess up or fail to achieve the outcome they were hoping for. A coach's challenge, then, is to remain patient until these and other types of "teachable moments" arise. The reward for such patience is athletes who are motivated to hear what you have to say and eager to incorporate your suggestions.

Good coaches know how and when to provide process-focused instructional assistance.

## *Capitalizing on the "Teachable Moment"*

Recent research has shown that learners benefit more from instructional feedback when they ask for it than when they don't think they need it. One interpretation of this finding is that learners prefer to solve their own problems, and they appreciate assistance only when they are unable to do so. The message for coaches here is to be alert to the "teachable moments" when athletes need assistance and then be prepared to capitalize on those moments by providing relevant, process-focused information. The opportunity may arise when an athlete is discouraged or at a loss as to what to do next. For example, a volleyball player may be having difficulty serving a "floater" because she is imparting spin on the ball by making contact some distance from the ball's center of gravity (Carr, 2004). Coaches can capitalize on this teachable moment by simply reminding the player to "hit through the center."

Teachable moments can also occur during competition, when athletes are prone to thinking about the score or the mistake they just made rather than about the processes necessary to achieve success on the next play. No matter how many times athletes hear their coaches say, "Let it go," when they make a mistake in practice, the real teachable moment more often comes during a big competition. Rather than becoming upset and voicing displeasure with an athlete when he makes a mistake, capitalize on that moment by reminding the athlete to refocus on the fundamental processes. You might tell a tennis player who has just double-faulted to lose the first set to "relax your grip and hit your targets" the next time she is serving; you might encourage a kicker who has just missed a field goal to "take a nice deep breath, focus on the ball, and stay smooth" before the next kick; or you might encourage a swimmer who is worried about her race to "focus on fluid turns and accelerating off the wall." Remember that every teachable moment represents an opportunity to provide athletes with the process-focused assistance they need. More important, it reminds them of the things they are in control of and encourages them to trust their preparation and enjoy the experience.

# SUMMARY

1. Learning is an internal state that is strengthened as a result of repeated practice. As such, learning is not directly observable.
2. Performing involves the observable behavior of athletes. Performance observations can be used to infer the present state of an athlete's learning.
3. To make reliable inferences about an athlete's learning, you must be able to identify performance characteristics that reflect that learning.
4. All learning and performing is made up of three basic ingredients: the athlete, the task, and the performance environment.
5. Each athlete possesses characteristics and experiences that can either facilitate or hinder learning or performing.
6. Different types of sport tasks present different demands and challenges for athletes.
7. Different performance environments pose different demands and challenges for athletes.
8. The key to providing effective instructional assistance lies in your ability to ask and come up with answers to process-focused questions.

# KEY TERMS

| | | |
|---|---|---|
| decision-making elements | learning | principle of specificity of training |
| implicit learning | motor control elements | process-focused instructional approach |
| intentional learning | performing | sensory-perceptual elements |

# REVIEW QUESTIONS

1. What is the relationship between learning and performing? Why is it important for coaches to be aware of this relationship?
2. What is the difference between intentional learning and implicit learning? Give an example of each type of learning from your sport.
3. What are the three basic ingredients of sport skill instruction? Why is it important to consider all three ingredients when attempting to provide instructional assistance?
4. What are the three categories of elements that make up most sport skills? Give an example of each element for one of the skills in the sport you coach.
5. Why is it important to allow athletes to spend some time practicing tasks before providing them with feedback or additional assistance? What might be some aspects of a sport task that athletes could discover or improve on their own?

# PRACTICAL ACTIVITIES

1. Select one task from the sport you coach and describe a practice activity for this task that illustrates the principle of specificity of training.
2. List five processes (i.e., thoughts, feelings, behaviors) necessary for successful performance of the task you selected in the previous item. For example, successful execution of the task

of passing a soccer ball using a lofted drive kick requires players to keep their eyes on the ball and their head steady, approach the ball from an angle, keep the plant foot behind the ball, strike the ball as low on its surface as possible, keep the foot extended and the ankle locked throughout the kick, and follow through after contact with the ball (Pronk & Gorman, 1985).

**3.** List three questions you need to consider when using a process-focused approach to teach athletes the task you selected in the previous activities. For example, a football coach might consider the following questions before teaching defensive linemen the swim move to improve their pass rush: Which processes should I instruct the players to focus on first? Which behaviors of the opposing offensive lineman should I encourage defensive linemen to focus on? Is there a specific sequence of movements defensive linemen should perform in order to successfully execute the swim move, or must they adapt the move to the actions of the opposing lineman? Should defensive linemen be relaxed or intense before initiating the swim move?

# 2

# *It All Starts With the Athlete*

© PhotoDisc

*When you finish reading this chapter, you should be able to explain*

1. the concept of individual differences and its relationship to athletes' learning and performance;
2. some of the learner characteristics athletes can be expected to differ on, including abilities, capabilities, age, previous experience, stage of learning, goals, and motivation; and
3. why you should avoid trying to predict an athlete's future success based on initial observations of his or her performance.

In the first chapter, you discovered that the most important ingredient of the learning process is the learner, which in your case is the athlete or team you work with or will work with. In this chapter, you'll learn more about some of the characteristics individual athletes possess that can influence the way they learn skills. People come in all sorts of packages, and it's important for you as a coach to be knowledgeable about the individual differences you will encounter in your athletes. Some learner characteristics you can expect your athletes to differ on include abilities and capabilities, age, previous experience, stage of learning, and goals. Perhaps the most important individual difference characteristic is the learner's motivation level. Athletes who are not motivated to learn are going to be difficult to teach. However, the more you know about the characteristics of your athletes, the better you will be at creating practice experiences that are beneficial and challenging. At the same time, you'll need to resist the temptation to predict who your best athletes are going to be based on one or two initial observations of their performance. Three reasons why predictions of future success can be problematic are given near the end of this chapter.

## Individual Differences

It doesn't take a rocket scientist to notice that people are different. They come in all shapes, sizes, and colors, and each person possesses a unique combination of strengths and weaknesses. The concept of **individual differences** is based on the assumption that people's performance on any task is due in part to differences in their respective backgrounds and personal characteristics. Background factors include cultural and social influences and previous movement opportunities. Personal characteristics are for the most part genetically determined or the result of early life experiences. They include body type, perceptual-motor abilities, personality, and learning style. Some examples of background factors and personal characteristics that might contribute to individual differences in the ways athletes perform and learn are shown in table 2.1. In the next section, you will discover more

about some of these characteristics and how you can recognize them in the athletes you coach.

## Learner Characteristics

Although many things make people different, several characteristics are particularly important when it comes to athletes' performance and learning. These include abilities and capabilities, age, previous experience, stage of learning, learning style, motivation, and goals.

### Abilities and Capabilities

Two important sources of athletes' individual differences are their abilities and their capabilities. Researchers define **abilities** as traits that are inherited and relatively stable. Research in motor learning indicates that many types of abilities exist and that different abilities serve different purposes. Some abilities are important for perceiving the environment, others are essential for making effective decisions, and still others are necessary for producing effective movements. An athlete who possesses excellent dynamic visual acuity (i.e., the ability to clearly see moving objects such as an approaching ball) should, all else being equal, be able to perform tasks requiring this ability (e.g., batting) more effectively than would an athlete with poor visual acuity. In a similar vein, an athlete with good explosive leg strength, sometimes referred to as leg power (i.e., the ability to rapidly contract the leg muscles), should be able to run faster and jump higher than an athlete with only average leg power.

**Capabilities** are similar to abilities but are considered modifiable with practice. For example, static strength (i.e., the maximum amount of force that can be applied to a heavy weight or a fairly immovable object) is considered a capability because it can be improved with practice (e.g., through a systematic weight training program). On the other hand, reaction time (i.e., the initiation of a rapid response to an unanticipated event) is not considered a capability because it is governed primarily by a person's nerve transmission time, which is relatively uninfluenced by practice. The important thing to remember

TABLE 2.1

## Individual Difference Factors That Can Influence Athletes' Performance and Learning

| Factor | Examples | Impact on learning and performance |
|---|---|---|
| **BACKGROUND FACTORS** | | |
| Cultural influences | Ethnicity, racial identity | Athletes from different ethnic or racial groups may demonstrate different styles of performance (e.g., more or less individuality, creativity, flair, intensity, emotion, discipline) |
| Social influences | Peer group, socioeconomic level | Reinforcement (or opposition) of peer group might enhance (or diminish) motivation; financial support (or lack of) might privilege or handicap skill development |
| Previous movement opportunities | Competitive, recreational | More (or less) previous exposure to the sport might be beneficial (or detrimental)<br>Competitive experience might be beneficial when performing under pressure, while recreational experience might promote a focus on personal skill improvement |
| **PERSONAL CHARACTERISTICS** | | |
| Body type | Lean, muscular, heavy | Impact would depend on type of sport and skill requirements (e.g., muscular body would be more beneficial for a wrestler than for a golfer) |
| Perceptual-motor abilities | Eye–hand coordination, speed, balance | Impact would depend on type of sport and skill requirements (e.g., balance would be more important for a gymnast than for a swimmer) |
| Personality | Outgoing, quiet | Impact would depend on type of sport and skill requirements (e.g., an outgoing personality might be beneficial for tasks requiring interactions with teammates for performance success, while a quiet personality might be more beneficial for individual sports requiring contemplation) |
| Learning style | Verbal, visual, kinesthetic | Verbal style would be beneficial for strategic aspects of competition, while visual and kinesthetic styles would be beneficial for gaining the desired look and feel of successful performance |

here is that capabilities can be improved with practice, while abilities tend to be more permanent or fixed in nature.

Different athletes have different upper limits, and these upper limits illustrate their level of ability. It is very likely that in young athletes, abilities and capabilities need some training to be performed at their fullest extent. An athlete may not exhibit a lot of flexibility or strength, but a coach can help the athlete train to reach her maximum level of flexibility or strength. At some point, athletes will reach the extent of their strength, flexibility, and stamina, and this level will differ depending on genetically dependent abilities.

Both the abilities and capabilities each athlete possesses will have some impact on the ultimate level of performance success the athlete is able to achieve. A basketball player who is learning how to rebound can improve his performance by improving his visual anticipation (i.e., the capability of predicting environmental events, which in this case might mean the way a basketball deflects off the rim and backboard). However,

## Personal Characteristics of Professional Football Players

Several years ago an interesting study was conducted with professional football players. The research was based on the assumption that the personal characteristics of offensive linemen are different from those of defensive linemen because of the nature of the respective tasks each must perform. The task of offensive linemen is to accurately carry out blocking assignments in a precise, orderly, and coordinated fashion. Defensive linemen, on the other hand, are expected to create havoc for the opposing team, throw caution to the wind, and play with near reckless abandon.

To determine whether these characteristics might be seen in other areas, the researcher obtained permission to inspect the lockers of the two groups. What he found was both revealing and humorous. The offensive linemen's lockers were neat and highly organized. All toiletries and clothing items were arranged in a systematic fashion. There seemed to be a place for everything, and everything appeared to be in its place. On the other hand, the defensive linemen's lockers were in a near state of chaos. In some cases, the contents of the locker spilled out onto the floor as soon as the researcher opened the door. Items that didn't spill out were often "stuffed" at random inside the locker. A bar of soap might be under a pile of clothes or inside a player's helmet. The results strongly suggest that the personal characteristics required for success in one sport task may be quite different from those required for success in another, and such differences may be seen in other forms of athletes' behavior, even down to the way they organize their lockers.

this player may never achieve the same level of rebounding skill as another player who possesses a similar level of visual anticipation but also has better manual dexterity (i.e., the ability to manipulate objects with the hands or feet). In some cases, athletes can compensate for their weaker abilities by possessing other abilities that are important for successful performance. Hall of Fame third baseman Brooks Robinson of the Baltimore Orioles was a very slow runner, but his extremely fast reaction time and excellent eye–hand coordination enabled him to become one of the best fielders in baseball history. Robinson's running ability (or lack thereof) may have limited his baserunning performance, but his reaction time and eye–hand coordination contributed to his fielding excellence.

It's not uncommon to hear coaches use the terms *ability* and *skill* interchangeably; however, the two terms actually represent different things. As mentioned earlier, ability or, more correctly, abilities (since there are actually many of them) are genetically determined characteristics that are relatively stable and that dictate to some extent an athlete's potential for performance

success. **Skill,** on the other hand, is the level of technical or tactical performance an athlete is able to demonstrate on a consistent basis (the next two chapters talk more about technical and tactical skills). Regardless of the patterns of abilities different athletes possess, all individuals can improve their technical and tactical skills as a result of practice. Your challenge is to create practice experiences that allow your athletes to maximize their abilities, improve their capabilities, and develop the skill(s) they need to achieve the best performance possible on a consistent basis.

As a coach, you should keep several things in mind when considering the abilities of your athletes. First, you should expect different athletes to possess different combinations of dominant abilities. Second, you should realize that each athlete's pattern of dominant abilities benefits that person's performance on some tasks more than on others. And third, you should have some idea of all your athletes' stronger and weaker abilities so that you can create practice experiences that allow each athlete to take advantage of strengths and improve on weaknesses.

## *Why a Mule Will Never Win the Kentucky Derby*

When asked to discuss the keys to athletic success, a famous college football coach once suggested the following formula (with the estimated percentage of success due to each factor shown in parentheses): strength of the athlete's abilities (90 percent), practice and training (5 percent), coaching strategies (3 percent), luck (2 percent). Although this coach was referring to athletes who had already achieved a high level of performance success, it is obvious he believed that the overwhelming determinant of athletic achievement was the strength of the performer's inherited abilities.

An old farmer expressed the same opinion when discussing the abilities of his prize mule. The farmer said, "Old Blue is the best mule in the county. He can pull a bigger load than any thoroughbred racing horse ever would. Course, no matter how hard or long I train Old Blue, he'll never win the Kentucky Derby." Clearly, the coach and the farmer agree that while practice is an important contributor to skill development, the potential for achievement in any endeavor also depends on whether the participant possesses a high level of the abilities necessary for successful performance.

© Rhoda Peacher

© Icon Sports Media

One way to experience the phenomenon of individual differences in athletes' abilities is to attend a local youth sport tryout session. Take a notebook and pencil with you, and see how well you can detect the dominant abilities of several of the participants. Refer to the list of abilities shown in figure 2.1, or come up with a list of your own. When you think you have identified each athlete's obvious strengths and weaknesses, write them down. To test the reliability of your initial perceptions, observe the athletes a second or third time before you leave. For each athlete, place a check mark by the strengths and weaknesses you noted during every observation, and scratch through those characteristics you failed to observe more than once. When you've completed this task, review the list and see what differences you can find in the dominant abilities of the different athletes. One way to do this is to circle athletes' strengths and underline their weaknesses. Think about how you would coach these athletes if you were their coach.

# Examples of Perceptual-Motor Abilities and Physical Proficiency Abilities

## Perceptual-motor abilities

- Multilimb coordination: the ability to coordinate the movement of a number of limbs simultaneously. This ability is important when serving a tennis ball or throwing a javelin.

- Control precision: the ability to make highly controlled movement adjustments, particularly where larger muscles are involved. This ability is important for synchronized swimming.

- Response orientation: the ability to make quick choices among numerous possible movements. A goalie in soccer or hockey, who must respond to various types of shots, would benefit from this ability.

- Reaction time: the ability to produce a single rapid response to a single unanticipated stimulus. This ability is important for the sprint start in track or swimming races.

- Rate control: the ability to continuously anticipate and adjust a response to a moving target or object. This ability is important for slalom skiing or a defender in water polo.

- Manual dexterity: the ability to manipulate relatively large objects with the hands and arms. An example is dribbling a basketball.

- Finger dexterity: the ability to manipulate small objects with the fingers. This ability is important for pitching a baseball.

- Arm–hand steadiness: the ability to perform slow and accurate movements. It is important for the sport of archery.

- Wrist–finger speed: the ability to rapidly move the wrist and fingers with little or no accuracy demands. An example is the overhead smash in badminton or tennis.

- Aiming: the ability to produce accurate hand movements under speeded conditions. This ability is important for a goalie in hockey or soccer.

## Physical proficiency abilities

- Explosive strength: the ability to expend a maximum of energy in one explosive act. It is advantageous in activities requiring performers to project themselves or some object as high or far as possible. Examples of tasks requiring explosive strength include the shot put, javelin, long jump, high jump, and 100-meter run in the sport of track and field.

*(continued)*

FIGURE 2.1    Which of these abilities are necessary in the sport you coach? Use this list to evaluate your athletes' strengths and weaknesses.

Adapted from E.A. Fleishman, 1964, *The structure and measurement of physical fitness* (Englewood Cliffs, NJ: Prentice-Hall), 155-160.

- Static strength: the ability to exert a maximum force against a relatively heavy weight or some fairly immovable object. It is important in weightlifting and wrestling.

- Dynamic strength: the ability to repeatedly or continuously move or support the weight of the body. Examples include performing on the high bar or still rings in the sport of gymnastics.

- Trunk strength: the ability to repeatedly or continuously contract the trunk and abdominal muscles. Tasks requiring trunk strength include leg lifts and the pommel horse in the sport of gymnastics.

- Extent flexibility: the ability to extend, or stretch, the body as far as possible in various directions. Aspects of many gymnastics routines depend on this ability.

- Dynamic flexibility: the ability to produce repeated rapid movements involving muscle flexibility. Gymnasts and springboard divers require high levels of dynamic flexibility.

- Balance with visual cues: the ability to maintain total body balance under conditions that allow the use of vision. This ability is important for gymnasts who perform on the balance beam.

- Speed of limb movement: the ability to rapidly contract limb muscles. It underlies tasks in which the arm(s) or leg(s) must be moved quickly, without the requirements of a rapid reaction. Examples include throwing a fast pitch in baseball or cricket or sprinting the final 100 meters of a 1,500-meter run.

- Gross body coordination: the ability to perform a number of complex movements simultaneously. Athletes needing this ability include ice hockey players who must skate and stickhandle at the same time.

- Stamina: the ability to keep the body moving for an extended time period. Athletes requiring stamina include distance runners and triathletes.

FIGURE 2.1   *(continued)*

In your own playing or coaching experience, you have probably noticed that different athletes seem to have a knack for doing a number of different things well. In baseball, some players are good fielders, others are good hitters, some are good baserunners, and the better ones are good at all these things. Although some athletes demonstrate better performance because they have practiced a skill more than their teammates, it is also possible that their performance is superior because the skill caters to their dominant abilities. For example, good fielders in softball or baseball likely possess higher levels of eye–hand coordination, manual dexterity, and force control than do average fielders. In a similar vein, good batters are likely blessed with superior eye–hand coordination, wrist–finger speed, and explosive arm strength. By expecting your athletes to possess different combinations of dominant abilities, you will more likely notice their assets when you see them in action and be able to anticipate the skills they will perform with little difficulty and the ones they will need to devote more practice to.

To determine the tasks that are best suited to each athlete's abilities, you must identify both the demands of the tasks and the abilities that contribute to successful performance. For example, heading a soccer ball requires the ability to make a quick decision about the direction the ball needs to be headed, the ability to make highly controlled movement adjustments, and the ability to maintain total body balance while visually tracking the approaching ball. One way to conceptualize the connection between athletes' abilities and task demands is to imagine a construction worker's toolbox. The tools in the toolbox are like the abilities the worker needs to perform different tasks. Depending on the demands of the task, the worker selects and uses the necessary tools. The tools that are important for laying a foundation are different from the ones necessary for installing plumbing or putting in electrical wiring, just as different abilities are needed for different sport skills. In addition, the quality of the tools designed to do a particular job may differ. An industrial-grade power saw is more sophisticated than a home power saw. Thus, the worker who possesses the industrial-grade saw would have an advantage over the worker who has the home model. In much the same way, the athlete who possesses a greater amount of explosive strength should be able to jump higher than the athlete who has lower levels of this ability.

To experience the challenge of connecting athlete abilities and task demands, take a minute and jot down a few of the demands of several sport tasks you are familiar with. The demands of a soccer goalie, for example, might include accurate perception of the path and speed of an approaching shot, effective decision making, and the execution of a coordinated movement that achieves the desired goal (e.g., passing the ball to a teammate, deflecting the ball over the crossbar, and so on).

After you've written down some task demands, look again at the strengths and weaknesses of the youth sport participants you observed earlier at the tryout session. See if you can determine which individuals would be better equipped to perform the different tasks you came up with. Don't be surprised if you discover that each individual is equipped to perform some tasks better than others.

Now apply this exercise to your own sport and the teams you coach. Identify the important demands of the different positions in the sport. Notice how these vary across position or sport. Then spend some time observing your athletes to determine their respective strengths and weaknesses. Compared with her teammates, one athlete might demonstrate a relatively faster reaction time, while another may have more foot speed, and a third may show more eye–hand coordination. If you are able to develop an abilities profile for each of your athletes, you can then design practice experiences that benefit all of them.

A good principle to keep in mind when creating effective practices is to always try to challenge athletes without discouraging them. You can do this by either having them practice advanced variations of an activity that tests their stronger

## *Specificity Hypothesis of Motor Performance*

Years ago, a physical education professor at the University of California at Berkeley proposed that all movement behavior is based on a very large number of abilities. More significantly, he contended that the abilities important for performing a particular task are highly specific to that task and are completely different from the abilities important for performing any other task. In addition, he predicted that people who are highly successful on one task might not be highly successful on other tasks unless, of course, they also possess high levels of the important abilities for the other tasks. Over the years, Franklin Henry's (1968) **specificity hypothesis** has received considerable experimental support and continues to be an important concept to keep in mind when providing instructional assistance. Among other things, this hypothesis suggests that athletes who possess the dominant abilities important for successful performance of a particular skill are the ones who are more likely to achieve success. Henry's hypothesis is also similar to the **principle of specificity of training,** which suggests that the most effective practice sessions are those that emphasize the activities and experiences needed for competition.

abilities or letting them practice simplified versions of a skill to compensate for their weaker abilities. For example, you might challenge a soccer player possessing relatively high levels of eye–foot coordination to practice a variety of advanced playmaking activities and challenge a player who has only average eye–foot coordination to play games that facilitate the development of ball-handling skills. Always remember that the higher the level of an athlete's abilities, the more demanding the practice repetitions need to be, and vice versa.

Another thing to keep in mind when designing practices is the kind of messages you want to send your athletes about the purposes of practice. You might impress on them the importance of practicing both the skills they perform well and the ones they don't. Moreover, you might encourage athletes to spend extra time practicing the tasks they don't perform as well instead of practicing the ones they do. A soccer goalie with a relatively low level of gross body coordination and a high level of leg power could be encouraged to spend additional time practicing skills that require gross body coordination (e.g., passing balls to teammates and stopping shots with both the hands and the feet) rather than skills that rely more on leg power (e.g., punting). When your athletes realize you are primarily interested in their skill development and not in perfect skill execution, they will be more open to practicing the tasks they are not as proficient at, they will be more willing to take risks, and they will not be afraid to make mistakes in order to improve their performance.

Here are some general guidelines for tailoring practice experiences to the abilities of your athletes:

- Identify the demands of the different tasks in your sport.

- Assess the stronger and weaker abilities of each of your athletes to determine which tasks they are going to be better at and which ones they will need to devote more practice to.

- Create practice experiences that are as gamelike as possible, that enable athletes to enjoy successful performance of the tasks they do well, and that challenge them to improve their performance of tasks they have more difficulty with. The concept of gamelike practices is explained further in chapter 7.

## Age

To create practice experiences that are challenging yet realistic, you must consider the characteristics of athletes of different ages. Remember that people develop at different rates, and considerable individual differences in maturational levels can be evident in some age categories (e.g., 13 to 15 years).

Generally speaking, people learn their basic motor skills during childhood and then gradually refine them or combine them with other skills to create more complex actions later on. If you are dealing with little league baseball players, it is a good idea to teach the fundamental skills of overhand throwing and two-hand catching before introducing different arm angles for making throws (e.g., three quarters, sidearm, underhand) or a wide variety of catching situations (e.g., ground balls, fly balls, balls coming from the left and right). During adolescence, people begin to acquire a wider variety of skills and improve their capability of adapting movements to meet the demands of different environments. For example, baseball and softball players become more adept at throwing to different targets and fielding balls while moving. Many athletes refine their skills during late adolescence and early adulthood, usually after having practiced them for months and years. In addition, athletes' performance may begin to peak in some sports requiring strength and speed because they are approaching their maximum levels of physical conditioning and skill. As athletes continue to age into their late 20s and early 30s, their performance slowly begins to diminish, forcing them to revise their goals and discover ways to adapt in order to continue to achieve task demands.

Here are some general guidelines you can use when coaching athletes of different ages:

- For young athletes (approximately 8 to 12 years of age), emphasize the development of foundational skills. For the sport of basketball, emphasis should be placed on the basic skills of dribbling, passing, rebounding, and shooting (including layups with either hand, jump shots, and free throws).

- For athletes in early adolescence (approximately 13 to 17 years of age), emphasize the continued refinement of foundational skills as well as the development of more complex skill combinations and the adaptation of movements to varying environmental demands. Again, for the sport of basketball, the emphasis might include combinations such as shooting off the dribble and rebounding followed by either a pass or, if on offense, a shot. An example of an adaptation to varying environmental demands is varying the type of pass used (e.g., two-hand chest pass, one-hand pass, bounce pass, overhead baseball throw) for different situations (e.g., quickly passing the ball around the perimeter of a zone defense, penetrating and dishing to a teammate, passing to a teammate driving for the basket at the end of a fast break, rebounding and throwing a long pass to a breaking teammate).

- For athletes in late adolescence and early adulthood (approximately 18 to 25 years of age), emphasize the development of task-specific skills and strategies for achieving optimal performance. For basketball players, you might emphasize the requirements of various offensive and defensive sets, the options available to each player within each offensive set, the responsibilities of each player within each defensive set, and the most effective offensive and defensive sets for different types of opponents.

- For athletes in mid- to late adulthood (approximately 26 years of age and up), emphasize the development of adaptive strategies that allow continued goal achievement in the face of gradually declining physical abilities and performance. Here you might stress the importance of boxing out on rebounds in order to compensate for players' diminished vertical jumping skills or encourage players to help each other on defense in order to minimize one-on-one situations against younger and stronger opponents.

## Previous Experience

Athletes come to your team with a wide variety of past experiences. The research literature shows that a person's social group, such as family and friends, exerts a significant impact

## *Scaling the Environment to Give Kids a Sporting Chance*

At the 1982 World's Fair in Knoxville, Tennessee, one exhibit gave visitors the opportunity to experience the typical home environment through the eyes of a child. Walking from room to room, viewers came upon standard furniture and appliances that appeared to be two or three times larger than normal size. In the "kitchen," visitors looked up to see the large handle of a frying pan extending out from one of the burners on top of an enormous stove. In a few short minutes, viewers were reminded of how large common objects in the home appear to a small child. In a similar vein, the environment of adult sport can be imposing for young athletes. To an eight-year-old basketball player, a goal situated 10 feet off the ground can appear to be miles away. Similarly, a regulation-size basketball can be cumbersome and heavy.

Two variables that typically differentiate younger athletes from older ones are size and strength. Therefore, when preparing for skill instruction, you need to be sure that your equipment and practice environment are scaled to the size and strength of your athletes. For younger children, equipment should be lighter and the practice environment more spatially compact. A little league baseball player who is learning how to field and throw correctly needs to use a ball and glove that are of manageable size and weight and needs to practice throwing and catching at distances from the target that encourage the development of proper mechanics. By scaling the practice environment to the size and strength of your athletes, you will encourage proper skill development regardless of the athletes' stage of maturation.

on the nature and frequency of his or her sport experiences. Therefore, it is helpful to obtain as much information as you can about your athletes' previous sport experiences to determine whether or not those experiences will be beneficial in their new situation. You should be able to obtain this information rather easily from older athletes, but you will probably need to contact the parents or guardians of younger athletes. One way to do this is by using a short questionnaire such as the one shown in figure 2.2.

By knowing something about the type and number of athletes' previous experiences, you can estimate which athletes might require more instructional assistance and which should be able to progress with greater ease. For example, if you are coaching basketball or ice hockey, you might expect that the youngster who possesses several years of soccer experience will acquire the skill of passing and receiving the ball or puck more easily than the player with no previous soccer experience. Assuming this is the case, you might expose the more experienced child to more advanced passing activities and provide the inexperienced player with more foundational exercises. This way both will enjoy success because each is being challenged to a degree that is commensurate with his or her respective level of previous experience.

---

## Previous Experiences in Sports Questionnaire

I look forward to helping your child develop the kinds of skills that will allow him or her to enjoy participation in the sport of _____. Since children's previous sport experiences can influence the ease with which they learn new skills, I would appreciate knowing a bit about your child's previous experiences so I can provide your child with the best instructional assistance possible.

Please list the sports your child has had previous experience in and the approximate length of time he or she has participated in each.

Child's name _____

| **Sport** | **Length of experience** |
|-----------|--------------------------|
| 1. _____ | _____ months/years |
| 2. _____ | _____ months/years |
| 3. _____ | _____ months/years |
| 4. _____ | _____ months/years |
| 5. _____ | _____ months/years |

I would appreciate your returning this information to me at your earliest convenience. Thanks.

FIGURE 2.2 You can give this questionnaire to parents to find out the previous sport experiences of their children.
From C.A. Wrisberg, 2007, *Sport skill instruction for coaches* (Champaign, IL: Human Kinetics).

Athletes bring different levels of past sport experience with them to a new learning situation.

## Stage of Learning

Just as you might expect your athletes to have different levels of previous sport experience when they join your team, you should also expect them to represent different **stages of learning** when it comes to the various techniques and tactics of your sport. Most of the literature in motor learning suggests that people pass through roughly three stages when progressing from beginning to advanced levels of performance. Different scholars assign different labels to these stages; this book refers to them as the mental stage, the practice stage, and the automatic stage.

### Mental Stage

The initial stage of skill learning is characterized by performance that is both awkward and hesitant. Athletes in the **mental stage** spend a lot of time trying to figure out the basic requirements of a movement technique and how they might go about performing it. Their primary goal is to achieve a general idea of the movement. During this stage, athletes engage in quite a bit of trial and error. Even when they do something correctly, they may not know how they did it. Since performance in this stage requires con-

siderable thought and reflection, athletes will usually appear hesitant and indecisive in their movements. However, once they have achieved a general approximation of the desired technique, they will begin practicing it more systematically. You can help athletes in this stage by keeping things simple and by providing them with occasional focus cues. A tennis player learning the overhead smash might benefit from a reminder to "point, transfer, and reach," which would emphasize the importance of watching the descending ball (by pointing at it with the opposite hand), transferring the weight from the back foot to the front, and reaching high to make contact with the ball.

### Practice Stage

In the **practice stage**, athletes spend most of their time refining the general movement pattern they have learned in the mental stage. They also become more adept at detecting and correcting their own errors and adapting the movement to meet the demands of their sport. You can help athletes in this stage by increasing the difficulty of practice experiences as you see their performance becoming more consistent. The tennis player who has achieved a consistent approximation of the correct technique for executing the overhead smash would benefit from practice sessions that involve hitting overheads from different locations on the court in response to different types of lobs (e.g., varying in height). The player might also try hitting the smash to different targets on the opposite side of the net. The practice stage is where most athletes spend the majority of their time, although a few may eventually become so advanced that their performance is virtually automatic.

### Automatic Stage

Athletes in the **automatic stage** demonstrate a level of performance that appears to be nonconscious and effortless. They have reached the point where they are able to produce their movements without paying attention to them and do so with little wasted motion. Because they spend little time or effort thinking about the mechanics of the action itself, athletes in this stage are able to devote their attention to other task-related information, such as tactical decisions or stylistic aspects of the movement. As you may have noticed, the best athletes in every sport seem to have their own "signature" form, or style, that sets their performance apart from that of others. The best way to help athletes in this stage is to provide as much variety as possible. For the tennis player, it might mean incorporating lobs at random moments during a simulated competition or asking a teammate to make occasional unfair line calls after a successful smash in an attempt to disrupt the player's focus.

Your role as a coach will be somewhat different for athletes in the different stages of learning. You will need to provide more instruction and feedback for athletes in the mental stage than for those in the latter two stages. Athletes in the practice and automatic stages will require less feedback from you but will need you to challenge them with creative practice activities. Thus, your effectiveness for athletes in the mental stage will be determined by what you say to help them understand the basics of skill performance. However, your effectiveness for athletes in the latter two stages will be determined less by what you say and more by the kinds of challenges you are able to create for their practice experiences.

## Learning Style

Considerable research shows that people learn in different ways, and this preference is referred to as their **learning style**. The three most common learning styles are visual, verbal, and kinesthetic. Visual learners learn best by watching something. In sport that "something" may be a demonstration by the coach or the movements of a skilled athlete. Verbal learners learn best by listening to instructions, and kinesthetic learners learn best by physically performing the task.

It's also true that instructors have preferred teaching styles that may or may not be compatible with the learning styles of their students. For example, a coach who prefers to teach by showing athletes what to do would be more helpful for athletes who are visual learners than for those who learn best by listening or physically practicing. Therefore, the best approach to sport skill instruction utilizes a variety of presentation methods. That way, regardless of the preferred learning style of different athletes, they all receive a type of instruction that should be helpful. An example might be the track coach who explains the hurdling technique, demonstrates it, and then allows athletes to practice it using modified mini hurdles.

Athletes who possess a kinesthetic learning style might have trouble standing still while listening to an explanation or watching a demonstration. Be careful not to label such athletes as "discipline problems." In reality, the "problem" may be a mismatch between the way you prefer to teach and the way the athlete learns best.

## Motivation

Perhaps the most important individual difference factor influencing athletes' performance and learning is **motivation,** or the reasons athletes do what they do. Why do athletes choose to participate in a particular sport? Why do athletes sometimes exhibit considerable enthusiasm and intensity when they practice and compete and other times appear listless or disinterested? Why do some athletes continue to participate in their sport for many years while others drop out after only a few? Most research suggests that the reason people choose to participate in sport in the first place is to have fun. Therefore, it's probably safe to say that if you make your practices fun and gamelike, your athletes will be more motivated than if practices are dull, repetitive, and boring.

Most athletes choose to participate in sport to have fun.

Athletes' motivation is influenced by both personal factors (e.g., personality, goals, interests) and situational factors (e.g., the coach, teammates, level of competition). The available research suggests that the main reasons young athletes participate in sport are to improve their skills, be with their friends, develop fitness, achieve success, experience a challenge, and have fun.

You should also expect different athletes to be motivated by different things and the same athlete to be motivated by different things from time to time. For example, personal achievement and improvements in performance might motivate one athlete, while competing with others might motivate another. In addition, the latter athlete might be more motivated if he thinks his opponent is someone he has a chance to defeat than if he thinks he has no chance to win.

As a coach you have more control over the situational factors that might influence your athletes' motivation than you do over the personal factors. To create an environment that adds to rather than detracts from athletes' motivation, find out as much as you can about what motivates each of your athletes. One way to do this is to observe what they like to do and what they don't. You might also ask your athletes to write down some reasons they want to be on your team or participate in the sport you coach. An example of a form you can use to obtain this information is shown in figure 2.3. Your observations and the athletes' responses to the first item on this form (Reasons I want to participate in this sport) should give you a pretty good idea of how to create practices that are challenging and fun.

It is also important to realize that an athlete's reasons for participating may not always be desirable. For example, an ice hockey player might be motivated to physically harm an opponent. With athletes like this you can use your influence to discourage the undesirable motive for participating and encourage the development of more desirable reasons (e.g., playing hard and clean). The best way to do this is by punishing behavior that is not appropriate and reinforcing behavior that is. For example, if a hockey player performs a dirty check during a practice or game he could be removed from the ice, but if the same player executes a clean check he could be given more playing time.

## Goals

Athletes' **goals** tell us a lot about what they would like to accomplish during their sport experience. To help them achieve their goals, it would be beneficial to have an idea of what your athletes' goals are. One way to find out is to ask them to complete the lower part of the form shown in figure 2.3. Chapter 6 talks more about the various types of goals athletes set for themselves, but for now here are some typical examples:

I'd like to improve my skills.

My goal is to be the best player I can be.

I want to become good enough to make the varsity team next year.

Once you have a sense of your athletes' goals, you can decide what types of practice experiences to provide for them and what forms of instructional assistance will be most helpful. In some cases you may need to encourage athletes to adjust their individual goals or think about how individual achievement will contribute to the team's success.

## Difficulties in Predicting Future Performance Success

The limited research examining the accuracy of coaches' predictions of athletes' success suggests that such predictions tend to be inaccurate. An athlete who shows promise at age 12 may or may not be one of the stars of the team when she reaches age 16.

Long-term predictions of an athlete's eventual performance success are problematic for a couple of reasons. For one thing, scientific evidence shows that the abilities required for successful performance during the mental stage of learning are not necessarily the ones that are important for success during the practice stage or the automatic stage. This is not surprising if you think again about the different characteristics of performers in the three stages of learning. Remember that learning in the mental stage is characterized by thinking and problem solving. Therefore, athletes who have more problem-solving ability will likely improve at a

# My Reasons for Participating in This Sport and Some Goals I'd Like to Achieve

People do things for different reasons. As your coach, I'm particularly interested in why you want to participate in the sport of _____.

Also, I would like to learn some goals you want to achieve this season. Please be as honest as possible. I will not share this information with anyone else but will use it to help you get the most out of your sport experience.

Name _____

## Reasons I want to participate in this sport:

1.

2.

3.

## Goals I would like to achieve this season:

1.

2.

3.

FIGURE 2.3 Use this questionnaire to learn the motivation and goals of your athletes.

From C.A. Wrisberg, 2007, *Sport skill instruction for coaches* (Champaign, IL: Human Kinetics).

faster rate and perform at a higher level during this stage than athletes who have lower levels of this ability. However, during the practice stage of learning where skill refinement occurs, athletes possessing higher levels of the physical and perceptual-motor abilities essential for task success may perform better than athletes possessing lower levels of those abilities. This shift in the abilities essential for performance success at different learning stages may be one reason Michael Jordan was cut from his high school basketball team yet eventually became one of the best players ever. And if you consider how athletes' goals can change at different times,

predictions of future success become even more problematic.

Instead of trying to guess which athletes will eventually be the best, it would be better to spend your energy providing the kind of coaching assistance that will help all of them develop their technical and tactical skills to the greatest extent possible. Regardless of their abilities, capabilities, age, previous experience, stage of learning, goals, and motivation, you can help your athletes the most by first getting to know as much about them as possible and then tailoring your instructions and feedback to meet the needs of each athlete.

# SUMMARY

1. Individual differences refer to the experiences and characteristics different athletes bring with them to the sport situation.
2. Athletes can differ with respect to their cultural and social background as well as their personal characteristics.
3. Depending on the demands of the task or sport to be learned, some background factors and personal characteristics may benefit athletes' performance more than others.
4. By identifying differences in the experiences and characteristics of athletes, you will be able to design practice activities that meet the needs of all participants.
5. Abilities are personal characteristics that are, for the most part, genetically determined.
6. Capabilities are like abilities except that capabilities can be improved with practice, while abilities remain relatively fixed over time.
7. Each athlete possesses a dominant pattern of abilities, with some abilities being stronger than others.
8. Depending on the athlete's dominant pattern of abilities, he or she has the potential to be more successful in some tasks than in others.
9. Although age can influence a person's potential for performance success, athletes of the same age can be considerably different with respect to maturational level, previous experience, stage of learning, goals, and motivation.
10. In the mental stage of learning, athletes are trying to get a general idea of the task or technique (i.e., figuring out what to do), and they make a lot of mistakes in the process.
11. Athletes in the practice stage of learning are attempting to refine their technique and adapt it to the demands of different situations.
12. Athletes in the automatic stage of learning are able to demonstrate high levels of accuracy, consistency, and efficiency of movement in a variety of competitive situations.
13. Athletes' motivation indicates something about the reasons they choose to participate in sport, play with different levels of enthusiasm, and continue playing rather than quitting.
14. Athletes' goals identify the outcomes they hope to achieve as a result of their participation.
15. Long-term predictions of performance success are difficult because the abilities that are important for success often change from the mental stage of learning to the more advanced stages.

# KEY TERMS

| | | |
|---|---|---|
| abilities | learning style | skill |
| automatic stage | mental stage | specificity hypothesis |
| capabilities | motivation | stages of learning |
| goals | practice stage | |
| individual differences | principle of specificity of training | |

# REVIEW QUESTIONS

1. Why is it important for you as a coach to understand the concept of individual differences?

2. What are two capabilities that can be improved with practice or training?

3. How might you determine the dominant abilities of different athletes?

4. Why should you consider athletes' previous experience, stage of learning, and goals, in addition to their age, when designing practices?

5. What are some observable behaviors you should expect to see from athletes in each of the three stages of learning?

6. Why is it important for you as a coach to know something about what motivates each of your athletes?

7. What are some goals you might expect an athlete to set if he or she is motivated to achieve success?

8. Why should you resist the temptation to predict which of your athletes will eventually achieve the greatest performance success?

# PRACTICAL ACTIVITIES

1. Describe one task or position from the sport that you coach (e.g., a point guard in basketball); list the abilities from figure 2.1 on pages 18 to 19 that you think are important for successful performance.

2. Observe two of your athletes, and list the dominant abilities of each.

3. Indicate which athlete you believe is better suited ability-wise for success on the task or position you described in activity 1 and explain why. Then discuss one or two activities the other athlete might practice in order to overcome an ability disadvantage and improve performance.

# PART II

# Skills Your Athletes Need

Regardless of the sport you coach, your athletes will need to develop technical, tactical, and mental skills to maximize their chances of success in competition. Technical skills are the fundamental movements of the sport, such as batting and pitching in baseball or softball, blocking and tackling in football or soccer, and serving and volleying in tennis or volleyball. Tactical skills are the plans and strategies athletes need in order to gain a competitive advantage over their opponents. Mental skills are the techniques athletes use to maintain their poise and concentration when the game is on the line. In part II, you'll learn how to classify the fundamental characteristics of technical skills, which will help you determine which ones to emphasize when teaching your athletes. You'll also learn how to help your athletes interpret the environment, prepare for a particular opponent, and improve their decision making in competition. Finally, you'll learn about the relationship between arousal, attention, and performance so you can help your athletes stay focused and in control of their emotions when performing under pressure.

# 3

# *Technical Skills*

## When you finish reading this chapter, you should be able to explain

1. the concept of technical skills, including the differences between *technique* and *skill,* and the definitions of technical skills, tactical skills, and mental skills;
2. different ways in which technical skills can be classified; and
3. the principle of speed–accuracy trade-off.

Chapter 2 examined some of the characteristics of athletes that can influence the way they perform and learn skills. This chapter takes a closer look at the skills themselves, in particular those referred to as technical skills. Movement scientists have used several approaches to classify technical skills. For each approach, a particular skill dimension will be examined, with some concrete examples to illustrate how that dimension is crucial for successful task performance. After that, you'll learn about the important trade-off between speed and accuracy that athletes must be able to manage when they perform certain kinds of technical skills.

## What Are Technical Skills?

In chapter 2, you learned the differences between abilities, capabilities, and skill. Abilities are genetically determined characteristics of individuals that are relatively permanent and not influenced that much by practice (e.g., reaction time). Capabilities are similar to abilities but, unlike abilities, they can be improved with practice or training (e.g., increases in strength and flexibility). **Skill**, on the other hand, is an indicator of one's current level of proficiency on a given task and represents a combination of the athlete's abilities, capabilities, and practice or experience with the task.

The word *skill* can also be used to describe a particular task or behavior. For example, water skiing, discus throwing, volleyball spiking, and baseball batting are all skills. Although it may be tempting to substitute *task* or *technique* for *skill*, there are a couple of important reasons not to do this. First, the word *skill* suggests a level of proficiency that isn't assumed for the words *task* and *technique*. The skill of passing a football implies that the performer is pretty good at passing under a wide range of conditions. On the other hand, the task or technique of passing deals more with the mechanics any person might use to produce a passing movement. Therefore, in this chapter and throughout the remainder of the book, the word *skill* will be used to describe the execution of a task in a proficient manner. Chapters 3, 4, and 5 take a closer look at three

different categories of skill: technical, tactical, and mental.

**Technical skills** require the effective execution of a particular movement technique, such as serving a tennis ball, rebounding a basketball, or performing a dismount from a high bar. **Tactical skills** refer to the kinds of decision making that enable athletes to gain an advantage over their opponents. **Mental skills** involve the effective mobilization of the thoughts and feelings athletes need in order to remain poised and confident while executing their technical and tactical skills.

This chapter talks about some of the dimensions of technical skills. Chapters 4 and 5 examine the important characteristics of tactical and mental skills, respectively. By knowing more about the various technical, tactical, and mental skills necessary for your sport, you should be able to create practice experiences that enable your athletes to improve those skills and, in so doing, enhance their prospects for successful performance in a variety of competitive situations.

## Classifications of Technical Skills

This section explains some of the ways movement scientists have classified technical skills. Specifically, we'll look at dimensions dealing with the mental and physical components of skills, the structure of skills, the stability of the environment in which skills are performed, and the way athletes use feedback to control their movements when performing different types of technical skills.

### Cognitive and Motor Components

One way to look at technical skills is to consider the amount of thinking that is necessary to perform the skill successfully. Some skills require relatively more thought than other skills do. For example, a gymnastics floor exercise follows a particular sequence of required and optional elements. The gymnast needs to have a clear idea of the progression of the elements she is going to perform and must remember the details of that sequence throughout the routine. Other sport skills are performed with relatively little thought (e.g., running, catching, skating, cycling, dribbling a basketball).

Notice that in the preceding sentence the word *relatively* describes the **cognitive components** (or mental demands) of skills. Most technical skills have a cognitive component, but the amount depends on the type of skill. Therefore, it's a good idea to consider the relative involvement of cognitive components and **motor components** (or movement demands) rather than the presence or absence of either one (i.e., a skill might involve a *relatively* greater emphasis on thinking than on doing). The mental demands of many technical skills diminish as athletes progress from one stage of learning to the next (discussed in chapter 2). That is, the amount of thinking required for successful performance is relatively greater during the mental stage of learning than during the practice or automatic stage. During the mental stage, swimmers learning the freestyle need to think about hand position, the flutter kick, and the synchronization of breathing, arm, and foot movements. Basketball players learning the jump shot have to think about holding the ball properly, squaring the shoulders to the target, timing the release of the ball to the peak of their jump, and following through. Baseball and softball batters need to think about the grip, stance, stride, and swing.

A good way to help athletes learn technical skills with a heavy cognitive component is to tell them to focus on just one part of the skill until they begin to feel comfortable with it (e.g., just the flutter kick, just the release of the basketball, just the stride) then move to another part (e.g., arm and breathing movements) or perhaps combine the first part with a second (e.g., the jump with the release of the ball, the stride with the swing). Part practice, which is discussed further in chapter 7, is a good way to reduce the mental demands of technical skills, particularly during the early stage of learning.

Other examples of skills with a substantial cognitive component are those requiring technical precision (e.g., springboard diving, figure skating, gymnastics) or a complex strategy (e.g., wrestling, tennis). Even advanced performers in those activities need to devote some thought to skill execution, either before or during performance. When coaching athletes who perform precise technical skills, you need to devote more time to skill analysis (e.g., perhaps using video) and to the planning of an effective "blueprint" for execution. For example, the diver might identify several components of a particular dive that represent the keys to successful execution. That way the athlete will have a good idea of what he should concentrate on during practice and in competition. When helping athletes in sports requiring more complex strategies, it is important to spend some time discussing the tendencies of different opponents and the possible strategies for maximizing performance against those opponents. Creating practice situations that simulate some of the possible situations that might arise in competition is a good way to help athletes prepare strategies for those situations and produce appropriate movements with little or no thought.

Athletes who perform technical skills with minimal mental demands don't need to devote much attention to the mechanics of the movement. Instead, they can focus on the desired outcome or feel of the movement. A basketball player shooting free throws might imagine the sight of the ball swishing through the basket and the feel of a smooth, fluid follow-through.

In summary, you should consider the following guidelines when helping athletes learn technical skills that require various amounts of cognitive and motor activity:

- For skills with a substantial mental component, emphasize the importance of skill analysis, effective strategy, attention to important environmental information, and advance planning. Examples include using video analysis of correct form in a gymnastics event, pointing out some simple focus cues for a pole-vaulter, directing a soccer goalie's attention to the movements of opposing players in order to enhance the goalie's response preparation, and helping a baseball pitcher develop a prepitch mental routine (see chapter 5).

- For skills with a greater motor component, emphasize the importance of the desired outcome and the feel of the movement. Examples include instructing a volleyball player to identify the target for a spike and then execute (and feel) the movement that produces the spike or helping a gymnast picture successful execution of a particular element and then perform (and feel) the appropriate action.

## Discrete, Serial, or Continuous Structure

Another useful way of classifying skills is with respect to the structure of the movement itself. Movements that have a defined beginning and ending point and that are produced in a very brief time frame are termed **discrete skills**. Examples of discrete skills include most throwing, kicking, striking, and jumping movements. When helping athletes perform discrete skills, it is important to emphasize the desired outcome and no more than one focus cue at a time. You might remind a softball pitcher to hit the catcher's glove (desired outcome) and to focus on her release point. Similarly, you could instruct a placekicker to make solid contact with the bottom half of the football (desired outcome) and to focus on a smooth leg action.

Skills that combine a sequence of discrete movements executed in a specific order are called **serial skills**. Sport examples of serial skills include the sequence of catching, pivoting, and throwing movements used by a shortstop during a double play and the sequence of discrete tumbling skills performed by a gymnast during a floor exercise. To help athletes develop their serial skills, emphasize the principle of one component at a time (e.g., catch the ball before pivoting, and pivot before throwing) while also encouraging them to begin preparing for the next skill in the sequence (e.g., catch the ball with the desired pivot in mind). That way, athletes are more likely to perform each skill cleanly while also making the transitions between skills quickly and smoothly. Here again, part practice of two adjoining skills (e.g., catching and pivoting) might be helpful until athletes are able to execute each skill and the transition between the skills. Once athletes are able to do this, they can add the next transition and skill in the sequence (i.e., catching to pivoting to throwing). Progressive part practice (or segmentation) techniques such as this are discussed in more detail in chapter 7.

Discrete skills such as a golf swing are characterized by their rather distinct beginning and ending points.

Serial skills such as the triple jump in track and field involve a structured sequence of discrete skills performed in a specific order.

Continuous skills are repetitive actions usually performed in a rhythmic fashion.

A third category of movement structure deals with actions that are repeated over and over in a rhythmic fashion and have no obvious beginning or ending point. These movements are called **continuous skills.** Performers can choose to begin or end the movement at any time during the repetitive cycle. Occasionally, an external object such as a wall at the end of a swimming lane dictates the end of the movement cycle. Sport examples include most running, cycling, skating, and swimming activities. Perhaps the most helpful assistance you can provide for athletes performing and learning continuous skills is to encourage them to focus on the rhythm they are trying to produce. If they can identify the rhythm of a song that matches the rhythm they want to achieve, they might sing that song to themselves as they practice. Sometimes athletes can identify focus cues for generating the desired rhythm. For example, during a recent regatta in the city where I live, the winning pair of rowers said they focused on the words *breathe* and *row* to achieve the rhythm they wanted to produce: "Breathe, row. . . . Breathe, row. . . . Breathe, row."

By now you may be thinking about the different ways the skills of your sport can be classified. If so, you are probably beginning to realize that at least some skills can be classified in several different ways. For example, the 110-meter hurdles event in track and field is a combination of discrete movements (the start and the hurdling action) and continuous movements (the running phase between the hurdles). Moreover, hurdling probably involves a greater mental demand than does running. In cases such as this, you will need to provide different types of instructional assistance for different aspects of the skill. You might instruct a hurdler to focus on exploding out of the blocks, achieving a rapid tempo and rhythm before and between hurdles, and anticipating and gliding over the hurdles.

Generally speaking, you should keep the following guidelines in mind when teaching discrete, serial, and continuous skills:

• For discrete skills, emphasize the desired outcome using only one or two focus cues. Examples include a smooth ball drop and acceleration of the kicking leg for a football punt, a high reach and a snap of the wrist for a tennis serve, and a smooth stride and swing for batting.

• For serial skills, emphasize the execution of one discrete skill at a time as well as smooth transitions between the skills. Examples include a solid pole plant, arm pull, and hip rotation in the pole vault or the setup, weight transfer, and ball contact in the overhead smash in tennis.

• For continuous skills, emphasize the preferred tempo or rhythm of the repetitive action. Examples include the arm and leg action of long-distance freestyle swimming or running.

## Closed and Open Environments

A third way to classify skills is according to the relative stability of the environment in which the skills are performed. Most performance environments are neither completely stable nor completely unstable. Instead, they vary in stability. Skills performed in relatively predictable and stable environments that allow athletes ample time to prepare their movements are called **closed skills.** The volleyball serve is generally considered a closed skill because the server has all the information necessary to determine the appropriate movement and has sufficient time to

Open skills require athletes to interpret and respond to an unpredictable or changing environment, often in a brief period of time.

plan the action. Even in beach volleyball where there are environmental influences (e.g., wind) not present in a gymnasium, the server still has time to consider those influences (i.e., allow for the wind) before hitting the serve.

At the other end of the stability continuum are **open skills.** These skills are performed in changing, moving, or unpredictable environments. Open skills often require performers to alter their movements—sometimes very quickly—according to variable properties of the environment. A linebacker in football, for example, must be able to quickly adjust to the movements of an approaching running back.

Another way to think about environmental stability is to consider the extent to which the sport environment waits to be acted upon during skill performance. From this perspective, golf is considered a relatively closed skill even though players must produce different types of shots. At the moment of performance (i.e., the swing), the environment waits to be acted upon (i.e., the ball lies motionless). On the other hand, hitting a baseball is classified as a relatively open skill because it is performed in an environment that dictates the batter's action. That is, a moving ball dictates the decision to swing as well as any adjustments that are made during the swing.

Compared with closed skills, open skills contain a wider range of demands because they

require athletes to quickly interpret a changing environment before selecting and executing their actions. A quarterback must be able to recognize whether a receiver downfield is open or covered before attempting to throw the ball his way. Similarly, a second base player must recognize the way a baserunner is approaching before deciding which type of pivot to use in executing a double play. When helping your athletes learn open skills, you should include practice experiences that challenge them to recognize important environmental cues and adapt their movements as needed. For example, the quarterback's recognition and decision-making skill could be improved by having him attempt passes against various types of defenses. In each case, his goal would be to determine whether the primary receiver is open, and if not, deliver the pass to an open secondary receiver or take a sack. Similarly, the infielder could practice against baserunners approaching the base in a variety of ways in order to improve her skill of selecting and executing the type of pivot that would allow her to elude the baserunner and make a successful throw to first.

Generally, it's a good idea to keep the following guidelines in mind when teaching closed and open skills:

• For closed skills, emphasize the key movement elements and the consistency of movement production. Examples include providing focus cues for athletes practicing movements such as field events in track (e.g., high jump, long jump, discus, shot put, hammer throw, pole vault, javelin), the serve in tennis and volleyball, the corner kick in soccer, and the free throw shot in basketball. In each case, pay particular attention to the anticipated outcome and the correct execution of key movement elements.

• For open skills, emphasize key environmental cues and the flexibility of movement production. Examples include a volleyball player practicing against different defensive formations and deciding which type of spike is most appropriate for each formation or a soccer goalie experiencing different attacking patterns and selecting and executing the most appropriate response to a shot (e.g., catch the ball, deflect the ball, or let the ball go out of play).

## Closed-Loop and Open-Loop Control

Still another system for classifying skills involves how performers use sensory feedback to initiate and regulate their movements. As you will learn in the next chapter, processing sensory information takes time. Therefore, whenever athletes have sufficient time to process such information, they can use it to control their movements. Scientists refer to this type of control as **closed-loop control** because the feedback that arises from the action can be used for adjustment purposes. It's like the type of control a driver uses when she sees her car drifting toward the right shoulder of the road and then makes a corrective steering movement to bring it back into its proper lane.

Open-loop control is needed to produce brief, rapid movements such as a tennis volley.

Some movements, however, are performed so quickly that athletes do not have enough time to use feedback to correct them. Scientists call the control needed for these types of movements **open-loop control** because once the movement is started, it must be produced without any additional adjustments. Sport movements that are controlled this way include those that last less than 200 milliseconds (i.e., one fifth of a second), such as a rapid bat swing in baseball or softball, the downswing during a golf tee shot, and the exchange from one bar to the other during a gymnastics routine on the uneven bars.

It's very likely that the technical skills in your sport are controlled using a combination of both types of control. The backswing in a golf shot is slow enough to allow for closed-loop control, but the downswing is probably too rapid to be controlled this way. The main thing to remember when determining which type of control your athletes will be using for a movement is the time it takes to complete the action. If it is very brief, athletes will not be able to use feedback to make any adjustments once they start the movement. Therefore, any corrections must be made on the next attempt. This means you will need to emphasize the importance of accurate anticipation, preparation, and execution in order to promote successful goal achievement. For example, a volleyball player needs to see the ball coming off the opposing hitter's hand in order to have the time to decide whether to respond and how to execute the desired response (e.g., dig, pass).

In most cases, you will need to estimate the extent to which your athletes will be able to use feedback to control their movements, unless you have the benefit of sophisticated timing devices. A figure skater probably has enough time to use feedback, such as the feel of her body and her location on the ice, to maintain proper balance and move toward an optimal position for executing each of the elements of her routine. However, certain rapid components of the routine (e.g., a double Lutz) need to be planned in advance and executed with little or no feedback adjustments. This is also the case for the quarterback who must plan his forward passes in advance (i.e., desired target, force required, release point) because he will not have much opportunity to make an adjustment once he begins the throwing movement.

Closed-loop control and open-loop control are possible in either a closed or open environment. A golfer operating in a relatively closed environment would use closed-loop control during the backswing, while a runner in a relay race (i.e., a relatively open environment) would use closed-loop control to position her hand for an accurate baton exchange. Examples of open-loop control in a relatively closed environment include the throwing action of a baseball or softball pitcher and the hitting action of a tennis player executing a serve. Open-loop control in an open environment would be used for a tennis volley and by a linebacker tackling a runner in an open field. It's important to identify which aspects of your athletes' performance require closed-loop and open-loop control so you can direct their attention to the sources of feedback necessary for adjusting their movements (in the case of closed-loop control) or to the factors they need to consider before initiating their movements (in the case of open-loop control).

In summary, then, you should consider the following guidelines when teaching athletes technical skills that are controlled in a closed-loop or open-loop fashion:

- For skills requiring closed-loop control, emphasize the importance of both internal and external feedback (e.g., the feel of the movement and the look of the environment), and encourage athletes to use this information to adjust their movements. A javelin thrower might use vision of the approaching foul line to practice adjusting the degree of shoulder extension before beginning the forward throwing motion, or a basketball player might use the feel associated with different degrees of knee bend to determine the one that promotes successful execution of the free throw shot.

- For skills requiring open-loop control, emphasize the advance planning of the entire movement (i.e., desired outcome, force, spatial pattern, and so on) to promote successful execution. A soccer player should practice deciding the appropriate force, trajectory, and direction of different types of throw-in passes before initiating the action. In an open environment, advance planning should be based on a careful reading of the situation. A defensive back in

## *Advantages of Motor Programs*

In many sports, athletes perform brief, rapid movements lasting less than a quarter of a second (e.g., hitting a tennis ball, kicking a football, shooting a hockey puck). Since these kinds of movements can't be corrected once they are initiated, performers need to have a clear idea of what they want to do before they begin the movement. Scientists refer to this type of control as open-loop control. One way athletes are able to control movements such as these is by using some sort of **motor program**—like a blueprint in the brain—that contains all the necessary details of the action, such as the order and timing of muscle contractions. According to motor program theory, performers are capable of developing general action blueprints that can be modified to meet the requirements of different situations. In a three-on-two fast break in basketball, for example, the attacking players may pass the ball to each other in a number of ways (e.g., chest pass, bounce pass, tip pass). Once a player decides what type of pass to make, he adjusts the details of the passing blueprint (e.g., force, release point, hand preference) and runs the program without interruption. Since the passer won't be adjusting the movement once he commits to it, he doesn't have to devote any attention to the mechanics of the pass while it's in progress. Therefore, he is able to not only produce the chosen pass smoothly and with little effort but also focus all his attention on the intended target (i.e., the anticipated position of the teammate receiving the pass).

football needs to read the movements of the approaching receiver as well as the path of the ball in order to determine how to break up the pass or intercept it.

## Speed–Accuracy Trade-Off

If you've coached for any length of time, you know there is a delicate balance between the speed and accuracy of skillful performance. When athletes are performing at their best, they seem to be moving at speeds that allow them to achieve maximum effectiveness without sacrificing accuracy. However, when they're not performing at their best, athletes can appear to be "out of control" or needing to slow down and "let the game come to them." For years, scientists have studied the relationship between speed and accuracy; they have found that the **speed–accuracy trade-off** is one of the most important principles of movement performance. Put simply, for any skill requiring both speed and accuracy, increases in speed are usually accompanied by decreases in accuracy, and vice versa.

Although the scientific literature mentions various versions of the speed–accuracy trade-off, the one that seems the most applicable to sport situations is when athletes attempt brief, rapid movements that must be performed with some degree of accuracy. A volleyball kill shot or overhead smash in tennis must be produced with an action that is forceful yet controlled enough to keep the ball within the boundaries of the opponent's court. Similarly, a gymnast must produce a rapid sequence of accurate hand movements during a pommel horse routine. For tasks such as these, available research suggests that as the speed of the movement is increased, spatial accuracy (i.e., the position of the hand or racket head as it enters the hitting area or the position of the gymnast's hands on the pommel horse) decreases. Only for very forceful actions, exceeding 80 percent of a person's maximal force, is spatial accuracy not diminished by further increases in speed. In those cases, athletes may actually be able to perform very rapid movements (i.e., in excess of 80 percent maximal force) more accurately than they do moderately

rapid ones (i.e., those produced with 40 to 60 percent of maximal force).

Since force seems to be an important factor in the speed–accuracy equation, you might try to think of situations when you should encourage athletes to produce their movements at near-maximal speeds. A baseball or softball batter who delays the start of the swing and produces it with greater speed (or force) would get the benefit of being able to watch the pitch longer before starting the swing yet would be just as likely to make solid contact with the ball as with a slightly slower swing.

Any time better performance is the result of movements being performed faster while still preserving accuracy, athletes should emphasize the speed of the movement. Examples include the long jump and triple jump in track and field; ground strokes and volleys in tennis; form tackles, hitting the hole (running backs), and long field goal kicks in football; long tee shots in golf; long throws by infielders and outfielders in baseball and softball; and shots on goal by soccer and hockey players.

When better performance is associated with faster speeds, athletes should focus on speed rather than accuracy.

For most tasks where better performance isn't necessarily associated with faster movements, athletes will need to experiment with different speeds or forces to determine the feel of the one that accompanies their best, and most accurate, performance. For example, a soccer player or football quarterback delivering a pass to a teammate must identify the force that produces the most rapid ball speed without overpowering the teammate.

In summary, then, you should keep the following speed–accuracy guidelines in mind when teaching athletes technical skills that require a combination of both factors:

- For skills emphasizing both speed and accuracy for goal achievement (e.g., passing a ball to a teammate), provide practice opportunities that allow athletes to identify the maximal speed or force of their movements that does not exceed accuracy requirements.

- For skills that allow near-maximal force production (e.g., baseball batting), encourage athletes to produce the movement with near-maximal force in order to optimize both the speed and accuracy of the action.

# SUMMARY

1. The word *skill* presumes the effective execution of a movement and thus differs from the words *task* and *technique,* which refer more to the mechanical features of the movement.

2. Technical skills refer to the effective execution of a movement technique or task.

3. Tactical skills require effective decision making that gives athletes an advantage over their opponents.

4. Mental skills involve the effective mobilization of the thoughts and feelings athletes need in order to remain poised and confident while executing their technical and tactical skills.

5. Technical skills can be classified along several dimensions, including the relative importance of the mental and physical components of the movement, the structure of the movement (e.g., distinctiveness of beginning and ending points, repetitiveness of the action, degree of sequencing), the stability of the environment in which the movement is performed, and the extent to which performers can use feedback to control their movements once they begin them.

6. Cognitive components of skills include strategies and other thought processes. Motor components involve various aspects of muscular activity and the feel of the movement.

7. Discrete skills are movements that have a distinct beginning and ending point (e.g., a golf swing). Serial skills are those made up of an ordered sequence of discrete skills (e.g., hop, step, jump). Continuous skills consist of repetitive and often rhythmical actions (e.g., swimming).

8. A closed environment is one that is stable and waiting to be acted upon (e.g., a golf course or swimming pool). Closed-skill performers usually are able to prepare their movements in advance without much time pressure.

9. An open environment is one that is relatively unpredictable. Open-skill performers must be able to respond to moving objects or changing events and adapt their actions in appropriate ways, often in brief periods of time (e.g., playing a tennis point).

10. Closed-loop control is possible whenever performers have the time to use feedback to adjust their movements (e.g., swimming laps, fielding a slow ground ball). Open-loop control is used for rapid actions that are planned in advance and carried out without the influence of feedback (e.g., a fast bat swing in softball).

11. For some tasks, athletes can develop general movement plans, or motor programs, to use when controlling rapid movements.

12. An important principle of movement performance is the speed–accuracy trade-off, which states that increases in movement speed are usually accompanied by decreases in accuracy, and vice versa.

13. One exception to the principle of speed–accuracy trade-off occurs when performers produce brief, rapid movements (e.g., an extremely fast bat swing or long field goal kick) that are performed at near-maximal force. In such cases, spatial accuracy does not diminish as speed or force is increased further.

# KEY TERMS

| | | |
|---|---|---|
| closed-loop control | mental skills | principle of speed–accuracy trade-off |
| closed skills | motor components | serial skills |
| cognitive components | motor programs | skill |
| continuous skills | open-loop control | tactical skills |
| discrete skills | open skills | technical skills |

# REVIEW QUESTIONS

1. How would you recognize an athlete's level of technical skill, keeping in mind the difference between technique and skill?

2. How would you explain the difference between tactical skills and mental skills? Give an example of each from your sport.

3. How is the demand different for athletes performing technical skills in an open environment and in a closed environment? Give an example of each type of skill in your sport.

4. What are some skills in your sport that athletes might control using a motor program?

5. How might an athlete adapt a flexible motor program from one movement attempt to the next when performing a closed skill? How might an athlete do this when performing an open skill?

6. What are some skills in your sport that have a speed–accuracy trade-off?

7. Which of the skills you identified in the previous question might athletes eventually perform better by emphasizing speed rather than accuracy when producing the movement?

# PRACTICAL ACTIVITIES

1. Give an example that illustrates effective execution of technical skill, tactical skill, and mental skill in a single athletic performance. For example, a basketball player shooting a contested reverse layup might demonstrate technical skill by taking off using the correct foot and by achieving full extension of the shooting arm, tactical skill by using the rim to prevent the defender from blocking the shot, and mental skill by maintaining a relaxed focus on the target.

**2.** Give three examples that illustrate how you might use your knowledge of several of the following dimensions of technical skills to create practice experiences that are beneficial for your athletes.

    **a.** The relative importance of mental activity (e.g., analysis, planning, feedback processing)

    **b.** The structure of the skill (i.e., discrete, serial, continuous, combined)

    **c.** The predictability of the environment (i.e., closed, open, combined)

    **d.** The type of control needed to perform the skill (i.e., closed loop, open loop, combination of the two)

**3.** Describe three situations in your sport (or another you are familiar with) where the principle of speed–accuracy trade-off might be an important consideration. For each situation, explain how you would use your knowledge of the principle to help athletes improve their performance.

# 4

# *Tactical Skills*

**When you finish reading this chapter, you should be able to explain**

1. the concept of tactical skills, including three categories of information athletes must process to perform effectively;
2. how you can help your athletes identify the tactical skills they need; and
3. how you can help them develop their tactical skills.

Chapter 3 talked about technical skills, the first of the three major categories of skills your athletes need to learn in order to perform well on a consistent basis. In this chapter, we'll look at the second important skill category your athletes need to develop to perform effectively: tactical skills. **Tactical skills** involve the decision-making aspects of the competitive situation. To provide a foundation for our discussion, the concept of information processing is presented first. Here you will learn that the three processing requirements for most types of sport are (1) the interpretation of the environment, (2) a decision about what to do, and (3) the execution of the most effective movement. Some sports require performers to successfully handle all three of these requirements, while others involve the processing of only one or two. Since athletes in some sports must be able

to process information in a very short period of time, the chapter also discusses some ways you can help them identify the tactical skills they need. Finally, you'll learn some ways to help your athletes develop these skills so they will be able to perform at their best in competition.

## Understanding Tactical Skills

A simple way to conceptualize tactical skills is to consider the types of information athletes must process in order to achieve their goals. According to the theory of **information processing**, athletes must process three categories of information in order to perform effectively: information in the environment, information affecting the decision about what to do, and information concerning how to do it. As shown in figure 4.1,

FIGURE 4.1    Effective information processing often involves (a) an accurate interpretation of the environment, (b) a decision about which of several possible responses to select, and (c) the execution of the selected action.

these three categories provide athletes with the information they need in order to answer the following questions:

- What is going on in the environment?
- What should I do about it?
- How should I do it?

First we will discuss each of these elements, and then we will look at several types of questions you can use during practice situations to help your athletes learn to process information quickly and effectively.

## Interpreting the Environment

The first type of information athletes must process deals with the current status or relevant aspects of the performance environment. To successfully interpret environmental information, athletes must use their vision, their hearing, and even the feeling of their bodies to obtain the necessary facts. A basketball player who is preparing to create an offensive play might hear instructions from the coach, observe the positioning of teammates and opponents, and feel the weight and texture of the ball in her hands. The athlete would also draw on her previous knowledge of the sport to interpret these sounds, sights, and feelings. Such knowledge includes the rules of the sport, an understanding of the strategy she has been taught for maximizing the effectiveness of her or the team's performance, and an appreciation of the nuances of the sport. For example, it would be helpful if the player knew that there is a shot clock, that her team has an offensive strategy that involves passing the ball to create an open shot, and that a zone defense is more difficult to penetrate than a person-to-person defense. The player would then use this knowledge to interpret the events going on in the environment. Once she does this, she needs to decide what she is going to do with that information.

## *Focal and Ambient Visual Systems*

Although many people view vision as a unitary system, it is actually made up of two systems—one that provides information for object identification and another that provides information for motor control. **Focal vision** is used whenever a person is consciously attempting to identify objects in the environment. This system spans a very narrow area at the center of the visual field, and its effectiveness is diminished when the lighting is poor. In short, the focal system allows performers to answer the question "What is it?" A second visual system, referred to as **ambient vision,** allows performers to detect the motion of objects in the environment as well as to determine their own position relative to those objects. This system spans the entire visual field, operates in a nonconscious fashion, and is relatively unaffected by conditions of poor lighting. Put simply, the ambient system provides performers with answers to the questions "Where is it?" and "Where am I in relation to it?" Researchers have discovered that ambient vision produces an "optical flow" across the retina of the eye that allows performers to perceive motion, position, and timing. Specifically, ambient vision provides people with information about the stability and balance of their movements, the speed at which they are moving, the direction in which they are moving, the movements of other objects in the environment, and the time it will take for them to make contact with objects that are either stationary or moving.

To illustrate how an athlete might utilize the two visual systems in a competitive sport setting, consider the task of a soccer goalie attempting to block an opponent's shot. The goalie would use focal vision to identify teammates and opponents and would use ambient vision to maintain proper balance, detect the movements of others, estimate how rapidly opponents are approaching the goal, and when the shot is taken, estimate its speed and time of arrival.

## Deciding What to Do

Once performers have interpreted the environment, they must select an appropriate action. Not surprisingly, experienced players are able to do this more rapidly and accurately than beginners because they have come to learn which responses are more successful for different sets of circumstances. More experienced athletes also have a better knowledge of their sport and of their own capabilities, thus allowing them to select the most appropriate option from among several possibilities. In the case of the aforementioned basketball player, an appropriate response might be to execute a head fake, penetrate the zone in order to draw defenders toward her, and then pass the ball to an open teammate for a jump shot. Once the player makes this decision, she must be able to execute the various movements necessary to achieve the desired goal.

## Determining How to Do It

The challenge of movement production includes organizing the motor system in such a way that the proper muscles are activated and the desired levels of force and timing are produced. For the basketball player, this might involve the following sequence: an up-and-down movement of the

head, a left-handed dribble penetration, and a one-hand bounce pass to the open teammate. Again, the more knowledge and experience the player has, the less attention she needs to devote to producing this movement sequence.

The extent to which the end result of all this processing is successful depends on how effectively the basketball player handles the information she encounters in each of the three stages. If the player accurately interprets all the relevant environmental information, chooses an appropriate response, and produces the movement in an effective fashion, the result will most likely be a successful pass. However, if she misinterprets the environment (e.g., doesn't notice the position of an opposing defender), selects an inappropriate response (e.g., decides to dribble into the heart of the zone and then shoot or perhaps pass to a teammate who is not open), or is unable to produce the action (e.g., loses control of the dribble because she has not achieved a sufficient level of technical skill with the left hand), the end result may be a blocked shot, an errant pass, or a loss of possession of the ball.

## Asking Timely Questions

When teaching your athletes tactical skills, it's a good idea to "put the ball in their court" occasionally by asking questions that make them think about the various types of information they should be looking for or considering when performing. When doing this, keep in mind the three categories of information processing that athletes are usually faced with: interpreting the environment, deciding what to do, and deciding how to do it.

### Interpreting the Environment Questions

Tennis players might be asked, "What are you looking for or noticing?" to determine how well they are interpreting an opponent's actions. The same question might be asked of soccer goalies, defensive play-

Selecting the most appropriate response in a particular situation is important for most types of tactical decisions.

© Associated Press

ers in football, volleyball players practicing their serve receive, baseball or softball batters, and basketball players working on a new person-to-person defense. The question might also be asked for a different reason of golfers, springboard divers, and football field goal kickers. For these athletes, environmental information is used to determine the most appropriate response for a particular situation. The golfer needs to observe the lie of the ball, the condition of the green, the placement of the pin, and the direction of the wind before deciding how to hit the most effective approach shot. The springboard diver needs to interpret the resistance of the board so she can make appropriate adjustments in board tension and in the force she needs to exert to achieve the desired leg drive for a particular dive. The field goal kicker needs to consider field and wind conditions to determine the best angle of approach to take for a particular kick.

### Deciding What to Do Questions

Athletes in every sport might be asked, "What are your options?" to determine how well they are able to generate appropriate solutions to a particular challenge. When facing a tough batter in an important situation, a baseball pitcher might decide that his options include going with his best pitch, using an assortment of pitches, or throwing all pitches just outside the strike zone. When asking athletes this type of question, it's a good idea to also ask them to provide some rationale for the option they think is the best at the time. For example, the pitcher might say he would prefer to challenge the batter with his best pitch if he believes that pitch is working particularly well that day. If he doesn't feel that way, the pitcher may say he prefers to mix up his pitches to keep the batter off balance or keep his pitches away from the middle of the plate in the hope that the batter will become impatient and chase a bad one.

### Determining How to Do It Questions

The purpose of this type of question is to find out what athletes are focusing on when it's time to produce their movements. In response to the question "How do you want to feel or be focused when performing?" the pitcher might say, "I want to feel in command and focused on the catcher's glove." The linebacker might say, "I want to match the intensity of the blocker and keep him away from my legs, read the hips of the ball carrier, and maintain balance in anticipation of the possible cut-back move." The swimmer might say, "I want to feel smooth and rhythmic, with my eyes focused on the approaching wall." When asking this question, make sure athletes tell you how they want to feel or focus rather than how they don't want to feel or focus (e.g., "I don't want my movement to feel jerky or to take my eyes off the ball"). When athletes think about *not* doing something, they tend to be more likely to do it. It's kind of like the problem a person has when instructed not to think about elephants. Suddenly that's all the person can think about.

## Asking Constructive Questions

When asking your athletes questions, be as constructive and positive as possible. Athletes should believe you are genuinely interested in their answers and in helping them get better at processing the various types of information they need in order to achieve success. If you are annoyed or upset with an athlete, hold the question, make a mental note of the situation, and discuss it with the athlete after taking a few deep breaths or after you have sufficiently calmed down. Also remember to expect less from younger or less experienced athletes than from older or more experienced ones. Regardless of your athletes' age level or experience, though, you can learn a lot about what they are paying attention to by simply asking them.

# Identifying Important Tactical Skills

To maximize your team's chances of success in competition, you need to be sure that each of your athletes knows what to do as well as how and when to do it. Athletes who have a good working knowledge of their sport and who can also accurately interpret environmental cues, prepare their responses in advance, and produce their movements more automatically are usually able to do the right things at the right time more quickly and effectively.

## Speeding Up the Processing of Information

Information processing takes time, but you can help your athletes improve their processing speed in several ways. The importance of sport-specific knowledge, strategy, and experience has already been mentioned. Another common practice of coaches and athletes in many sports is the scouting of an opponent. By watching an opponent perform under competitive conditions, athletes can observe the opponent's behaviors and movement tendencies. A basketball or football team might spend hours reviewing game video in order to detect predictable patterns in the behaviors of an upcoming opponent. By doing this, the team can focus on relevant cues to watch for when playing that opponent. Being able to anticipate the opponent's actions enables athletes to speed up their interpretation of the environment.

Once athletes have a good idea of what their opponent is likely to do, they can also speed up their decision making by reducing the number of possible responses. For example, a low post player in basketball who knows that the opposing player she will be guarding prefers a spin move when driving for the basket can prepare a response to thwart that move. Similarly, a defensive back who knows an opposing quarterback typically throws a quick out pattern on third down and short yardage situations can prepare a response that involves a rapid movement toward the sideline.

When it comes to how the movement should be performed, the best way to enhance processing speed is to practice the action as often as possible in situations that closely simulate the actual competitive environment. By having teammates simulate the movements of the offensive player and the quarterback mentioned previously, the low post player and defensive back could practice each of their responses to those movements, respectively. Once athletes are able to produce their movements more automatically, they can execute them quickly and accurately (i.e., "just do it") without needing to devote much processing time to the "how." Chapter 7 discusses a games approach to practicing skills that you can use to help your athletes improve their speed of information processing.

However, you can help your athletes speed up this learning process in several ways. To begin with, you might ask yourself the three questions posed in the previous section. If you were one of your athletes, how would *you* know what to look for in the environment, what to do, and how and when to do it in different situations? If you spend some time contemplating those questions, you will probably find at least three general categories of information your athletes need in order to develop their tactical skills: knowledge of the sport, understanding of team strategy, and awareness of variable factors.

### Knowledge of the Sport

When it comes to athletes doing the right things, there is little substitute for knowing as much as possible about their sport. **Tactical knowledge** can include everything from the rules of the sport to the ways of playing it to the impact of various types of environmental conditions on how the sport is played. For example, in the game of baseball, the infield fly rule states that when there are runners on first and second base or on first, second, and third base and fewer than two outs, a batter who hits a fly ball that can be caught by an infielder is automatically out, and baserunners may advance only at their own risk. A baserunner who knows this rule—and who is a fast runner, plays for a coach who likes runners to be aggressive on the bases, notices that the wind is swirling and that the ball will be difficult to catch, and knows that the infielder trying to catch the ball is not a good fielder and does not have a strong throwing arm—may try to score from third base if the fielder drops the fly ball. If the player doesn't know the infield fly rule or does not contemplate the other factors, he will not be as prepared to take tactical advantage of the situation.

## Team Strategy

Depending on your philosophy of coaching, you will have your own opinions as to the best ways to maximize your athletes' chances of success. The **team strategy** you come up with will depend on the skill level of your athletes and the anticipated strengths and weaknesses of your opponents. Athletes who have a clear understanding of their team's strategy will have a better sense of the kinds of tactical decisions that are consistent with that strategy. A soccer team with slower than average foot speed might have a team strategy that encourages players to maintain closer spacing in order to advance the ball by using shorter passes. If players understand that strategy, they will be less tempted to try long passes their teammates are unable to catch up to.

## Variable Factors

Tactical decisions do not occur in a vacuum but are always made within the context of a particular competition. That context usually varies from one competition to the next because of a number of factors, including the quality of the opponent, field conditions, weather conditions, time left in the game, and score differential. In tennis, it is not a good idea to hit lob shots on a windy day because the longer the ball is in the air, the more likely it will be blown out of bounds. Sometimes tactical decisions vary at different times within a single competition. In baseball, as the adage goes, the visiting team should play for the win when it is behind in the ninth inning, while the home team should play for the tie. Presumably, the reason the home team should play more conservatively is because it always bats last. Therefore, if the game goes into extra innings, the home team always has one more chance to tie or win the game should it fall behind.

## Helping Your Athletes Develop Their Tactical Skills

It has been said that "experience is knowledge acquired too late." As a coach you want to do all you can to speed up your athletes' learning of tactical skills rather than wait for them to learn by experience. The best way to do this is by exposing them to information and experiences

Sometimes variable factors such as weather conditions must be considered when making tactical decisions.

that will enhance their decision-making capabilities. Pass on to your athletes the rules of the sport, a clear presentation of your own team strategy, an understanding of their individual roles on the team and their individual strengths and weaknesses, an understanding of the strengths and weaknesses of opponents, competition-like experiences during practices, and reminders of the keys to success before and during competitions.

## Teaching the Rules

Depending on the age and experience level of the athletes you coach, you may need to alert them to certain rules. Football players need to know that a kickoff fielded in the end zone does not have to be advanced. However, if the ball is advanced outside the goal line, it is in play. In addition to the formal rules of the sport, there may be informal rules you need to alert your athletes to before competitions. Wrestlers need to know that a referee might stop the match whenever he sees either wrestler venture outside the circle because the size of the apron is too small for safe combat. To help your athletes gain an understanding of the rules of your sport, you must obviously know the rules yourself as well as which ones your athletes may not be familiar with. Once you know which rules your athletes need to learn, you should both verbally explain them and physically demonstrate them as clearly as possible.

It's a good idea to simulate a situation in which the rule applies and then have several athletes demonstrate what should be done (or avoided) in each case. After your athletes have observed the demonstration and been allowed to ask questions, give them opportunities to experience the rule in competition-like practice situations. In softball and baseball, when there are fewer than two outs, baserunners need to be sure a batted ball contacts the ground before they attempt to advance. Players could strengthen their knowledge of this rule during batting practice by running to first base after they have completed their turn at bat and then gradually advancing around the bases as the subsequent players practice batting. Each time the next batter makes contact with the ball, the runner would wait until she sees it hit the ground

before advancing to the next base. If the batted ball were caught on the fly by an infielder, the runner would stay at first base.

## Presenting Your Team Strategy

The importance of devising a global strategy that maximizes the strengths of your athletes and minimizes their weaknesses was discussed earlier. Depending on the maturity of the athletes you work with, it is a good idea to obtain feedback from some of your players before sharing your strategy with the entire team. Once you and your team leaders have settled on a strategy you think the team can commit to, it is essential to present that strategy in as clear a fashion as possible and then reinforce it on a regular basis. In this way the strategy becomes your team's "identification badge." A team strategy might include components such as "swarming on defense" or "patience on offense." Once you've communicated the strategy to your athletes, remind them of the key ingredients at timely moments during practice sessions, or devise other tangible symbols, such as signs placed in the locker room that they will see on a regular basis. For example, if offensive players are experiencing frustration when running their plays during a football scrimmage, it would be a good time to remind them to "stay patient." Similarly, signs posted in the locker room that read "Stay patient" or "Victory goes to the team that is patient" can serve as tangible reminders of this strategy.

## Clarifying Individual Roles and Identifying Strengths and Weaknesses

Your athletes will have a better idea about the most appropriate tactical decisions they should make during competitions if each has a clear understanding of his or her role on the team and an appreciation of his or her individual strengths and weaknesses. You can clarify these issues in individual meetings between you (or perhaps an assistant coach) and each of your athletes. Be consistent in what you say and what you do by giving each of your athletes a role that conforms to his or her strengths. In addition, you can demonstrate a sincere desire to see your athletes improve by suggesting some ways each might work on specific weaknesses. A basketball player who demonstrates good vertical jumping ability but is not a particularly good shooter might be given a role that primarily involves rebounding and setting picks. Thus, this player's tactical decisions would primarily pertain to the various ways she might achieve effective rebounding position or set effective picks. However, you could also encourage the player to spend some extra time on her shooting and obtain additional coaching assistance to improve that technical skill.

## Identifying the Strengths and Weaknesses of Opponents

In some sports it is important for athletes to know something about each of their opponent's strengths and weaknesses. A basketball player would benefit from knowing that the person he will be guarding is left-handed, always likes to drive to his left, and doesn't dribble well with his right hand. In other sports, knowing something about an opponent's tendencies can eliminate some surprises an athlete might otherwise encounter when she faces the opponent in competition. A distance runner who knows that a particular opponent likes to sprint off the start line and take the lead during the first part of the race will be less likely to panic and lose her focus when the opponent does that during a track meet. By gaining knowledge about their opponents' tendencies in various types of situations, your athletes will be better able to anticipate the opponents' actions and prepare their responses in advance.

You can also provide valuable practice experiences by simulating the various actions of opponents and teaching your athletes the best ways to respond in each case. In the example of the basketball player, a left-handed teammate might simulate the moves of the upcoming opponent so that the player who will be guarding the opponent can develop an anticipation of those moves when he encounters them in a game. Similarly, a teammate of the distance runner might serve as a "rabbit" during a simulated race so that the runner can practice resisting the tendency to lose focus and to abandon her own race plan when she encounters an opponent's fast start during a track meet.

## Providing Competition-Like Experiences During Practice

As mentioned earlier, a games approach to practicing skills will be discussed in chapter 7. Basically, this approach is grounded in the notion that the best practice experiences place athletes in the kinds of situations they can expect to encounter during actual competitions. In the sport of soccer, for example, the center forwards, wingers, and halfbacks might practice various and random three-on-two scoring opportunities to test the quality of their tactical decisions about when to pass and when to shoot. Of all the ways you might help your athletes develop their tactical skills, using the games approach is the most productive.

## Emphasizing the Keys to Success

You can never emphasize the tactical keys to success too much with your athletes. Before each practice and competition, review each of the keys and emphasize again the important components of your team strategy. In addition,

Pat Head Summitt reminding Shanna Zolman of her roles and responsibilities for the next possession.

encourage your athletes by providing them with positive tactical reminders throughout the course of a competition. You might remind the batter who has struck out during his previous two times at bat because he tried to pull an outside pitch to "just hit the ball where it is pitched."

Tactical "keys" can pertain to general principles such as the one illustrated in the previous example or to specific decisions that are appropriate for particular situations. Pat Head Summitt, one of the most successful collegiate basketball coaches of the past 30 years, uses time-outs near the end of games to remind each player of her role and of the tactical options she will have during the upcoming possession. By periodically reminding your own athletes of the keys to success, you can greatly facilitate their development of tactical skills. Then when they find themselves in the midst of the most heated competitions, your athletes will be more likely to do what they have been practicing all along.

## Creating a Blueprint of Tactical Options

As Aristotle once said, "We are what we repeatedly do. Excellence, then, is not an act but a habit." In much the same way, there is no shortcut to the development of tactical skills. Rather, athletes develop those skills by repeat-

edly encountering tactical situations and doing the things that give them the best opportunity to achieve success. Table 4.1 contains a blueprint for developing specific tactical skills for a distance runner and a basketball team. You should use this type of blueprint or something like it to identify the tactical decisions your athletes will likely face in various competitive situations. Then you should incorporate those situations on a regular basis in your training sessions. Since the tactical options may be different for different athletes depending on their respective strengths and roles on the team, create tactical blueprints for each of your athletes as well as for the team as a whole.

By equipping your athletes with both the technical and tactical skills of your sport, you will enhance their chances of success (i.e., the appropriate and effective execution of technical skills in any and all situations) every time they compete. Notice that the emphasis here is on effective execution, not on winning the game, finishing first in the race, or beating an opponent. When it comes to tactical decisions, the only thing your athletes have control over is the choices they make at any given time. However, if their decisions are based on a clear understanding of the rules of the sport, a knowledge of team strategy, an awareness of their respective roles and capabilities as well as the capabilities of their opponents, and an appreciation of miscellaneous variable factors, they are more likely to make the right decisions.

TABLE 4.1

### Blueprint for Tactical Skill Development

| Situation | Relevant knowledge | Options available |
|---|---|---|
| Middle segment of 1,500 m run | Runner's race plan<br>Weather conditions<br>Phase of training<br>Previous days' rest | Maintain tempo<br>Draft behind other runners<br>Surge for 100 m |
| Last 30 seconds of first half in basketball | Score differential<br>Player matchups<br>Number of personal fouls on key players | Play for last shot<br>Take first open shot<br>Attack opposing player in foul trouble |

# SUMMARY

**1.** The notion of information processing is a useful conceptual framework for understanding tactical skills.

**2.** The stages of information processing include interpreting the environment, deciding what to do, and determining how to do it.

**3.** The quality of information processing depends on the knowledge and previous experience of the athlete.

**4.** Focal vision provides athletes with information about the identity of an object (e.g., the center of the catcher's glove), while ambient vision provides information about where athletes are in relationship to those objects (e.g., the location of teammates and opponents during a fast break in basketball).

**5.** The speed with which athletes are able to process information increases as they learn to anticipate and focus on the most relevant environmental cues, prepare their responses in advance, and automate their movements.

**6.** Tactical skills pertain to an athlete's capability of knowing what to do as well as how and when to do it.

**7.** Three categories of information athletes need in order to develop their tactical skills are knowledge of the sport, understanding of team strategy, and awareness of variable factors, such as the quality of the opponent and environmental conditions.

**8.** The learning of tactical skills can be enhanced by teaching athletes the rules of the sport; presenting and reinforcing basic team strategy; clarifying each athlete's role, strengths, and weaknesses; identifying the strengths and weaknesses of opponents; exposing athletes to competition-like experiences during practices; and reminding athletes of the keys to success before and during competitions.

# KEY TERMS

| | |
|---|---|
| ambient vision | tactical knowledge |
| focal vision | tactical skills |
| information processing | team strategy |

# REVIEW QUESTIONS

**1.** How would you explain tactical skills from an information processing perspective?

**2.** What are the three categories of information athletes need to process in order to perform effectively?

**3.** Explain how the speed and quality of information processing might be different for a less experienced and more experienced athlete in your sport.

**4.** What are three questions athletes need to have answers for in order to make the most effective tactical decisions?

**5.** Discuss one example of how an athlete's knowledge of the sport, understanding of team strategy, and awareness of a particular variable factor (e.g., quality of opponent, environmental conditions) might influence his tactical decision making.

**6.** Explain how an athlete's awareness of her own strengths and weaknesses and role on the team might affect the athlete's tactical decision in a specific competitive situation.

**7.** Why is the games approach to practice the most productive way for coaches to help athletes develop their tactical skills?

# PRACTICAL ACTIVITIES

**1.** Choose a technical skill in your sport and give one example of a situation in which an athlete would need to interpret the environment, decide what to do, and prepare a movement for execution. Explain how you might help the athlete understand what to look for, what to do, and how to do it.

**2.** Think of a situation that frequently occurs in the sport you coach and draw a tactical blueprint similar to the one shown in table 4.1 on page 54. List the relevant knowledge necessary for a tactical decision and the possible options available to the athlete or athletes.

# 5

# *Mental Skills*

© Icon Sports Media

**When you finish reading this chapter, you should be able to explain**

1. the role of emotional arousal in athletic performance,
2. the role of attention during sport competition,
3. the connection between arousal and attention,
4. the role of memory in performance preparation,
5. how athletes can use mental skills to maximize their performance of technical and tactical skills, and
6. how athletes can combine mental rehearsal and physical rehearsal when learning and performing technical and tactical skills.

Chapters 3 and 4 covered some of the ways you can help your athletes develop the technical and tactical skills they need in order to be successful. This chapter discusses another category of skills that can be a powerful tool for improving the consistency of athletes' performance. Because these skills deal with how athletes attempt to control their thoughts and feelings before and during performance, they are usually referred to as mental skills. The foundational elements of mental skills include adjusting emotional arousal, focusing attention, and retrieving relevant past experiences from memory. The chapter begins with a discussion of these elements and suggests some ways you can help your athletes develop them. We'll then look at various aspects of the performance environment as well as some characteristics of different sports that represent different types of mental challenges for athletes. These include relevant and irrelevant environmental information, spectators, type of sport (individual or team), action requirements of the sport (consistent or varied), and the nature of athletes' interactions with opponents (alongside or against). Here you will learn how these factors, alone or in combination, have the potential to either facilitate or impair athletes' performance and how you can help your athletes develop the mental skills they need in order to meet different challenges. Finally, the chapter suggests some ways your athletes can use mental skills to rehearse the technical and tactical skills of their sport.

## Emotional Arousal in Athletic Performance

There is little doubt that emotion plays an important role in most types of sport performance. If an athlete is either emotionally "flat" or overly anxious, his performance usually suffers. In motor skill literature, the word used most often to describe people's emotional state is *arousal*. **Arousal** is conceptualized as a state of activation of the nervous system that lies along a continuum from a very low level (e.g., sleep) to a very high level (e.g., excitement). The curvilinear relationship between arousal and performance is best represented by the **inverted-U principle**

shown in figure 5.1. As you can see from the figure, performance is usually best when arousal is at a moderate level rather than when it is too low or too high.

Although the inverted-U principle has been shown to be valid for the performance of most technical skills, the optimal arousal level for any particular performance depends on the specific characteristics of the performer, the demands of the task, and the participant's perception of the situation. Perhaps the most important characteristic you need to keep in mind is your athletes' general mental and emotional makeup. As you are probably aware, athletes differ in how they respond to different situations. Some are more "laid back" and relaxed, while others are more analytical and nervous. The general tendency of people to differ along the mental–emotional continuum from "relaxed" to "tense" is a characteristic referred to as **trait anxiety**. Athletes who fall closer to the "relaxed" end of this continuum are less likely to interpret situations as threatening and would be labeled "low trait anxious." Conversely, athletes falling closer to the "tense" end of the continuum are more likely to perceive situations as threatening and would be considered "high trait anxious."

In addition to an athlete's normal level of trait anxiety, a second factor that must be considered when trying to determine the optimal arousal level for a particular type of performance is the

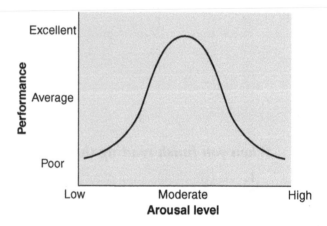

FIGURE 5.1    The inverted-U principle. Increased arousal improves performance up to a point, after which further increases in arousal diminish performance.
Reprinted, by permission, from R.A. Schmidt and C.A. Wrisberg, 2004, *Motor learning and performance*, 3rd ed. (Champaign, IL: Human Kinetics), 68.

## *Different Strokes for Different Folks*

Anxious athletes are more likely to wilt under pressure than calm athletes are. However, there is also such a thing as being too calm, or "flat." How you provide assistance for anxious and bored athletes needs to be different. Strategies for helping athletes who appear anxious include anything that directs their attention to the process of performing (and to things that are under their control) rather than to the end result. A simple focus cue (e.g., telling an anxious baseball batter to "just watch the ball and put the fat of the bat on it" or reminding an anxious swimmer to "just focus on the rhythm of your stroke"), an instruction to take a few deep breaths and relax the body, or a reminder to "just do the same things you do every day in practice" are the kinds of assistance most anxious athletes need in order to regain control of their thoughts and reconnect with the feeling they like to have when they are performing.

On the other hand, underaroused (i.e., flat or bored) athletes usually need something to elevate their arousal level. A good way to help them do this is to emphasize the importance of the end result of their performance (e.g., by challenging the batter to "try to go four for four today" or telling the swimmer she is "ripe for an upset in this race"). Another strategy you can use with underaroused athletes is to create special challenges for them. You might challenge a volleyball player who is trying to develop a jump serve to use it more frequently when she serves against a weaker team. This strategy will not only increase the player's arousal level for that match, at least when she is serving, but also provide her with an opportunity to improve an aspect of her game that could be beneficial against stronger opponents in future matches.

demand of the technical skill in question. Some skills are more complex (e.g., hitting a baseball) or require a higher degree of fine motor control (e.g., putting a golf ball). Others contain fewer mental demands but require higher levels of muscular force (e.g., throwing a javelin, rebounding a basketball, tackling a ball carrier in football).

Generally speaking, the more complex or mentally demanding the technical skill, the more relaxed the athlete should be to perform it. A complex skill, such as hitting a baseball, would be performed better by a relatively relaxed athlete than by a more tense player. Therefore, a batter who is high trait anxious and who tends to overanalyze situations or fall closer to the "tense" end of the relaxed–tense arousal continuum would benefit from a reminder to "just look for the ball coming out of the pitcher's hand, and try to put the fat of the bat on it" when coming up to bat in a crucial game situation. This reminder changes the batter's perspective from "I have to get a hit or we're going

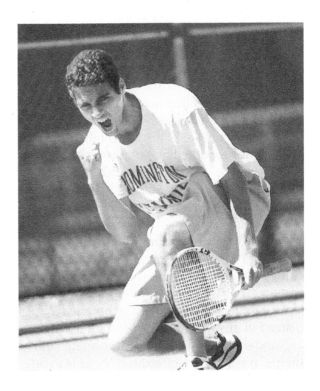

Emotion plays an important role in most types of sport performance.

to lose this game" to "All I need to do is watch the ball and try to hit it hard somewhere." As a result, the batter's arousal level will likely be lowered, making successful execution a more likely prospect.

The final factor to consider when determining the optimal arousal level for effective performance is the nature of the situation in which the technical skill is executed. In actuality, it's the athlete's interpretation of the situation, rather than the situation itself, that's important here. For example, a free throw shot in basketball requires a player to shoot the ball from a standing position to a circular target located 15 feet away and 10 feet above the ground. However, this technical skill can be performed in an empty gym in the middle of the afternoon or in the presence of thousands of spectators during the last few seconds of a tied championship game. Thus, a player could perceive the demands of those two sets of circumstances differently even though he is theoretically performing the same technical skill in both situations. Remember the scene in the film *Hoosiers* where the coach demonstrates to his small-town team that the dimensions of the free throw lane and the height of the basket in the gym where they are going to be playing for a state championship are the same as in their little gym back home? Among other things, this coach was trying to adjust his players' perception of the situation so that it would appear less threatening.

Obviously, the easiest way to deal with athletes who are not well suited, mentally and emotionally, for a particular situation is to remove them from the situation. However, it is better to resist this simple fix; try instead to think of ways you might help those athletes achieve an arousal level that is better suited to the demands of the situation. One of the best things you can do is help them develop the mental skill of attention control, which is discussed further in the next section. That way, you will empower your athletes to manage their own thoughts and feelings instead of always looking to you for assistance.

Another way to facilitate appropriate adjustments in your athletes' arousal levels is to alter the demands of the task or situation through your coaching advice. If your skilled, laid-back tennis player is competing against an inferior opponent, your player's arousal level will likely be lower than optimal, basically because she feels bored. One thing you might do in this situation is instruct the player to attempt some things during the match that she would be unwilling to do against a stronger opponent. If she normally likes to play from the baseline, you could challenge her to attack the net more often and try to hit more volleys. By increasing task demands in this way, you are increasing the player's arousal to a level that is more optimal for this opponent and situation. The point is that you can do things as a coach, such as increasing or decreasing task demands or adjusting your athletes' perception of the demands of a situation, to prompt increases or decreases in their arousal levels, which in turn should improve their chances of success.

By keeping in mind the personal characteristics of your athletes (particularly their trait anxiety levels), the demands of the technical skills they need to perform, and the way they interpret the situation they are performing in, you should have a pretty good idea of what, if anything, you should do to help them achieve a level of arousal that will enhance their performance.

## Attention During Sport Competition

**Attention** is like the lens through which individuals view their world, and where athletes direct their attention is known as their **focus**. Athletes must be able to focus on (i.e., pay attention to) only those thoughts, feelings, or environmental information that are essential for effective performance. For a basketball player it might mean visually focusing on the front of the rim before shooting a free throw, while for a springboard diver it might involve focusing on one or two technical aspects of a particular dive (e.g., head in, tight twist).

An important principle of attention is that people can focus on only a limited amount of information at any one time. Perhaps you've experienced the frustration of trying to drive your car, listen to a newscast on the radio, and carry on a conversation with a friend, all at the same time. In such instances, something's got to give (let's hope it isn't the driving!). This is just one practical illustration of the **principle of limited attention capacity**. In chapter 4, you learned that information processing involves interpreting the environment, deciding what to do, and preparing and executing the desired movement. Because of their limited attention capacity, athletes need to find ways to focus only on those pieces of information that are essential to performance.

According to one popular theory, attention is made up of two general dimensions. In combination, these dimensions represent four possible types of focus an athlete might adopt at any particular time. The first dimension deals with the width of the focus. An athlete uses a **broad focus** to attend to a number of cues simultaneously. A **narrow focus** involves attending to no more than one or two cues. The second dimension pertains to the direction of the focus. An **external focus** means the athlete is directing his attention toward information contained in the environment. An **internal focus** indicates that the athlete is directing attention to her own thoughts or feelings. In figure 5.2, the four possible combinations of these two dimensions are illustrated, along with an example of each combination for a soccer player.

When it comes to managing their attention, athletes must first learn how to identify the focus that is most appropriate at a particular moment and then be able to achieve that focus as quickly as possible. For a quarterback in football, the following sequence of shifts in focus might occur during the course of a single pass play:

1. Look to the coach on the sidelines for the hand signal that indicates the desired play. (narrow external)

2. Think about how to communicate the entire play and the snap count to teammates in the huddle. (broad internal)

3. While walking to the line of scrimmage, look over the opposing team's defense. (broad external)

4. Recall the precise snap count. (narrow internal)

5. While retreating to set up for the pass, locate the desired receiver and deliver the ball to the target. (narrow external)

In sport, the principle of limited attention capacity is important because of the various types of information that compete for athletes' attention. The various demands of sport situations and technical skills are discussed later in the chapter, and some suggestions for how you can help your athletes use their mental skills, including focusing their attention, to meet those demands are offered.

## Connection Between Arousal and Attention

One explanation for the inverted-U principle (figure 5.1) is the **cue utilization hypothesis**. According to this view, when athletes are underaroused they are more prone to being distracted by a wide range of environmental cues, some of which are irrelevant to their performance (e.g., the lackadaisical basketball player dribbling up the floor and noticing the opposing team's logo painted on the wall). As a result, underaroused athletes may miss a relevant cue (e.g., the defender's sudden attempt to steal the ball) and experience a performance breakdown (e.g., the ball being stolen). On the other hand,

**Width of focus**

| | Narrow | Broad |
|---|---|---|
| **Internal** | Imaging the desired corner kick | Rehearsing a strategy for a particular opponent |
| **External** | Watching the approaching ball | Looking over the defensive alignment of several opposing players |

**Direction of focus**

FIGURE 5.2 Examples of the four possible combinations of attention focus for a soccer player.

when athletes are overaroused their attention narrows dramatically, limiting the number of environmental cues they are able to focus on. If the cue they select is irrelevant to their performance (e.g., the heckling of a particularly loud spectator), a breakdown may again occur (e.g., the ball being stolen) but for a different reason. Under conditions of extremely high arousal, anxious athletes may even exhibit a "deer in the headlights" look because they are focusing on a single thought, feeling, or cue. Ideally, you want your athletes' arousal to be near optimal so that their focus is only on the most relevant cues for their performance.

In addition, the relationship between arousal and attention is a two-way street. Although shifts in arousal can produce adjustments in attention, shifts in attention can also produce adjustments in arousal. A field goal kicker who feels extremely anxious (i.e., highly aroused) before entering the game can focus his attention on the keys to his performance (e.g., picturing the line of ball flight, keeping the head down,

and following through). By shifting his attention to game-relevant cues, the kicker can lower his arousal to a level that is more conducive to producing a relaxed and smooth movement. The kicker could also direct his focus to his body, taking several deep breaths to lower his arousal and release muscular tension. Both these examples illustrate the strong connection between arousal and attention and the importance for athletes to use mental skills, such as focusing and arousal management, to achieve the thoughts and feelings that accompany their best performance.

A helpful activity to emphasize the importance of the right feel and correct focus is to ask your athletes to complete a form similar to the one shown in table 5.1. In this example, a softball pitcher has identified the feel and focus she needs to have between innings, before each batter, before each pitch, and when delivering the pitch. The objective of this activity is to increase athletes' awareness of the best feel and focus for different situations. Once they have done this, they can begin developing ways of achieving the desired feel and focus during scrimmages and in competition. If the pitcher knows, for example, that before each pitch she needs to be relaxed but intense and focused on the type of pitch she intends to throw, she can begin working on a prepitch routine that includes using her breathing to adjust her arousal level and creating an image of the feel and desired outcome of the pitch.

## Memory in Performance Preparation

The third foundational element of mental skills is memory. In psychological literature, memory is conceptualized as the capacity to retain and utilize previous information in various ways. The two memory systems that seem to have the greatest relevance for sport performance are working memory (sometimes referred to as short-term memory) and long-term memory.

### Working Memory

**Working memory** is analogous to a mental workspace that people use when attempting to

To achieve performance success on a consistent basis, athletes must be able to effectively manage their arousal and focus their attention.

TABLE 5.1

## How I Want to Feel and What I Need to Focus On

| When | Feel | Focus |
|------|------|-------|
| Between innings | Relaxed, arm warm | Tendencies of upcoming batters |
| Before each batter | Alert, poised | Game situation; what to do if the ball is hit to me |
| Before each pitch | Relaxed, intense | The pitch I'm going to throw (type, velocity, location) |
| When delivering the pitch | Relaxed, confident | Catcher's glove |

achieve a particular goal. In preparation for sport performance, an athlete brings into this workspace any information that might be relevant to goal achievement. A soccer player may remind herself of the tendencies of the scheduled opponent, the strategies she will use in executing the game plan, and the strengths and weaknesses of different teammates. The softball pitcher from table 5.1 might remind herself, before facing each batter, of several things pertaining to the game situation, such as the score, the number of outs, the number of runners on base, and the batter's strengths and weaknesses.

Working memory, like attention, shares the feature of limited capacity. Research clearly shows that people can maintain only five to nine "chunks" of information in working memory at a time. By *chunk*, researchers mean a single identifiable unit of information. Thus, the more information your athletes are able to store in each chunk, the more information they will have at their disposal. The golfer who is able to "chunk" the wedge shot as a single action would have more available space in working memory for other pieces of information (e.g., reminders about the potential trouble spots on a particular course) than the golfer who needs to remember several components of the shot (e.g., the stance, the angle of the club face, the swing, the follow-through).

The other limiting feature of working memory is the short length of time that information remains available for the performer's use. Information that is not used on a regular basis can disappear from the workspace in as little as 30 seconds. Remember those times when you thought about something one moment and then minutes later realized you'd forgotten it? This happens because other events capture your attention long enough for the information to fade away.

Since working memory is limited in capacity and duration, your athletes must be selective when choosing what to put in their mental workspaces and must use that information as soon as possible. One way you can help them keep information "fresh" is by providing either verbal or nonverbal reminders. You could verbally remind a softball pitcher to focus on her release point when throwing the rise ball, or you could encourage her to wear a wristband that serves the same purpose. Each time the pitcher sees the wristband, she is reminded of the correct release point.

## Long-Term Memory

The other memory system athletes use when preparing for performance is **long-term memory**. This system is analogous to a storage bin that contains all the information people have acquired over their lifetimes. Unlike working memory, long-term memory is thought to be unlimited in capacity and duration. Sometimes people have difficulty retrieving information from long-term memory (e.g., the name of a teacher they had in the third grade), but at other times they are able to remember things even years after they last attempted them (e.g., how to ride a bicycle).

To provide the best assistance possible to your athletes, it would be helpful to have an idea of their previous life experiences. However, athletes can add whatever information they want to their long-term memories as long as they are willing to spend the time and effort to do so. Your job is to give them useful information, and theirs is to rehearse it. During his days as an all-American quarterback at the University of Tennessee, Peyton Manning was well known for his dedication to game preparation. He spent countless hours reviewing video of his opponents as well as of himself performing. By devoting considerable time and energy to this activity, Manning was able to amass considerable information that he then used when practicing and competing. Even athletes who are not as dedicated to their mental preparation as Manning might be convinced to treat practices more seriously if they were periodically reminded that practice is the time to learn the things they need to know if they want the opportunity to play.

In addition to rehearsing and storing information in long-term memory, athletes must be able to retrieve that information at a moment's notice. The best way to improve your athletes' retrieval capabilities is to create competition-like practice situations that force them to practice memory retrieval. For example, offensive linemen who must retrieve different ways to effectively pass-block an aggressive opponent need to experience different pass-blocking practice situations against an aggressive pass rusher. These linemen could also practice memory retrieval by mentally rehearsing their blocking assignments between practice repetitions or while observing other offensive linemen during a pass-blocking situation.

## Using Mental Skills to Maximize Performance

Arousal adjustment, attention focusing, and memory retrieval are all extremely important mental skills for athletes to develop, particularly if they want to perform at their best on a consistent basis. This section discusses two aspects of the performance environment, along with several characteristics of different sports that athletes should be aware of in order to maximize their chances of success. In each case, suggestions are given to help athletes effectively use their mental skills.

## Demands of the Performance Environment

When considering the competitive sport environment, at least two things stand out. First, every sport situation contains information that is either relevant or irrelevant to athletes' performance. Second, every situation includes spectators of some kind or other. Therefore, when preparing your athletes—mentally and emotionally—for competition, you need to keep both of these aspects in mind.

### Relevant and Irrelevant Information

Aspects of the performance environment may be theoretically classified as either relevant or irrelevant to goal achievement. For the gymnast performing a high bar routine, the feel of the apparatus represents **relevant environmental information,** while the actions of other competitors is **irrelevant environmental information.** However, the mere knowledge that something is relevant or irrelevant doesn't guarantee that athletes will attend to the relevant informa-

One way to improve athletes' mental toughness is to encourage them to remember the right feel and focus for each task. This will improve their confidence even in pressure situations.

tion and ignore the irrelevant. Therefore, you should identify the demands of competitive situations and then create training experiences that challenge your athletes to respond to those demands by focusing only on the most relevant information.

You can help athletes prepare to focus by reminding them of some of the things they learned from previous experiences (i.e., by promoting memory retrieval). The information in table 5.1 represents examples of relevant information (in the form of feelings and focus cues) a softball pitcher might have remembered from past experiences. By practicing memory retrieval and attention focusing, athletes will become more adept at preparing for performance and paying attention to relevant environmental cues. This should give them the confidence they need for actual competition. If, before each pitch, the pitcher feels relaxed and intense and is focused on the pitch she intends to throw, she won't have to hope she's ready to compete, she will know she's ready.

### Spectators

Spectators are another aspect of the sport environment that presents a mental demand for athletes. In some sports, spectators are permitted to engage in behavior that has the potential to influence athletes' performance. Positive spectator behavior (e.g., cheering) is usually intended to encourage or motivate athletes, while distractive behavior (e.g., booing, whistling) is designed to disrupt athletes' performance. In sports such as baseball, basketball, football, and soccer, spectators are allowed to shout and make nonverbal gestures (e.g., wave their arms, stomp their feet) at virtually all times. In sports such as golf, gymnastics, and tennis, spectators are more passive. In many

## *Developing Mental Toughness in Practice*

Competitive athletes experience pressure to perform well on a regular basis. This pressure can come from parents, friends, or other significant people in their lives. To help your athletes learn how to deal with various types of pressure, create practice situations that simulate competitive conditions and then reward your athletes for effective execution. For example, if you coach volleyball, you might simulate a match point situation and award the serving team one point if they set up the block in the appropriate way and the receiving team one point if they devise and execute an effective attacking strategy. Moreover, a player who hits a serve that is difficult for the opposing team to handle should be rewarded for doing so, regardless of whether the opponent wins the point; an outside hitter who stays aggressive and hits the ball with authority to different targets should be rewarded for doing so, even if the opposing team is able to successfully dig the ball and keep it in play. Consistently rewarding your players' execution sends the message that all you expect them to do are the things they have control of (e.g., retrieving the most relevant information, adjusting their arousal, focusing on task-relevant cues, and executing their movements to the best of their ability). Knowing this, your athletes are likely to remain poised and focused when competing, even during pressure situations.

To simulate the pressure athletes feel to not let their teammates down, you could create a "crucial" match situation and reward all players on the serving team one point if the serve is executed in the desired fashion and reward everyone on the receiving team one point if the player receiving the serve executes an effective pass. This activity will help your athletes learn how to do the right things even when their teammates are counting on them. At the end of the season, you might present athletes who achieve the most points in pressure situations with a plaque or certificate symbolizing their mental toughness.

cases, social convention discourages them from making noise or other nonverbal gestures while athletes are performing.

During a normal sport season, athletes will compete at their home facility (i.e., stadium, pool, arena) approximately half the time and at the facilities of their opponents the rest of the time. The experiences athletes encounter in these two situations are usually different. A basketball player who is shooting a free throw shot in his home arena in front of supportive spectators can expect the crowd to be quiet before and during the shot, cheer after a successful shot, and groan or be silent after an unsuccessful shot. Conversely, when shooting a free throw in an opposing team's arena, the player can expect considerable noise and nonverbal gesturing from spectators before and during the shot, silence after a successful attempt, and cheering or jeering after a miss.

Ultimately, the effect that observers have on athletes depends on the athletes' perceptions. A gymnast may see one of her competitors watching her and think the opponent is trying to disrupt her concentration. Regardless of who is watching, however, and whether these people are active or passive, knowledgeable or naive about the fine points of the sport, athletes should be coached to ignore them and focus their attention on the relevant aspects of their own performance.

You can help your athletes achieve optimal arousal and a task-relevant focus in the presence of spectators by creating practice settings where people (acting as spectators) engage in the various kinds of behaviors normally seen in that setting. Golfers might practice in the presence of spectators who simply stand and observe, baseball players might practice in the presence of spectators who watch while engaging in normal conversation, and soccer players might practice in front of spectators who continually demonstrate a variety of behaviors (e.g., singing, cheering, shouting). Regardless of the situation or the behavior of spectators, an athlete's goal is to adjust arousal and focus on task-relevant cues. You can help your athletes do this more automatically by verbally reminding them of techniques for reducing their arousal (e.g., "Take some deep breaths" or "Relax your hands"), increasing their arousal (e.g., "Challenge yourself" or "Pick up the tempo"), and focusing on important cues (e.g., for a free throw shooter in basketball, the front of the rim and putting the ball just over it; for a swimmer, "hot walls" to emphasize quick turns).

## Diminishing the Influence of Competitive Distractions

For years psychologists have studied the responses of people who are repeatedly exposed to the same external stimulus. These studies have consistently shown that the size of the response diminishes with increased exposure to the stimulus. This phenomenon is known as **habituation.** As a coach, you can take advantage of the habituation phenomenon by repeatedly exposing your athletes to the kinds of irrelevant stimuli they can expect to encounter during competition. In addition to including the usual sights and sounds (e.g., spectator harassment, poor judgments by an official), you can repeatedly remind your athletes of the score or the fact that a lot of people are counting on them to perform well. With increased exposure to potentially distracting stimuli over many practice sessions, your athletes should become more adept at ignoring those stimuli and maintaining their focus on relevant cues under the most intense competitive circumstances. Former University of Tennessee basketball player Tony White said he was able to hit two free throws with less than one second left and his team trailing by one point in an important game against the University of Georgia because he did the same things he always did before attempting his shot: take a deep breath; focus on a point in the center of the rim; and say to himself, "Just over" (the rim).

## Demands of Different Types of Sports

In addition to aspects of the competitive environment, a number of other characteristics of sports represent unique mental and emotional demands for athletes. These include individual and team sports, the action requirements of different sports, and the nature of athletes' interactions with their opponents.

### Individual and Team Sports

Most sports can be classified as either individual or team. Individual sports require athletes to compete alone—either alongside other opponents, as do runners and swimmers in a race, or in direct opposition to the opponent, as do tennis players and wrestlers. Team sports involve the collective efforts of one group of athletes directed against those of another group. Examples include soccer, basketball, and volleyball. Individual and team sports often entail different mental demands as well. The arousal level of athletes competing alone (e.g., gymnasts) is likely to be different from that of athletes competing alongside (e.g., swimmers) or against (e.g., wrestlers) their opponents.

In addition, some team sports contain particular tasks that emphasize the efforts of a single player. Punting or placekicking in football and free throw shooting in basketball represent activities that accentuate the performance of an individual. By the same token, some individual sports include events requiring the joint efforts of several teammates. Examples include relay races in track and swimming and doubles play in tennis. Thus, the arousal and attention demands of the punter or placekicker are different from those of a running back or defensive lineman; and the demands of a runner, swimmer, or tennis player vary depending on whether they are performing events as individuals or in coordination with other teammates.

By keeping in mind the different demands of individual and team sports, you can create practice experiences that will mentally prepare your athletes for the specific situations they are likely to face in competition. For individual sports, your primary emphasis should be on developing and performing the necessary skills for goal achievement. Gymnasts must learn and be able to execute each of the required movements for their respective events. Similarly, tennis players must practice the basic shots of the game (i.e., service, forehand and backhand ground strokes, volleys) so they can effectively employ them in a variety of ways during competition. However, athletes in these types of sports also need to realize that at times their performance will determine whether their team wins or loses (e.g., the team event in gymnastics, Davis Cup play in tennis). Therefore, it is essential that they be periodically confronted with competition-like scenarios that have team implications (e.g., displaying the respective "team scores" alongside the athlete's individual scores; having other team members standing and watching the athlete as she finishes the event or match). Practices like this will help athletes learn how to maintain their poise and concentration even when they know their teammates are counting on them to win.

Team sport performers must practice synchronizing their movements during training sessions to ensure effective group coordination during competition.

In addition to learning and performing the basic skills of their sport, athletes in a team setting must learn how to synchronize their actions with those of their teammates. Offensive linemen in football must not only be able to execute each type of block but also know how to coordinate the timing of their blocks with those of other offensive linemen. Similarly, ice hockey players must not only have the necessary skills to control and pass the puck but also be able to judge the movements of teammates and opponents to ensure that their passes are successfully received and not intercepted. Thus, when synchronization is important for performance success, athletes should practice paying attention to their teammates' mannerisms and movements, which will help them become better at anticipating each other's actions.

One principle to keep in mind when planning practice sessions is that the greater the demand for coordination among team members, the greater you need to emphasize activities that require athletes to synchronize their movements. It's okay for a punter in football to devote the majority of his practice time to perfecting the different types of kicks he needs to produce in the game. However, defensive linemen should not only practice their different pass rushes but also spend some time coordinating their moves with those of other linemen. Coordinated practice enables athletes to develop a memory of each other's movements so that in competition they are able to "act as one" rather than as a bunch of individuals.

## Action Requirements of Different Sports

In some sports, athletes attempt to produce movements that are as similar as possible from one attempt to the next. Gymnasts and springboard divers, for example, want to produce a consistent movement pattern for each event or dive. In other sports, athletes are called on to produce wide variations of one or more movements. Infielders in baseball and softball must make different types of throws of different distances, speeds, and trajectories; and tennis players must hit a variety of shots to targets all over the opponent's court.

In chapter 2, you learned the differences between technical skills performed in open and closed sport environments (referred to as open and closed skills, respectively). Sports performed in open environments require athletes to selectively attend to a variety of changing and moving environmental cues so that they can adapt their movements appropriately. Soccer players must constantly observe the changing activity patterns of teammates and opponents in order to anticipate the responses that are most effective in different situations.

Sports that take place in closed environments allow athletes to preplan their movements and produce them when the athletes are ready. For example, before beginning his routine on the parallel bars, a gymnast stands near the apparatus (which remains fixed and waiting to be acted upon) and then, when he is ready, signals his intent to officials.

When teaching the technical skills of your sport, consider ways of structuring practice sessions that will help your athletes produce their movements in the most effective manner. If the sport includes skills that require varied responses to changing environmental information, introduce as much variety into the practice environment as possible. A tennis player needs to experience a variety of different environmental conditions when practicing her ground strokes (e.g., different opponents, different surfaces, different weather conditions) to learn how to adapt her strokes and achieve performance success during competition. She also needs to practice variations of ground strokes, volleys, and serves so that she can produce each whenever she needs to during matches.

If, on the other hand, your athletes must perform technical skills requiring the same movements or produce skills within closed environments, you should create practice situations that allow them to experience those types of circumstances. A pole-vaulter should practice the same sequence of behaviors each time he attempts a vault—stretching, finding his mark, increasing his arousal with energizing focus cues (such as "Do it" and "Time to soar"), and using simple focus cues before beginning his approach ("Easy speed") and planting the pole ("Push the pole high"). The pole-vaulter might also practice waiting longer between attempts in order to prepare for the intermittent lulls he will experience during competition.

The task of a field goal kicker requires a rather consistent action (i.e., kicking the ball from a point on the ground, over the outstretched arms of defenders, above the crossbar, and between the goalposts). The environment is also relatively predictable as long as the holder places the ball down in approximately the same way before each kick. However, one competitive circumstance that can be a problem for field goal kickers is the time they are given to prepare for the kick. The rules state that the play clock begins when the official places the ball on the ground and blows the whistle. At that moment, the offensive team has 25 seconds to initiate a play or be penalized for delay of game. In game situations, it may take the head coach several seconds to decide to send in the field goal team. The longer the coach waits to make this decision, the less time the kicker has to run onto the field, line up the kick, and signal to the holder that he is ready. By creating unpredictable situations during practice, coaches can help kickers learn how to prepare themselves while waiting for an opportunity to kick. For example, the kicker could start planning the kick (e.g., estimating the distance and angle, checking the wind) before the official starts the clock so that whether the coach signals for the field goal team or not, the kicker is mentally prepared before he runs onto the field.

### Nature of the Interaction With Opponents

In some sports opponents compete alongside, but not in direct contact with, each other. In other sports opponents compete directly against each other. Each situation presents different types of challenges for athletes.

When athletes compete alongside each other, victory usually goes to the one who achieves the best performance relative to some external standard or to that of other competitors. Participants in a golf tournament play 72 holes under similar conditions, and the winner is the player who achieves the lowest total score for four rounds. Similarly, in gymnastics and springboard diving, all athletes compete on the same apparatus, with the winner being the person who achieves the highest total score (as determined by a panel of judges). In the sport of track and field, athletes who compete in events such as the discus, shot put, pole vault, long jump, high jump, triple jump, and javelin win by achieving the highest score (i.e., distance or height) in their respective events. Athletes in running events compete alongside their opponents, shift their focus back and forth from their own performance to that of other competitors, and try to determine the best possible strategies for winning or finishing near the front of the group.

If you coach a sport where your athletes compete alongside other athletes, try to create practice experiences that challenge athletes to remain primarily focused on their own performance and "tune out" that of others. Golfers need to practice focusing on their own shots, one shot at a time, while ignoring the shots and scores of their opponents. Gymnasts and divers need to practice focusing on their own actions while ignoring the judges' ratings for other competitors.

Some athletes find it more difficult to ignore their opponents' actions. This is okay as long as they don't become too caught up in what their opponents are doing. If runners or swimmers devote too much attention to their opponents' performance, they can easily lose focus on their own race plan. A useful practice strategy you can employ with athletes such as this is to have them focus on the timing and rhythm of their own movements until they achieve the feel they are looking for. Once they settle into their preferred tempo, they might briefly switch their attention to the rhythm of a nearby opponent. If the two rhythms are similar, the athlete might decide to use the sound of the synchronous pace to help maintain that tempo for a period of time. However, as soon as the athlete notices that the rhythms are becoming different, she should switch back to her own tempo in order to stay in touch with her individual race plan. The challenge becomes even greater when runners and swimmers are approaching the finish line and find themselves in an all-out race. During these moments, athletes need to resist the temptation to focus on their opponents' actions and must devote all their attention to what they need to do to maximize their own finishing speed (e.g., staying relaxed, increasing stride or stroke frequency).

Some athletes need to focus on their opponents' actions, while other athletes need to focus only on their own.

In contrast to sports that require athletes to compete alongside each other are those that necessitate a direct confrontation between athletes. In these sports, strategy is particularly important because winning depends on maximizing one's own performance while minimizing that of the opponent. Examples of these sports include basketball, football, hockey, rugby, soccer, wrestling, and tennis.

If you coach one of these "confrontational" sports, you need to design practices that include opportunities for athletes to refine their basic movement skills and develop general strategies for defeating opponents. During competition, encourage your athletes to adopt strategies that enable them to do the things they do best while, at the same time, preventing their opponents from doing the things they like to do. You might instruct a tennis player with a strong forehand who is playing against an opponent with a weak backhand to hit more shots to her opponent's backhand. In this way she should get weaker returns from her opponent, allowing her to hit her own forehand shot more often. Athletes in these types of sports should also practice adapting their strategies when something isn't working or when their opponent has adjusted to the initial strategy. A basketball team facing an opponent that overplays the passing lane needs to adjust by using more ball fakes when passing or by running more backdoor cuts that exploit the opponent's defensive aggressiveness.

## Combining Mental and Physical Rehearsal

A growing body of research suggests that athletes should develop their mental skills at the same time they develop their technical and tactical skills. For example, the blocking assignments of an offensive lineman in football or the responsibilities of a point guard on a set play in basketball represent tactical skills that players can acquire through mental rehearsal as well as through physical rehearsal. Two mental skills athletes can incorporate during the physical practice of a technical skill are the mental rehearsal of procedural details and mental imagery of the skill itself.

## Facilitating Team Sport Athletes' Appreciation of Diverse Skill Demands

Too often, team sport athletes understand the skill demands of their own position but fail to appreciate those of other athletes. In an attempt to solve this problem, one little league baseball coach in Michigan devised a creative system for teaching his players the demands of all defensive positions. Each player would begin a scrimmage at a particular position. However, after the first inning, the players would rotate to another position. For example, the shortstop moved to third base, the third baseman moved to left field, and the left fielder moved to center field. By running the practice in this way, the coach helped his players appreciate the technical and tactical demands of all positions on the field. Therefore, the center fielder would be more likely to throw the ball to the shortstop in a way that made it easier for the shortstop to catch because the center fielder now knew what type of throw he would like to receive if he were playing shortstop. Occasional practices like this can keep team sport athletes motivated while deepening their understanding of the various technical and tactical skills of their sport.

## Rehearsal of Procedural Details

As mentioned previously, the procedural aspects of some technical skills lend themselves to mental rehearsal. Recall from chapter 2 that the beginning stage of technical skill learning is a time when athletes are trying to grasp the basic idea of task requirements, such as the fundamental structure and rhythm of the action. During this stage, athletes obtain instructions, watch demonstrations, attempt the skill, process feedback from their movements, receive the coach's feedback, and refine their strategies. Most instructions include a sequence of steps the athlete needs to remember when practicing the skill. You might tell a soccer player that the chip pass is a good technical skill to use whenever he wants to pass the ball over the head of an opponent. To perform the chip pass, the player needs to remember the following sequence:

1. Approach the ball in the direction you want it to go.
2. Place your nonkicking foot alongside and slightly in front of the ball.
3. Keep your eyes on the ball and your head directly over the ball.

4. Contact the underside of the ball by producing a stabbing action with the kicking foot.

To speed up the player's learning of this skill, instruct him to mentally rehearse the correct sequence before each practice attempt. To avoid overloading the player with too much information, you could simplify the sequence by giving him the following verbal cues to rehearse:

Approach
Foot alongside
Head over ball
Stab underneath

## Mental Imagery of Technical and Tactical Skills

Once athletes improve their technical skills to the point that they are able to perform the desired movements on a consistent basis, they can begin using **mental imagery** to rehearse the look and feel of the movements. In some cases athletes might use an **internal imagery perspective** by "seeing and feeling" themselves performing the skill in exactly the same way they experience it during physical rehearsal. A basketball player might "see" the basket and rim in the distance and "feel" the extension of the legs during the jump shot. In other situations, athletes might use an **external imagery perspective,** as if they were watching themselves on television or through the eyes of another person. A springboard diver might "see" the mechanics of her dive from the perspective of a judge sitting by the side of the pool. Athletes for whom movement form is an important aspect of their performance (e.g., divers, figure skaters, gymnasts) seem to benefit more from an external perspective than from an internal perspective. However, it's up to the individual athlete to determine which perspective to use. Therefore, it's a good idea to introduce both perspectives to your athletes so they can determine which one generates the look and feel they want to achieve during actual performance.

Athletes can also use imagery to rehearse emotional and tactical aspects of their performance. For example, they might use imagery to rehearse the kinds of emotions they want to experience during competition (e.g., relaxed and focused under pressure) or to reinforce a particular tactical strategy they intend to use (e.g., exploiting an opponent's weakness). In addition, athletes can use imagery to

- manage their arousal level (e.g., by imagining themselves walking on a quiet beach to decrease arousal or paddling a whitewater canoe to increase arousal),
- mentally prepare themselves for an important competition (e.g., by imagining themselves at the competition site along with teammates, opponents, coaches, officials, and spectators), and

- mentally "see and feel" themselves successfully performing exactly the way they intend to.

As is the case with technical and tactical skills, mental skills get better with practice. However, shorter bouts of mental rehearsal (i.e., less than 15 minutes) are preferable to longer ones. Several advantages to mental rehearsal are that it can be done at just about any time and place, it doesn't place a physical burden on the body, and it requires no special equipment. To improve their imagery skill, all athletes need to do is close their eyes and take themselves in their minds to the practice environment or the competitive setting. Once they are "there," they can practice seeing and feeling themselves retrieving important information from memory, adjusting their arousal level, focusing their attention on the most relevant performance cues, and performing flawlessly.

With consistent practice, brief bouts (less than five seconds) of imagery can also be incorporated into athletes' preperformance routines for tasks such as placekicking and punting in football, pitching in softball and baseball, gymnastics routines, springboard dives, serving in tennis or volleyball, penalty kicks in soccer, and most field events in track (i.e., the pole vault, long jump, high jump, discus, hammer, javelin, and shot put). Such imagery might also be included during a time-out in basketball once the coach has diagrammed the desired play. In this case, each player would imagine the successful execution of her respective assignment (e.g., setting a pick, moving without the ball, running an opponent into a screen, taking the shot, positioning for the possible offensive rebound, and so on).

# SUMMARY

1. The relationship between emotional arousal and motor performance is curvilinear. The inverted-U principle states that increases in arousal are accompanied by increases in performance up to a point, but beyond this point further increases in arousal lead to diminished performance.

2. Three factors that determine the optimal arousal level for performance success are the personality of the athlete, the mental and physical demands of the task, and the extent to which the performer perceives the environment as threatening.

3. Generally speaking, the more complex or mentally demanding the technical skill, the lower the level of arousal needs to be for optimal performance.

4. An important principle of attention is that of limited capacity. This principle states that people are able to attend to only a few pieces of information at any one time.

5. Athletes should use both working memory and long-term memory to prepare for performance situations.

6. All sport environments contain sources of information that are either relevant or irrelevant to successful performance.

7. An important challenge for athletes is learning to identify and focus on relevant environmental information while ignoring irrelevant information.

8. Athletes can learn to manage the stress of competition by practicing their technical and tactical skills under conditions that closely approximate those of competition.

9. When competing alongside opponents, athletes should focus primarily on their own performance and ignore that of others.

10. When competing directly against opponents, athletes should focus on optimizing their own performance and diminishing that of opponents.

11. Imagery is an important mental skill that athletes can use to rehearse their technical and tactical skills.

12. The best practices are those that combine the rehearsal of technical, tactical, and mental skills.

# KEY TERMS

arousal

attention

broad focus

cue utilization hypothesis

external focus

external imagery perspective

focus

habituation

internal focus

internal imager perspective

inverted-U principle

irrelevant environmental information

long-term memory

mental imagery

narrow focus

principle of limited attention capacity

relevant environmental information

trait anxiety

working memory

# REVIEW QUESTIONS

1. Generally speaking, what is the relationship between arousal and sport performance?

2. What is the connection between arousal and attention?

3. What is trait anxiety, and how is it related to arousal?

4. What is the principle of limited attention capacity, and how is it related to the concept of focus?

5. What is the difference between an internal focus and an external focus? When might an internal focus be advantageous in your sport? When might an external focus be more effective?

6. What is the difference between relevant and irrelevant environmental information? How might each type of information affect an athlete's performance in a pressure situation?

**7.** What is the difference between working memory and long-term memory? How might an athlete in your sport use each type of memory during a performance?

**8.** What is the difference between an internal and external imagery perspective? What would an image of the same event in your sport be like from the two perspectives?

# PRACTICAL ACTIVITIES

**1.** Using table 5.1 on page 63 as a guide, describe three different performance situations in your sport and list the feelings and focus cues that might produce effective performance.

**2.** For each of the three previous situations, describe a practice activity that would help athletes improve their mental skills.

**3.** For one of the three situations, write a brief imagery script an athlete might use to mentally rehearse successful performance.

# PART III

# Designing Practice Sessions

Good coaches take a systematic approach to designing practices. They maximize the effectiveness of each practice by clearly defining their goals and by emphasizing the target behaviors athletes need to work on in order to perform at their best. Good coaches employ a games approach to practice that makes practices more competition-like, both physically and mentally, and that incorporates a variety of instructional techniques to promote skill learning. They know not only how and when to provide feedback but also how to challenge athletes to become their own problem solvers. Finally, good coaches know that the best practices focus on essential skills, challenge each athlete to improve his or her performance, are relevant to competition, and are fun. In part III, you will learn how to use the goal-setting process to develop an effective blueprint for your practices; to incorporate a games approach that encourages the development of the essential technical, tactical, and mental skills of your sport; to provide feedback that is relevant and timely; and to design practices that prepare your athletes for competition and give them the confidence they need for any challenge they might face.

# 6

# *Skill Analysis: Deciding What to Teach*

**When you finish reading this chapter, you should be able to explain**

1. how to identify the skills your athletes need to learn,
2. the principles of effective goal setting,
3. the difference between outcome goals and performance goals,
4. the process of technical skill analysis,
5. the three elements of technical skills,
6. the concept of target behaviors, and
7. how to use target behaviors to help your athletes achieve the proper focus during practice and in competition.

Chapters 3 through 5 discussed the three categories of skills that athletes need to master in order to achieve their performance potential on a consistent basis—technical skills (chapter 3), tactical skills (chapter 4), and mental skills (chapter 5). In this chapter, we'll look at several factors to consider when helping athletes develop these skills. First, the importance of identifying the skills your athletes need to learn is discussed, followed by the goal-setting process and the principles of effective goal setting. Here you'll discover the important distinction between outcome and performance goals. Next, the chapter focuses on the process of technical skill analysis and identifies the three major elements that make up most technical skills. Finally, the concept of target behaviors is explained, and you will learn how to use target behaviors to focus your athletes' attention during practices and in competition. By the end of this chapter, you should have a good idea of how to identify what to teach, whether you are planning a season, a week, or one practice session.

## Identifying the Skills Your Athletes Need to Learn

The three skill categories emphasized in this book are technical skills, tactical skills, and mental skills. Chapter 5 briefly discussed the relationships between these skill categories and suggested some ways you might combine them in your practice activities. Keep these relationships in mind when you're identifying the skills your athletes need to learn. It's also important to remember that your athletes' level of physical conditioning (e.g., strength, endurance, flexibility) can restrict their capability of learning certain technical skills. Where this is the case, you will need to consider the relative emphasis to place on physical training and skill development during practice sessions. For example, a basketball coach would not be able to devote as much practice time to full-court pressing defenses and fast break situations early in the season when her players are still improving their physical conditioning as she would after her players achieve sufficient fitness levels. For more discussion of physical training skills as

well as other skill categories you might want to consider when determining practice priorities (e.g., communication skills and character skills), see the book *Successful Coaching* by Rainer Martens (2004).

A good way of determining which skills to emphasize during instruction is to first identify the technical, tactical, and mental demands of your sport. Some examples of these three types of demands are shown in table 6.1. As you look at these examples, think about the ones that might be more important for your athletes. If you coach a team sport, you might notice that the demands differ depending on the requirements of a player's position (e.g., linebacker versus wide receiver in football, outside hitter versus setter in volleyball). For both team and individual sports, the demands can differ depending on the nature of the technical skill (e.g., free throw shooting versus rebounding in basketball, pole-vaulting versus long jumping in track and field). Remember as well to consider the competitive circumstances under which your athletes will be performing and how those circumstances might change from one competition to the next (e.g., playing at home versus playing on the road) or over the course of a single competition (e.g., early and late in a long race, when the score is tied or lopsided, during the first few minutes and the last few minutes of a game, and so on).

When deciding which technical skills your athletes need to learn, you should differentiate essential skills from advanced skills. Essential skills are the foundational skills of your sport, while advanced skills represent either advanced forms of the essential skills or more sophisticated or complex actions. Examples of essential skills include blocking and tackling in football; shooting, rebounding, and defending in basketball; digging, passing, serving, hitting, and blocking in volleyball; serving, volleying, and hitting forehand and backhand ground strokes in tennis; and batting, fielding, throwing, and baserunning in baseball and softball. The essential skills of athletes in sports such as track and field differ depending on the event (e.g., pole-vault, long jump, distance events, shot put, javelin, sprints, hurdles, discus, or high jump). The freestyle stroke is an essential skill for

TABLE 6.1

## Assessing the Technical, Tactical, and Mental Demands of Skills

### TECHNICAL DEMANDS

Speed
Accuracy
Strength
Power
Eye–hand coordination
Total body coordination
Flexibility
Anticipation
Timing

### TACTICAL DEMANDS

Movement strategies
Team strategies
Positional strategies
Strategy adjustments
Opponent's tendencies
Importance of competition
Conditions of competition (weather, noise levels, spectators)

### MENTAL DEMANDS

Focusing attention
Shifting attention
Controlling arousal
Achieving or dictating tempo
Managing energy
Managing pain
Staying aggressive
Exercising patience

most swimmers, but some may learn additional strokes for specific events (e.g., breaststroke, butterfly, and backstroke). Golfers and springboard divers must learn variations of one or more essential skills (e.g., driving, pitching, chipping, and putting; twists and somersaults in both front and back dive positions). Examples of advanced skills include jump serving in volleyball, hitting the ball to all parts of the field in baseball and softball, and hitting the overhead smash or drop volley in tennis. Later in this chapter, we'll discuss some of the elements of technical skills you

need to consider when teaching your athletes the technical skills of your sport.

Once you have identified the essential and advanced technical skills of your sport, you should make a list of the relevant tactical and mental skills. For example, relevant tactical and mental skills for effectively executing the technical skill of open-field tackling in football are a proper pursuit angle and a high level of emotional intensity, respectively. Therefore, to optimize players' open-field tackling performance, all three skills should be introduced and practiced together. Similarly, tennis players should practice the tactical and mental skills of hitting to an opponent's weaker side and focusing on the seams of the ball, respectively, when working on their forehand and backhand ground strokes. Chapter 9 discusses some more ways of simultaneously facilitating technical, tactical, and mental skill development to improve your athletes' performance and enhance their prospects for competitive success.

Table 6.2 provides a format you can use in deciding which skills to include in your practice plans. For each of the three skill categories—technical, tactical, and mental—determine which are the most important; your athletes' present level of proficiency; and, if their proficiency is low, their level of readiness for learning the skills. Once you've completed your assessment, you should have a good idea of your priorities as a coach for either the upcoming season or for an individual practice session. Skills rated as 1 in importance should receive the highest priority and be taught first, while skills rated as 2 or 3 are less essential and can be taught after your athletes demonstrate an adequate level of proficiency in the essential skills.

Determining what skills to emphasize in your practices is an ongoing process. Once you make a list of the relevant technical, tactical, and mental skills of your sport and determine which ones your athletes need to develop first (either individually or as a team), create practice experiences that emphasize those skills and pay close attention to how well your athletes perform them. It helps to keep a notebook and record your observations of each athlete's performance. Depending on the size of your team and the number of support staff available, you might

TABLE 6.2

## Format for Deciding What Skills to Emphasize During Practice

| Skills | Importance (circle one) | | | Proficiency (circle one) | | | Readiness (circle one) | |
|---|---|---|---|---|---|---|---|---|
| **TECHNICAL** | | | | | | | | |
| 1. | 1 | 2 | 3 | High | Moderate | Low | Yes | No |
| 2. | 1 | 2 | 3 | High | Moderate | Low | Yes | No |
| 3. | 1 | 2 | 3 | High | Moderate | Low | Yes | No |
| 4. | 1 | 2 | 3 | High | Moderate | Low | Yes | No |
| 5. | 1 | 2 | 3 | High | Moderate | Low | Yes | No |
| 6. | 1 | 2 | 3 | High | Moderate | Low | Yes | No |
| **TACTICAL** | | | | | | | | |
| 1. | 1 | 2 | 3 | High | Moderate | Low | Yes | No |
| 2. | 1 | 2 | 3 | High | Moderate | Low | Yes | No |
| 3. | 1 | 2 | 3 | High | Moderate | Low | Yes | No |
| 4. | 1 | 2 | 3 | High | Moderate | Low | Yes | No |
| 5. | 1 | 2 | 3 | High | Moderate | Low | Yes | No |
| 6. | 1 | 2 | 3 | High | Moderate | Low | Yes | No |
| **MENTAL** | | | | | | | | |
| 1. | 1 | 2 | 3 | High | Moderate | Low | Yes | No |
| 2. | 1 | 2 | 3 | High | Moderate | Low | Yes | No |
| 3. | 1 | 2 | 3 | High | Moderate | Low | Yes | No |
| 4. | 1 | 2 | 3 | High | Moderate | Low | Yes | No |
| 5. | 1 | 2 | 3 | High | Moderate | Low | Yes | No |
| 6. | 1 | 2 | 3 | High | Moderate | Low | Yes | No |

From C.A. Wrisberg, 2007, *Sport skill instruction for coaches* (Champaign, IL: Human Kinetics).

assign evaluation responsibilities to assistant coaches. Periodically assess athletes' progress to determine which skills they are performing well, which ones require further practice, and which additional skills they might be ready for. If you have access to video equipment, you might want to supplement your written notes with videos of your team's practices. This will allow you to replay particular aspects of athletes' performances to determine which skills to emphasize in subsequent practices.

By identifying the skills your athletes need to learn, prioritizing those skills when you design your practices, and systematically evaluating your athletes' skill proficiency, you should be able to create practice experiences that are both challenging and productive. However, to maximize your athletes' skill development, you must help them identify specific goals to focus on. That way they will be able to see the relationship between goal achievement and success in competition.

## Setting Goals

An important prerequisite of skill learning is **goal setting.** Considerable research in the field of motor behavior has shown that people who systematically set goals develop their skills more rapidly and perform them more consistently than individuals who don't. There are two useful ways to conceptualize goals: as targets and as roadmaps. Goals are like targets because they provide athletes with a specific focus, and they are like roadmaps because they represent the paths athletes need to follow in order to achieve their ultimate destination—performance success.

When assisting your athletes with goal setting, keep the following four principles in mind. Effective goals are always

- challenging,
- attainable,
- realistic, and
- specific.

Notice that the first letter of each of those words forms the acronym **CARS.** As long as you remember this acronym, you will be able

to evaluate the effectiveness of your athletes' goal setting.

- **Goals should be challenging.** Athletes are always more stimulated by goals that are challenging than by ones that are not. A challenging goal requires a consistent and concerted effort. Moreover, when athletes achieve a challenging goal, they are more motivated to set and strive for higher goals. Challenging goals are designed to encourage athletes to achieve something they have not achieved before or have not achieved as consistently as they would like to. For example, a challenging goal for many individual sport athletes is to set a personal best in an event (e.g., a cross country runner breaking her previous best time on her home course) or a particular activity (e.g., a tennis player increasing his first serve percentage from 50 to 55 percent).

- **Goals should be attainable.** To achieve their goals, athletes must have the necessary time, opportunity for practice, equipment, and environmental conditions. A soccer player in her first year on the team may have the potential to score 10 goals in a season, but because she is probably going to get less playing time than her more experienced teammates, she may not have the opportunity to do so. Similarly, a distance runner may be capable of setting a record in his event during a cross country meet, but extremely cold and windy conditions would make it unlikely for him to do so. Goals that are attainable allow athletes to experience success under any conditions, which in turn will motivate them to continue their efforts. For example, the goal of keeping the feet moving after initial contact with a defender is attainable for any running back in football, regardless of the number of opportunities the player has to carry the ball. Goals that are unattainable prevent athletes from receiving the kind of reinforcement they need to keep striving for goal achievement. A running back who sets a goal of rushing for more than 100 yards against an opponent that has the best rushing defense in the league is setting himself up for failure. Athletes who set attainable goals are more likely to keep striving for improvement, while those who set unattainable goals are more likely to be demotivated by repeated failure and want to quit.

• **Goals should be realistic.** Effective goals are also realistic, although you need to remember that the word *realistic* is a relative term. What might be realistic for one athlete may not be realistic for another. To determine whether or not a particular athlete's goals are realistic, you need a sense of that athlete's past performance or present capabilities. For a basketball player who has never attempted a hook shot, the goal of making 8 out of 10 hook shots during the first practice session would be unrealistic. However, for an experienced player, 8 successful shots out of 10 attempts in a practice session and a 70 percent shooting percentage for the season might be very realistic.

• **Goals should be specific.** Vague wording is a frequent problem for athletes when attempting to set goals. A volleyball player might say, "My goal is to be the best hitter on the team," or a swimmer might say, "My goal is to win the race." In each of these examples, the athlete sets a goal that is difficult to evaluate because it isn't clear what behaviors are required for goal achievement. Examples of more specifically worded goals include to "increase my kill percentage from 60 to 70 percent and decrease my number of unforced errors from 10 to 7 in a three-set match" and to "lower my time in the 100-meter freestyle by 0.3 seconds." Helping your athletes state their goals in specific terms lets them evaluate their progress more accurately. When they do this, athletes are more likely to see the value of their goals and less likely to abandon them.

## Outcome Goals

The most common types of goals athletes set for themselves are **outcome goals**. Outcome goals represent the results an athlete hopes to achieve for a particular performance or over a period of time. Examples of outcome goals include winning a batting title in baseball, finishing no lower than third place in the high jump competition at a conference track meet, achieving a free throw percentage of 70 percent over the course of a basketball season, and swimming 100 meters in a time of 1:15 during a training session.

Outcome goals represent the results an athlete hopes to achieve, such as winning a race in track.

Outcome goals allow athletes to easily assess their skill improvements, and the goals can be quickly evaluated by using available statistics (e.g., batting average, free throw percentage, race times, and so on). However, the downside to many of these statistics is that they indicate little about the athlete's actual performance. A baseball player's batting average reveals nothing about how frequently the player made solid contact with the ball during a given number of at-bats. Similarly, a high jumper may not place among the top three competitors at a track meet, although her score may be a personal best. Thus, in addition to setting outcome goals, your athletes need to set goals that represent a more accurate assessment of their actual performance. As you might guess, these types of goals are called performance goals.

## Performance Goals

**Performance goals** enable athletes to evaluate improvements in their own performance, irrespective of the outcomes they achieved or how they did relative to other athletes or opponents. A punter might set a performance goal of increasing his punting average from 38 to 43 yards over the course of a season. Or an 800-meter runner might set a performance goal of improving her previous best time by two seconds in the next meet.

Athletes can also use performance goals to evaluate improvements in the behaviors necessary for goal achievement. A basketball player might set a performance goal of visually focusing on the middle of the rim before each shot. In this case, the performance goal reflects the athlete's desire to improve the mental skill of attention focusing. A high jumper might set performance goals of driving the lead leg across the body at takeoff and looking down the bar when attempting to clear it. In this example, the jumper's first goal concerns a particular element of the technical skill (i.e., the leg action), while the second involves improving the mental skill of focusing.

The main advantage of performance goals is that they call for behaviors that are completely

Performance goals describe task-relevant behaviors that contribute to successful skill execution, such as focusing on the middle of the rim during a free throw shot in basketball.

under the athlete's control. The downside of performance goals is that these behaviors are sometimes difficult to evaluate. How, for example, does the basketball player measure the quality of his visual focus on the rim or the high jumper measure the quality of the movement of her lead leg across her body? One way is to assign a subjective rating to the behavior itself. For example, the basketball player might rate the quality of his visual focus on a scale from 1 to 3, with 1 being "unacceptable," 2 being "acceptable," and 3 being "outstanding." The high jumper could do the same thing, except she might rate her form by watching a video of each of her attempts during a high jump competition.

In addition to encouraging your athletes to rate their own behaviors, you should rate their behaviors as well. You can then share your ratings with each athlete to see which aspects of performance you both believe are in need of particular attention. If you have access to portable video equipment, you could tape the athlete's performance and then review it together to determine how well the athlete appears to be achieving the desired behavior (e.g., visual focus on the rim, lead leg crossing). If you don't have access to video equipment, you will need to evaluate the athlete's behavior during actual performance. In either case, you should position yourself (or the video camera) in a location that provides the best viewing perspective for evaluating the behavior.

Since goals are an individual matter, it is important to individualize the goal-setting process as much as possible. That way all your athletes will be more motivated to work on the things they need to improve in order to achieve success. Remember to use the CARS criteria (figure 6.1) when helping athletes set their goals, and encourage them to set performance goals as well as outcome goals. A baseball player, for example, might set an outcome goal of achieving a .300 batting average for the season and a performance goal of hitting the ball with the "fat" part of the bat. To achieve his performance goal, the player might also set mental goals of relaxing his body and focusing his attention on the seams of the approaching ball on every pitch. By setting goals that pertain to the process of performing, athletes become more aware of the keys to their success. Moreover, they are more likely to

FIGURE 6.1   Keep the CARS criteria in mind when helping athletes set their goals.

remain motivated when they don't achieve their outcome goals. If the aforementioned player doesn't get any hits during a practice or in a game but stays relaxed at the plate, maintains a sharp focus on the seams of the ball, and makes solid contact with the ball, he knows he is achieving the performance goals that will eventually help him achieve his outcome goal.

## Analyzing Technical Skills

You have identified the technical, tactical, and mental skills you want to teach and have helped your athletes set the kinds of goals that should motivate them to develop their skills. However, to evaluate their progress you must also be proficient in **skill analysis**. When it comes to analyzing technical skills, the first step is to identify the elements of the skill that must be mastered in order to achieve success. Generally speaking, **technical skill elements** fall into three categories: movement elements, perceptual elements, and conceptual elements.

An important movement element of technical skills is the relative timing pattern of body and limb segments, such as the differences in the speed of the lower arm action and upper arm action when throwing.

### Movement Elements

All technical skills possess distinctive **movement elements**—a unique pattern of coordinated activity among several combinations of joints and muscles. The leg stride and arm swing elements of the tennis ground stroke; the repetitive and alternating arm and leg actions of freestyle swimming; the leg thrust and arm pull in rowing; and the running approach, foot plant, and arm extension in the javelin throw are illustrations of such **coordination patterns**. Another important feature of all coordinated movements is the **relative timing pattern** of body and limb segments. In throwing a ball, the upper arm moves at a slower speed than the lower arm, and the lower arm moves at a slower speed than the wrist. Put another way, the wrist action is faster than the

lower arm action, and the lower arm action is faster than the upper arm action. In fact, it's this pattern of progressive acceleration of the arm from shoulder to wrist that provides the forces necessary for successful projection of the ball toward its target. The relative timing pattern of technical skills can be viewed more simply as the rhythm of the action.

Although you do not need to know all the biomechanical properties of the technical skills of your sport, you do need to be aware of the basic rhythm and coordination pattern of each. An excellent source for this type of information is Gerry Carr's book *Sport Mechanics for Coaches*. Table 6.3 contains some examples of movement elements for the preparation, execution, and follow-through phases of the tennis forehand

TABLE 6.3

## Examples of Movement Elements for Two Technical Skills

| Tennis forehand volley | Basketball jump shot |
|---|---|
| **PREPARATION** | |
| Knees bent, short backswing, eyes level with ball | Knees bent, elbows in, ball held high between ear and shoulder |
| **EXECUTION** | |
| Forward step made with opposite foot, wrist firm at contact | Shooting elbow extended, wrist and fingers flexed forward |
| **FOLLOW-THROUGH** | |
| Short follow-through, balance quickly recovered | Shooting hand palm down, balance maintained on landing |

volley and the basketball jump shot. Your challenge is to know the movement elements essential for effective performance of the technical skills of your sport and, when you see errors in those elements, to provide your athletes with appropriate focus cues for correcting errors. In many cases, the elements themselves represent the best candidates for focus cues (see table 6.3 again). For example, a tennis player who is taking a long backswing when preparing to hit a volley might be told to "shorten the backswing."

## Perceptual Elements

In addition to the important movement elements of technical skills, **perceptual elements** are sometimes crucial for successful performance. In chapter 4, you learned that information processing includes the interpretation of the environment. To achieve performance success in some sports, particularly those performed in open environments (chapter 3), athletes need to attend to and interpret relevant environmental cues. A soccer goalie must watch the movements of opposing players and the flight pattern of the approaching ball in order to prepare and execute an appropriate response at the correct moment.

Subpar technical skill performance is sometimes due to an inaccurate interpretation of environmental cues rather than improper execution of the movement pattern. A softball batter may produce a mechanically sound swing yet miss the ball because she failed to identify the pitcher's release point or was unable to interpret

the speed and trajectory of the approaching ball. Similarly, a wrestler might execute a mechanically sound maneuver but fail to achieve the desired result because he misinterpreted his opponent's actions.

To provide the best assistance for your athletes, you must identify the environmental cues that are most important for performance success. Once you have done this, you should repeatedly emphasize those cues and encourage your athletes to focus on them whenever they are performing. Examples of perceptual elements include detecting the speed and spin of the approaching ball (for baseball and softball batters, volleyball players, and tennis players), estimating the time of arrival at the wall (for swimmers executing a flip turn), and reading the breaks and speed of a green (for golfers). To enhance the detection of some of the preceding perceptual elements, you might instruct volleyball players to watch the ball come off the server's hand, backstrokers to look for the flags marking the end of the lane, and golfers to bend down or kneel in order to visually detect the slope of the green that inclines toward the hole.

## Conceptual Elements

**Conceptual elements**, the third category of technical elements, refer to the strategic and rule-bound aspects of the skill. In tennis it is important that performers hit their shots deep in order to keep their opponents as far from the net as possible. The player who positions herself nearer the net is better able to control the pace and tempo of the point. This type of conceptual element is strategic in nature and is relevant to the successful execution of technical skills such as volleys and ground strokes. Rule-bound conceptual elements represent the things athletes need to know in order to avoid penalties or to execute certain strategies while performing their technical skills. For example, one tennis rule states that any ball that passes outside the net post and below the top of the net and that lands within the boundaries of the opponent's court is in play. Players familiar with this rule would know that the execution of a ground stroke that satisfies those criteria is an option whenever the opponent moves them outside the sideline of their own court.

Following are some examples of conceptual elements from other sports:

- Maintaining court or field balance in basketball or soccer (because maximum coverage requires players to be situated at all points on the court or field)

- Staying inside the sideline boundary when running a pass route in football (because the player becomes an ineligible receiver if he steps outside the sideline at any time before catching a pass)

- Keeping the trajectory of throws from the outfield in baseball or softball as low as possible (because this enables an infielder to intercept, or "cut off," a throw if it is off target)

- Achieving a stationary defensive position before contact with an approaching offensive player in basketball (because this is the criterion officials use to determine whether the defensive player has committed a blocking foul or the offensive player is guilty of charging)

As a coach, you obviously must know the basic strategies and rules of your sport and be able to convey them as clearly as possible to your athletes. The best way to do this is to discuss a particular strategy or rule when it is relevant to the execution of technical skills your athletes are practicing. For example, the offensive foul rule in basketball should be discussed when players

The conceptual elements of technical skills include strategic aspects such as running near the inside boundary of a lane in track.

are practicing the technical skill of "taking a charge." If you are working with more advanced athletes, check their knowledge of a particular conceptual element by asking them questions at random moments in a workout (e.g., during a water break, ask a more experienced baseball player to explain the infield fly rule, catcher's interference, or the proper execution of a rundown play).

## Identifying Target Behaviors

Once you have determined the important technical skill elements and tactical and mental skills of your sport, you need to identify which ones your athletes need to focus on in order to maximize their prospects for success. In chapter 5, you learned that attention is limited and that athletes can only be expected to focus on one or two things at a time when they are performing. Thus, when coaching your athletes, make sure they focus only on those behaviors that will give them the best chance of succeeding. One strategy is to think of those behaviors as **target behaviors** because they are the objects of athletes' focus. By focusing on producing the important target behaviors, athletes will give themselves the best opportunity to achieve both their performance goals (e.g., the improved synchronization of arm strokes and breathing in the 100-meter freestyle) and their outcome goals (e.g., achieving a time of 1:15 or better in a training session).

Remember that each athlete's performance depends on the successful execution of certain target behaviors. A soccer player's perfectly timed pass to a moving teammate may be due to his focus on executing specific technical elements, such as a smooth kicking motion (movement element); his accurate judgment about his teammate's running speed (perceptual element); or his appropriate application of the principle of "leading" the receiver (conceptual element). In addition, the player's passing success may have been due to effective employment of a tactical

skill (e.g., a correct decision as to the type of pass to use against a particular opponent) or mental skill (e.g., remembering the speed of the opponent, shifting attention from the anticipated target to the seams of the ball during contact, maintaining a relaxed intensity).

Conversely, an athlete's failure to produce the desired response may be the result of a lack of focus on the essential target behaviors or a focus on nonessential ones. A beginning swimmer in her first competitive race should probably not focus on advanced race tactics (i.e., tactical skills); instead, she should focus on the execution of correct stroke mechanics (i.e., movement elements of the technical skill). In a similar vein, an experienced swimmer in a championship race should probably not focus on stroke mechanics because it would take her technical skill off of "automatic" and put her at risk of "paralysis by analysis."

For your athletes to feel confident when performing, they must be focused on the target behaviors they know will give them the best chance of achieving success. As mentioned previously, these behaviors may differ for different athletes at different times. To provide the most helpful instruction, you must be aware of the various target behaviors necessary for success in the different skills of your sport. One way to do this is by creating a checklist like the one shown in figure 6.2, which contains possible target behaviors athletes might focus on to produce effective topspin ground strokes in a tennis match.

A tennis coach could periodically use the chart in figure 6.2 to evaluate a player's ground strokes during scrimmages or actual matches. The coach would place a check mark beside those skills or skill elements he or she sees the player executing well and an "x" beside those that appear to be in need of further improvement or that are difficult to assess. At a convenient time, the coach could share his or her evaluation with the player and then ask the player which target behaviors he was focusing on when hitting his ground strokes, which ones he felt were the most effective, and which ones he might want to focus on during the next match. A blank version of a checklist for target behaviors is provided in figure 6.3. Use figure 6.3 to list the target behaviors for various skills in the sports you coach.

© PhotoDisc

Skill improvements require a focus on the execution of essential target behaviors, such as the follow-through that is necessary to produce a topspin forehand ground stroke in tennis.

## *Obtaining Athletes' Perspectives on the Most Effective Target Behaviors*

Since the athletes are the ones doing the performing, it is helpful to know which target behaviors they are focusing on when they practice and compete. Keep in mind that at times your athletes may be focused not on any relevant target behavior but on thoughts of coming through in the clutch or not screwing up. A soccer player attempting a penalty kick might be focused on the irrelevant thought of how terrible he will feel if he fails to score and lets his teammates down instead of on any of a variety of relevant target behaviors (e.g., executing a smooth and solid follow-through, anticipating the goalkeeper's movements, determining the desired target to shoot for, staying relaxed). Although you might be able to detect the player's focus by watching his eyes and observing his body language, the best way to corroborate what you observe is to obtain feedback from the athlete. At an appropriate time, share your observations with him, and ask him what he remembers focusing on and whether he felt the focus was effective. Regardless of the player's response, you will have a much better idea of what kinds of assistance to offer than if you did not obtain his feedback.

Of course, your athletes will be open to provide you with honest feedback only if they trust you and feel comfortable sharing their thoughts and feelings. Their trust and comfort level will depend on your ability to develop the kind of communication that allows them to share their experiences without the fear of ridicule or reprisal. The next chapter discusses some ways you can develop open, two-way communication with them.

Even in game situations, you can discuss target behaviors with athletes.

# Target Behaviors for Effective Topspin Ground Strokes in Tennis

Technical skill: _Topspin ground strokes_

## Technical skill elements

MOVEMENT ELEMENTS

*Preparation phase*

__Draw racket back early

__Turn side to net

__Step toward target

*Execution phase*

__Shift weight forward

__Swing parallel to court

__Minimize wrist movement

*Follow-through phase*

__Continue swing after ball contact

__Swing out, across body, and up

PERCEPTUAL ELEMENTS

*Preparation phase*

__Watch arm action of opponent

__See ball come off opponent's racket

__Observe speed and trajectory of ball

*Execution phase*

__Try to visually follow the ball to contact point

*Follow-through phase*

__Observe speed and trajectory of ball

__Watch preparatory movements of opponent

CONCEPTUAL ELEMENTS

*Preparation phase*

__Consider possible target options

__Take racket back early

__Keep feet moving

*Execution phase*

__Keep the ball deep

__Emphasize both speed and accuracy

*Follow-through phase*

__Briefly evaluate effectiveness of outcome

## Tactical skills

__Speed up the tempo when winning, slow down when momentum seems to be shifting to the opponent

__Identify opponent's strengths, weaknesses, and preferences

__Exploit opponent's weaknesses and anticipate opponent's preferences on big points

## Mental skills

__Maintain primary focus on seams of ball during points

__Use relaxation breaths to decrease arousal level

__Refocus during change-overs

FIGURE 6.2 Sample checklist of target behaviors.

# Checklist for Target Behaviors

Technical skill: _____

## Technical skill elements

### MOVEMENT ELEMENTS

*Preparation phase*

__1. _____
__2. _____
__3. _____

*Execution phase*

__1. _____
__2. _____
__3. _____

*Follow-through phase*

__1. _____
__2. _____
__3. _____

### PERCEPTUAL ELEMENTS

*Preparation phase*

__1. _____
__2. _____
__3. _____

*Execution phase*

__1. _____
__2. _____
__3. _____

*Follow-through phase*

__1. _____
__2. _____
__3. _____

### CONCEPTUAL ELEMENTS

*Preparation phase*

__1. _____
__2. _____
__3. _____

*Execution phase*

__1. _____
__2. _____
__3. _____

*Follow-through phase*

__1. _____
__2. _____
__3. _____

## Tactical skills

__1. _____
__2. _____
__3. _____
__4. _____
__5. _____

## Mental skills

__1. _____
__2. _____
__3. _____
__4. _____
__5. _____

FIGURE 6.3   Use this blank checklist to identify the target behaviors for a technical skill in the sport you coach. When observing athletes, place a check mark beside the technical skill elements, tactical skills, and mental skills you see the player executing well and an "x" beside those that appear to be in need of further improvement or that are difficult to assess.

From C.A. Wrisberg, 2007, *Sport skill instruction for coaches* (Champaign, IL: Human Kinetics).

To emphasize the importance of target behaviors, ask your athletes to do the following:

1. *Before practice:* identify the technical, tactical, and mental target behaviors they think are essential for performance success (some examples are shown in table 6.4)

2. *During practice:* try to focus on those behaviors on a consistent basis

3. *After practice:* evaluate the effectiveness with which they achieved the desired focus and produced the desired behaviors

4. *Before and during competitions:* remember their key target behaviors, try to focus on them throughout the competition, and keep focusing on them even if something goes wrong

By emphasizing a focus on relevant target behaviors, you will teach your athletes two important lessons:

1. Success is the result of consistent execution of task-relevant behaviors.

2. They are in control of the behaviors they choose to focus on.

TABLE 6.4

## Examples of Technical, Tactical, and Mental Target Behaviors

| **TECHNICAL TARGET BEHAVIORS** |
| --- |
| Reading the speed of an approaching ball in sports such as soccer, tennis, baseball, softball, and volleyball |
| Producing the correct relative timing pattern for a particular technical skill (e.g., the pattern of arm, head, and leg movements for the breaststroke in swimming) |

| **TACTICAL TARGET BEHAVIORS** |
| --- |
| Increasing tempo when momentum is in the athlete's favor during a tennis match and slowing down when momentum seems to be shifting to the opponent |
| Forcing opponents to do things they don't do well (e.g., getting back quickly on defense to force a fast-break oriented basketball team to run their half-court offense) |

| **MENTAL TARGET BEHAVIORS** |
| --- |
| Taking a relaxation breath and remembering a relevant focus cue after an error, a bad break, or a poor call by an official |
| Using the same preperformance routine before every practice repetition of a closed skill such as field goal kicking, free throw shooting, and tennis serving |

# SUMMARY

1. When deciding which skills athletes need to learn, consider tactical and mental skills as well as technical skills.

2. Goal setting is an essential prerequisite for effective teaching and learning.

3. The most effective goals are challenging, attainable, realistic, and specific.

4. Outcome goals pertain to the desired results (e.g., winning the race), while performance goals describe the improvements athletes would like to achieve in their own behaviors or performance (e.g., maintaining a consistent stroke tempo or improving the speed of flip turns).

5. Athletes' achievement of outcome and performance goals is often dependent on the effective execution of technical, tactical, and mental skills.

6. The evaluation of outcome and performance goals requires an accurate identification of the skills and skill elements necessary for successful performance.

7. When teaching or analyzing technical skills, three categories of technical skill elements need to be considered: movement elements, perceptual elements, and conceptual elements.

8. Two critical movement elements of all technical skills are the fundamental coordination pattern and the relative timing pattern.

9. Perceptual elements are an important component of technical skills performed in open environments.

10. Conceptual elements involve rule-bound aspects of technical skills.

11. Target behaviors are the technical skill elements, tactical skills, and mental skills athletes must focus on to give themselves the best chance of succeeding in their sport.

12. Target behaviors should be emphasized during skill instruction and discussed with athletes when evaluating their performance.

# KEY TERMS

| | | |
|---|---|---|
| CARS | movement elements | relative timing pattern |
| conceptual elements | outcome goals | skill analysis |
| coordination pattern | perceptual elements | target behaviors |
| goal setting | performance goals | technical skill elements |

# REVIEW QUESTIONS

1. What are the four principles of effective goal setting? Explain why all four principles are necessary for a goal to be beneficial.

2. Why are performance goals more effective than outcome goals in promoting athletes' skill development?

3. How would you describe the coordination pattern and relative timing pattern of a technical skill in your sport?

4. What is the difference between the perceptual elements and the conceptual elements of technical skills?

5. What are target behaviors, and how might you use them in providing instructional assistance to your athletes?

# PRACTICAL ACTIVITIES

1. List some of the key movement elements, perceptual elements, and conceptual elements of a technical skill in your sport.

2. Using figure 6.3 on page 90, develop a checklist of possible target behaviors for a particular technical skill in a sport you are familiar with.

3. Using the checklist you developed in the previous activity, list three target behaviors you might instruct an inexperienced athlete to focus on during a practice session. Then list three target behaviors you think an experienced athlete should focus on before or during a critical moment in an important competition. Explain the rationale for each of your choices.

# 7

# Deciding on the Content and Structure of Practice

When you finish reading this chapter, you should be able to explain

1. the games approach to practice;
2. how to set the stage for learning by opening communication with your athletes, helping them determine their goals, and helping them identify target behaviors;
3. how to use verbal instructions, visual demonstrations, and physical guidance to help athletes gain an initial grasp of technical skills;
4. how to modify the practice of technical skills using part practice and slow-motion practice;
5. how to structure technical skill practice by blocking, varying, and randomizing repetitions;
6. how to help your athletes develop anticipation for environmental events; and
7. how to use the games approach to prepare your athletes for competition.

Chapters 3 through 6 focused on what to teach, and the rest of the book explains how to provide effective learning experiences for your athletes. This chapter describes the games approach to skill practice and explains how you can use this approach to prepare your athletes for the various challenges they will face in competition. You'll learn how to set the stage for instruction by opening two-way communication with athletes; providing helpful verbal instructions, visual demonstrations, and physical guidance; and modifying practice by breaking skills down into parts and rehearsing them in slow motion.

Next, you'll learn how to structure the practice of technical skills in ways that maximize skill learning and promote the development of athletes' anticipation of environmental events. Finally, the chapter suggests some ways you can use the games approach to help your athletes transfer what they learn in practices to competitive situations.

## Games Approach to Skill Practice

"If practice makes perfect, what will my athletes be perfecting in practice today?" The preceding question is one you should contemplate every time you plan a practice session. Since the purpose of practice is to prepare athletes for competition, you need to design your practices to achieve this purpose. The question is, how?

In his book *Successful Coaching,* Rainer Martens suggests that the traditional approach to sport practice may not be the best way to equip athletes for competition. According to Martens, the real issue is whether practice improves athletes' skill, assuming *skill* means "the proficient use of techniques and tactics to play the sport" (2004, p. 170). The traditional approach to practice typically begins with some form of physical warm-up, followed by an introduction of the skill or skills to be rehearsed that day. Once the plan is announced, athletes practice the various skills in drill-like fashion, and the coach provides feedback as needed, either for individuals or the entire team. A scrimmage is sometimes included to give athletes the opportunity to practice their skills in an environment that resembles competition in some way. A period of physical conditioning may be added at the end of a practice if the coach thinks it's necessary. On the surface, this approach appears to make sense. Moreover, the majority of coaches have followed this approach over the years. However, Martens points out several drawbacks to the traditional approach that diminish its effectiveness as a tool for skill development. These include

- an overemphasis on technical skills and an underemphasis on tactical and mental skills;
- an overemphasis on a command style of teaching and an underemphasis on athletes' problem-solving skills;
- repetitive drills that have little or no resemblance to competition-like situations; and
- frequent boredom, particularly when athletes spend more time waiting in line than practicing.

As an alternative to the traditional approach, Martens recommends the **games approach**, which emphasizes skill learning through competition-like practices. The conceptual rationale for this approach is that it helps athletes achieve an appreciation of the technical, tactical, and mental skills of their sport because they practice them in ways that are more relevant to competition. Table 7.1 provides a summary of the advantages of the games approach to practice.

TABLE 7.1

### Advantages of the Games Approach to Sport Practice

- Skills are taught through competition-like activities.
- Athletes learn to appreciate the main purposes of their sport as well as the relevant technical, tactical, and mental skills.
- Athletes are taught to think for themselves.
- Two-way communication exists between athletes and the coach.
- Practices are athlete centered and focused on athletes' needs.
- Practices are fun, relevant, and challenging.

Adapted from R. Martens, 2004, *Successful coaching*, 3rd ed. (Champaign, IL: Human Kinetics), 180.

In table 7.2, you can see how the traditional approach and games approach compare in the sport of baseball. Notice that the traditional approach is more fixed, rigid, and coach centered than the games approach. Drills are typically performed in the same way and often in the same order day after day, little attention is devoted to the development of individual players, and players get the message that the way to improve is to "do what I tell you to do, and the more often you do it, the better you'll get." In the games approach, practices resemble the demands of competition in that players are constantly being challenged technically, tactically, and mentally. Moreover, they are actively involved in the decision-making process and in assisting one another. This athlete-centered environment sends a more positive message:

"You are capable of making good decisions and getting the job done. So go for it!"

As a coach, you need to do three things when implementing the games approach in your practices. First, shape the play by creating opportunities for **relevant practice**—teach only those skills and activities that are relevant for competition. Second, focus the play by directing your athletes' attention to the key elements of the sport. And third, enhance the play by creating practices that are challenging, motivating, and enjoyable. In the remainder of this chapter, you'll learn some methods to shape, focus, and enhance your athletes' practice experiences. To do any of these things well, you must first establish good communication with your athletes, so let's take a look at how you can do that.

TABLE 7.2

## Traditional Approach and Games Approach to Practicing Baseball

| **Traditional approach** | **Games approach** |
| --- | --- |
| **Drills are used to practice technical skills.** Batting practice consists of each player attempting 3 bunts and then 15 full swings. Other players are positioned around the infield and outfield, talking to each other and returning balls hit to them toward the pitcher's mound. | **Drills are used to teach both technical and tactical skills of the sport.** During batting practice, players are stationed at each fielding position; any additional players serve as baserunners to create gamelike situations. The batter, baserunner(s), and fielders then practice executing the most appropriate technical and tactical response for each situation (e.g., with a runner on second and no outs, the batter tries to hit the ball toward the first base side, infielders try to hold the runner at second before making a play to first, and outfielders hit the correct cutoff person with their throws). |
| **Specific skills are taught in isolation and then combined later.** Isolated bouts of batting practice, fielding practice, and baserunning practice are culminated with a competition-like scrimmage. | **The sport is taught as a whole, and the parts are refined as necessary.** Batting, fielding, pitching, and baserunning are practiced together in competition-like situations as much as possible. The coach then provides feedback to players about the specific technical and tactical skills they need to target for further improvement. |
| **Instruction is coach centered and often ignores the individual needs of athletes.** The coach stops batting practice to lecture the entire team on how to hit pitches to the opposite field because one batter is having difficulty doing so. | **Instruction is athlete centered.** The coach targets feedback to individuals and addresses the entire team only when discussing information that is pertinent to everyone. |

*(continued)*

TABLE 7.2

## *(continued)*

| Traditional approach | Games approach |
|---|---|
| **Practices are often boring and unmotivating.** During batting practice, most players are standing around doing little more than fielding an occasional ball and softly tossing it toward the pitcher. | **Practices are fun, challenging, and relevant to the demands of competition.** Players are challenged to refine their technical and tactical skills in a variety of competition-like situations (e.g., base-runners practice advancing from first to third rather than stopping at second whenever they see an outfielder fumble a batted ball). |
| **Players are highly dependent on the coach.** Players don't dare deviate from the coach's directions and instructions. An outfielder who needs to improve the accuracy of his throws to third base avoids doing so during batting practice because the coach has instructed all players to softly toss balls they field toward the pitcher's mound. | **Athletes take an increasingly active role in the learning process and become less dependent on the coach.** The shortstop and second base player converse about the different types of throws and pivots that might work best for different types of double play situations. |
| **The coach strives to develop automaticity of technical skill execution through extensive and repetitious drills.** Players engage in the same batting, fielding, and base-running drills day after day. | **Practices are designed to promote creative thinking and effective decision making.** The infielders, pitcher, and catcher confer about what each will do in a particular situation during batting practice (e.g., runners on first and second with no outs in the ninth inning, with the game tied and a left-handed power hitter at bat). |
| **The coach makes all decisions with little or no player input.** The coach decides which of two batters a pitcher should face in a close game with runners on second and third and two outs. | **Athletes are encouraged to provide input to the coach in decision making.** The coach asks a pitcher which of the next two batters he would rather face in a close game with runners on second and third and two outs. |
| **Players are not encouraged to help each other.** An outfielder who sees a flaw in his teammate's throwing doesn't mention it to the teammate because he's not the coach. | **Athletes are encouraged to help each other master the skills of the sport.** A skilled bunter helps a teammate who is having difficulty executing a successful bunt. |
| **The coach prefers a command style where he or she makes all the decisions.** The coach does all the talking, and the players are expected to do exactly what they are told to do. | **The coach prefers a cooperative style that strikes a balance between directing athletes and allowing athletes to direct themselves.** The coach confers with a pitcher and catcher about the best way to pitch to a particular batter, and they go with the decision they all agree on. |

Adapted from R. Martens, 2004, *Successful coaching*, 3rd ed. (Champaign, IL: Human Kinetics), 180.

## Establishing Two-Way Communication

All sport practice has a starting point. Since the games approach calls for the creation of an athlete-centered practice environment, it's important to "get off on the right foot" with your athletes. To do this you need to develop good communication with them, help them define their goals, and identify relevant target behaviors for them to work on. Goals and target behaviors were discussed in chapter 6; this section focuses on communication.

Skill learning can be an intimidating experience. Attempting new things they're not good at can make athletes feel vulnerable and self-conscious, creating a barrier to learning. The

To provide the most effective instructional assistance, try to establish open, two-way communication with your athletes.

best way to ease athletes' anxieties is to establish open, **two-way communication.** You can encourage this by spending some time getting to know your athletes, making them believe their perspectives are important, and inviting them to ask you for help when they need it. Whenever possible, try to talk with your athletes individually about things going on in their lives as well as issues pertaining to your sport. Let them know that your instructions and feedback are intended to help them improve their skills and enjoy their athletic experience.

## *Communicating Without Words*

Effective communication involves more than words. How you convey the things you say (e.g., tone of voice, volume) is at least as important as what you say. To experience this for yourself, say, "Good job," in two different ways. First, say it with energy and enthusiasm. Now, say it in a sarcastic, derogatory fashion. If your athletes hear a sincere and enthusiastic "Good job," they will be encouraged to continue to give a good effort. However, if they hear a sarcastic and disgusted "Good job," they will wonder what you are unhappy about and may become more anxious or frustrated.

Your body language is another important ingredient of communication. To illustrate this point, repeat the previous exercise, this time while looking in a mirror. Notice how your facial expression reflects the tone you use when you say, "Good job," in the two different ways.

An athlete who tries her best and then sees you frowning or shaking your head gets the message that her best effort isn't good enough for you.

As with spoken communication, **unspoken communication** is a two-way street. Therefore, you also need to pay close attention to your athletes' body language to determine how they might be feeling. Athletes with their heads down and shoulders slumped are probably not feeling very good about themselves, whereas those who walk with their heads up and a spring in their step are probably feeling confident about how they are performing. The discouraged athlete needs your assistance and encouragement, while the confident athlete requires additional challenges and the opportunity to demonstrate or continue to improve his skills.

Chapter 8 identifies the various types of feedback you might choose from, but for now remember that most of what you say to your athletes will take the form of either knowledge of results or knowledge of performance.

**Knowledge of results** is information about the outcomes of technical skills or tactical decisions. You might tell a high jumper that the height she achieved in her last attempt was 1.6 meters or a tennis player that 80 percent of his second serves were to the opponent's backhand. **Knowledge of performance** is information about the process of skill execution, regardless of the outcome. You might tell a softball player that she needs to field ground balls more in front of her body than off to the side so that if the ball takes a bad hop, she is still able to block it. When communicating these two types of information to your athletes, use plain and simple language, providing no more than one or two suggestions at a time. It's also a good idea to ask them if they understand what you are saying or better yet ask them to explain to you what they heard you say. If they can tell you what you said, you can be pretty sure they heard you and are capable of using the feedback to improve or adjust their subsequent performance. When listening to your athletes, show them you are interested in what they are saying by maintaining eye contact and allowing them to finish speaking before you respond.

Most important, match your actions to your words. I'm from Missouri (the show-me state), and I have been known to remind people that others will be more impressed by what you show them than by what you tell them. If you tell your athletes to be patient when things don't go well, you must demonstrate patience when things don't go well for you.

## Instructions, Demonstrations, and Guidance

As mentioned at the beginning of this chapter, one of the things you'll need to do when using the games approach in your practices is focus your athletes' attention on relevant information. Three techniques you can use to do this are verbal instructions, visual demonstrations, and physical guidance.

## Verbal Instructions

**Verbal instructions** can include everything from the key elements of the sport to descriptions of the various tactical and mental skills essential for success to explanations of the mechanics or the relative timing pattern of technical skills.

Instructions can also convey information about the feelings your athletes can expect to experience when performing a technical skill. You might alert a gymnast to the pulling feeling she will experience in the arms and shoulders when practicing on the uneven bars. Or you might tell a running back to briefly take note of the feel of maintaining good balance while exploding through an opening in the line.

By providing advance information about the mechanics of a technical skill or the kinds of thoughts and feelings that accompany performance, you can diminish athletes' anxiety and make them feel more in control of their practice activities. Athletes might also appreciate instructions that help them connect past experiences with the present situation. A verbal reminder that the weight shift from rear foot to front foot when hitting a tennis forehand is similar to that used in batting would be helpful for aspiring tennis players with previous baseball or softball experience.

Before providing athletes with verbal instructions, consider the following three questions:

- Can the point I'm about to make be accurately described in words?
- Will it convey an appropriate amount of information?
- Does it represent a relevant learning cue?

Regarding the first question, skills that involve some thinking or mental analysis lend themselves more to verbal descriptions than do skills that primarily rely on vision or feel. For example, verbal instructions would be more effective for focusing a springboard diver's attention on the sequence of movements in a complex dive than for focusing a gymnast's attention on the feel of walking on the balance beam. Verbal descriptions would also be helpful when focusing athletes' attention on the relevant tactical skills and mental skills of your sport.

# Using Learning Cues to Focus Athletes' Attention

Effective coaching often involves saying the right thing at the right time. Timely and relevant learning cues direct athletes' attention to the thoughts and feelings that contribute to successful performance. Here are some examples from several sports.

## Baseball

Look for the seams, keep the hands inside the ball, stride and hit (for batters), hit the catcher's glove, follow through, just this pitch (for pitchers)

## Basketball

Make sharp cuts (on offense), keep the shoulders square (when shooting), quick slide steps (on defense)

## Football

Run to daylight (for ball carriers), keep your head on a swivel (for special-teams players running downfield), finish the kick (for placekickers)

## Swimming

Keep the legs tucked (on the flip turn), explode (off the blocks), relax and maintain rhythm (throughout each length during a distance event)

## Tennis

Hit the ball on the rise (for ground strokes), firm grip at contact (for volleys), lift and release (for the ball toss on the serve)

Keep in mind that athletes need to be given some time to try out new strategies and evaluate feedback on their own. More instructions are not always better. Therefore, it's important to resist the temptation to "overcoach," and one way to do this is through the timely use of learning cues.

Of relevance to the second and third questions are the concepts of limited attention capacity and working memory (chapter 5). Remember that most athletes are able to attend to or hold in working memory only a few pieces of information at one time. Excessive information is particularly problematic for athletes who are hearing an instruction for the first time. Therefore, restrict the amount and length of your verbal instructions to ensure that your athletes focus on the most relevant elements of the skill you are teaching them. A short, precise statement such as "Stay smooth and follow through" would be more helpful for a basketball player attempting a free throw shot than "Keep your weight evenly distributed, shooting elbow

in, eyes on the rim, knees bent, and shoulders relaxed" (see figure 7.1).

It is also a good idea to prioritize the information you want your athletes to focus on, emphasizing the fundamental concepts first and providing no more than one or two new points at a time. During the initial stage of technical skill practice, you should provide instructions that direct athletes' attention to the relative timing pattern of the movement. For a batter, this might be "Make your hands move faster than your arms" if you want to focus the batter's attention on the rapid wrist action he needs to achieve. Once athletes have acquired the basic relative timing pattern, use instructions to point out ways they might adjust the action. For the

FIGURE 7.1   Keep verbal instructions simple, and emphasize no more than two key points at a time.

batter, an example might be "Try to make contact with the ball out in front of the plate" or "Step with your front foot in the direction you want the ball to go."

You can also use verbal instructions to assess your athletes' understanding of important tactics and strategy or to determine how they are thinking or what they are focusing on at a particular moment. Martens suggests

## Short and Sweet

The best instructions are short and to the point. They focus athletes' attention on what they should be trying to do (e.g., look for the seams, relax the shoulders, stay smooth) rather than on what they should be trying to avoid doing (e.g., don't pay attention to the spectators, don't tense the shoulders, don't be stiff). Verbal cues are miniature versions of instructions that direct athletes' attention to a particular aspect of a skill in one or two words (e.g., *brace* and *punch* might be good verbal cues if you want to focus a soccer player's attention on the keys to heading the ball).

a focusing technique he calls the "freeze replay" in which the coach stops practice (by saying, "Freeze!") and asks athletes to describe such things as what they just did correctly, what they are focusing on at this moment, what the tactical options of the present situation might be, which option they would choose and why, and so on. By doing this, you encourage your athletes to be active participants in the learning process.

## Visual Demonstrations

Another technique you can use to focus your athletes' attention during practices is **visual demonstrations**. Here are the questions you need to ask yourself:

- What is it I want my athletes to see in this demonstration?
- Which viewing angle(s) will enable them to pick up those things?
- How often do I need to provide the demonstration?

When it comes to deciding what you should demonstrate, the answer should always be relevant to successful performance in competition. Examples include the pre-serve receiving position of volleyball players on the back row, the relative timing pattern of a successful back handspring, or the correct location of the pitcher during a sacrifice bunt.

When determining the viewing angle(s) that will give your athletes the best perspective for picking up relevant information, it is a good idea to observe a demonstration yourself from several angles before making the final decision. In some technical skills (e.g., shooting a basketball, punting a football, serving a tennis ball, performing a front somersault on a balance beam), one relevant feature of the skill might be better detected from a side view, while another might be more accurately detected from a front or rear view.

When it comes to deciding how often you should provide a demonstration, the answer

The most effective demonstrations of technical skills clearly convey the desired pattern of relative timing.

ponents. One way to simplify demonstrations is to emphasize one part of the skill at a time. For example, when teaching the correct mechanics of the soccer kick, you might demonstrate the proper placement of the plant foot by itself. Once athletes understand that aspect of the skill, the kicking action can be shown in isolation. The only time you need to demonstrate more than one part at a time is when the parts are closely linked rhythmically. The toss and swing in the tennis serve require rhythmical coordination of the two hands. Therefore, it would not be helpful to demonstrate the two parts separately. For skills like this, try to think of other ways to simplify the demonstration (e.g., tossing the ball with one hand and catching it with an overhand motion of the other hand).

Another way to simplify demonstrations is to perform them in slow motion. When demonstrating technical skills that appear similar but consist of an important difference, a slow-motion presentation is a good way to emphasize the distinction. The curve ball and slider, for example, are two baseball pitches that appear to be delivered in the same way, yet one involves a rotation of the wrist (the curve ball) and the other does not. A slow-motion demonstration that illustrates this subtle difference would be particularly helpful for pitchers who are trying to add the two pitches to their repertoire.

## Physical Guidance

In some cases, technical skill learning requires additional **physical guidance** in order for athletes to achieve a general idea of the desired movement pattern. Two ways you can provide physical guidance are by manually "steering" the athlete's limbs through the desired plane and by limiting or restricting the athlete's own movements. When using **assistive guidance,** you do most of the moving while the athlete remains relatively passive. An example is a gymnastics coach guiding an athlete through a back handspring for the first time. When using **restrictive guidance,** you physically define the boundaries of the movement, and the athlete moves until he "discovers" the boundaries. An example of restrictive guidance is a golf coach standing behind a golfer learning the correct backswing

depends on the athletes' skill level and preference for assistance. Studies suggest that more experienced athletes need fewer demonstrations and are able to detect the key features better than less experienced athletes can. Recent research also indicates that learners benefit more from demonstrations when they ask for them, perhaps because people are more motivated to watch something they want to see than something they don't think they need. Consistent with the games approach to practice, tell your athletes to request a demonstration any time they think it would be helpful.

As is the case when providing verbal instructions, you will sometimes need to keep your demonstrations as simple as possible so as not to overload athletes with too much information. This is particularly true for less experienced athletes and when you are demonstrating technical skills that consist of a number of important com-for a half wedge shot. The coach holds a golf club at a point representing the height of the desired backswing and then instructs the golfer to slowly move her club back until it contacts the club he is holding. In this way, the coach is restricting the length of the golfer's backswing, thereby helping her identify the correct stopping point.

In general, assistive guidance is less effective than restrictive guidance and should be avoided whenever possible. There are three reasons for this. First, assisted movements have a different "feel" than unassisted movements. Second, athletes are not as attentive to the movement, or they attend to different cues when they are being moved than when they are doing the moving. And third, athletes have no opportunity to detect and correct their errors because they are always being guided through the desired move-

Guidance procedures should be used only as long as it takes athletes to gain a basic understanding of the movement.

ment plane. Although assistive guidance may occasionally be necessary for unskilled athletes having difficulty comprehending the correct movement pattern, it should be used sparingly and withdrawn or interspersed with bouts of unassisted practice as soon as possible to promote maximal skill development. A football coach might move an offensive lineman's hands and arms through the desired movement plane of a pass-blocking technique to give the player a general idea of the correct action. However, after a repetition or two of assisted guidance, the player should be allowed to attempt the movement by himself a few times. If necessary, a few repetitions alternating between assisted and unassisted movements could then be practiced until the player is consistently producing the correct movement pattern on his own.

Restrictive guidance may be used with both unskilled and skilled athletes any time they are able to produce the required movement on their own but perhaps require assistance for safety purposes or to fine-tune their coordination. A skilled gymnast who is attempting to add an additional somersault to a dismount might initially need restrictive guidance that prevents her from overrotating and perhaps injuring herself upon landing. Once she has mastered the dismount, restrictive guidance should no longer be necessary.

## Modifications of Technical Skill Rehearsal

Two other ways to focus your athletes' attention on the key elements of a technical skill are to ask them to practice parts of the skill and to rehearse the skill in slow motion.

### Part Practice

Some technical skills are so complex that athletes have trouble focusing on all relevant features at one time. In such cases you might want to let them practice the skill in more manageable units. By using **part practice**, athletes can focus on the key features of the skill until they are able to perform it in its entirety. A pole-vaulter or long jumper might practice the approach in isolation before attempting the pole plant or takeoff maneuver, or a basketball center might

Some complex technical skills may initially need to be broken down into more manageable units for practice.

practice posting up and catching the ball before attempting a drop-step baseline power move.

Before using part practice, you should consider the following questions:

- Is the skill really too complex for the athlete to practice all at once?
- If so, which part(s) can be isolated for focused practice, and which parts need to be kept together to preserve the relative timing pattern of the skill?

Encourage athletes to practice technical skills in their entirety whenever possible. That's the best way to become familiar with the fundamental pattern of relative timing. Practicing the skill as a whole obviously makes more sense for skills that involve rapid, discrete actions (e.g., throwing or kicking a ball, swinging a bat, shooting a basketball, passing a volleyball, jumping as high as possible). Whole-skill practice should also be encouraged whenever part practice would change the dynamics of the skill. For example, the backswing and downswing of the entire golf shot involves a fluid sequence of muscle lengthening and shortening. Practicing either component in isolation would create a swing dynamic (i.e., an abrupt stopping of the backswing or an abrupt starting of the downswing) that differs from the dynamics of the whole shot. Thus, you need to be sure that modifying the practice of a technical skill will preserve (or at least not diminish) the fundamental dynam-

ics (e.g., the relative timing pattern or the mechanical properties of the muscles and joints) of the entire action.

If you decide to use part practice, determine what portions of the skill would benefit from this approach. Sometimes one part of a skill can be practiced by itself, but other parts may need to be practiced together. The freestyle stroke in swimming involves arm movements, head movements (for breathing), and leg movements. The repetitive leg action, which is not as highly related to either of the other parts, can be practiced in isolation. However, since the relative timing of arm and head movements is crucial for performance (i.e., the head is turned and breaths are taken at particular points in the arm cycle), these two parts should always be practiced together.

Part practice can also be an effective way to teach some types of serial skills (previously discussed in chapter 3) in which the action of one component is not tightly connected to the action of other components. A second base player in baseball or softball could perform any of the following sequence of parts when practicing the pivot and throw on a double play:

1. Run to second base.
2. Catch the throw.
3. Tag the base and pivot to avoid the sliding baserunner.
4. Throw the ball to first base.

However, the player would also need to spend some time practicing the entire sequence to learn how to make rapid adjustments in any of the components. For example, if the player takes more time to get to the base, she would have less time for the catch, pivot, and throw.

Occasionally, you might want to have an athlete return to the part practice of an isolated component for the purpose of error correction or skill refinement. If the second base player's pivots are getting sloppy, a brief bout of part practice might be needed to focus the player's attention on more precise execution of that component.

## *Part Practice Techniques*

You can structure the part practice of complex technical skills in several ways in order to focus athletes' attention on key components. In motor learning literature, these techniques are called fractionization, segmentation, and simplification. **Fractionization** involves practicing a single component by itself. A football linebacker might practice reading the quarterback's eyes and dropping into pass coverage by itself before attempting to break up or intercept a pass, or a volleyball player might practice the tossing component of the jump serve in isolation before attempting the entire serve. **Segmentation** (also known as progressive part practice) involves practicing one component and then progressively adding others until the entire skill is being performed. A track athlete learning the triple jump might first practice running to the takeoff board. Once the athlete is comfortable with the basic running component, she would add the hopping component and practice the two together. In the same fashion, she would add the stepping and jumping components until she is able to perform the entire run, hop, step, and jump together. Unlike fractionization and segmentation, **simplification** is a part practice technique that enables athletes to reduce the complexity of technical skill practice by modifying a particular aspect of the skill in some way. For example, a take-down maneuver in wrestling might be simplified by having the wrestler practice the maneuver in slow motion. In this way he would have more time to recall the ordering of the parts as well as to focus on the relative timing pattern of each.

## Slow-Motion Practice

As suggested previously, another way to modify the practice of technical skills is to perform the movements in slow motion. Because they are moving at a slower rate, athletes can control their actions more effectively and, in some cases, perform them with greater accuracy. The important thing to remember is that **slow-motion practice** must preserve the relative timing pattern (i.e., rhythm) used when performing the skill at full speed. A tennis server can practice a topspin serve at a slower speed as long as the relative timing of the toss and hit is the same as what she would use in the full-speed serve.

If athletes slow their movements down too much, they risk practicing a relative timing pattern that is different from the one they need when performing the skill at full speed. Such a possibility exists for technical skills that contain a speed–accuracy trade-off (see chapter 3). A tennis player who practices slowing down the speed of her ground strokes in order to keep the ball inside the boundaries may encounter problems when she tries to speed up her swing later on. This happens because the dynamics of very slow tennis swings are substantially different from those of swings produced at full speed. In situations such as this, the player needs to practice her swings at full speed from the beginning. Athletes may be reluctant to trade off accuracy for speed because it will affect their control. When this happens, tell them you don't expect their accuracy to be consistent until after they master the coordination of the full-speed movement.

Another excellent use of slow-motion practice is during the rehearsal of new plays, routes, or strategies. Basketball players could rehearse the various movements of a new inbounds play, or a trio of wide receivers might practice running different routes in a new pass play. By slowing down their actions during group rehearsal, athletes are able to focus on what they need to do as well as on coordinating their movements with those of their teammates.

## Practice Structure

When using the games approach, you can shape and enhance your athletes' practices by doing what Martens (2004) calls "teaching through the game." By this he means that practices need to be structured so that athletes are able to rehearse their technical, tactical, and mental skills in the ways they use them during competition. In other words, your practices must provide athletes with experiences that allow them to achieve mastery of the technical skills of their sport (e.g., the fundamental patterns of relative timing, spatial patterning, and so on) and develop the tactical and mental skills necessary for effective performance in competition.

The true measure of the effectiveness of any practice structure is the quality of athletes' performance in the competitive setting. It's useless for them to be "great in practice but lousy in games." Therefore, when choosing a practice structure, keep in mind the nature of your sport and the demands of the technical skills your athletes must learn. Depending on those two factors, there are three types of practice structure you can choose from: blocked practice, varied practice, and random practice.

## Blocked Practice

One of the key axioms of learning is that "practice makes perfect." Without practice, there is rarely any improvement in skill. On the other hand, it is easy to fall into the trap of thinking that practice is primarily an issue of quantity (i.e., the more people practice, the better their skills will be). Sadly, there are many examples of athletes who have devoted thousands of hours and incredible amounts of effort to practicing their technical skills, only to fail miserably when they try to perform them in competition.

For years, movement scientists have contended that the best way to strengthen a behavior is to repeat it. A **blocked practice** structure involves repeating the same skill over and over. Certainly the early stages of technical skill learning seem suited to this type of practice. The best way for athletes to initially get an idea of a technical skill is to simply "do it." My own high school football coach definitely believed this because he frequently made us repeat a task over and over until we got it right.

Unfortunately, the problem with numerous repetitions of the same skill is that, after a period of initial practice, training becomes repetitious to the point of mindlessness. Skill practice that is repetitious is not only boring but can be deceptive as well. Athletes who practice the same skill under the same sets of conditions over and over can become deceived into thinking they are getting pretty good at it. The real question is, "Will this repetitious form of practice produce the same kinds of results in competition?" Since so few competitive sport settings allow athletes to perform their skills in a repetitive fashion under constant conditions, a blocked practice structure is not a good idea. In most cases it should be used only sparingly, especially after athletes achieve a satisfactory level of technical skill proficiency.

## Varied Practice

A better way to enhance the relevance of some types of technical skill practice is through **varied practice.** Chapter 3 discusses the concept of general motor programs—that is, general plans of action that contain all the details of a movement and are adaptable to meet the demands of different situations. These programs contain structural features of the action that do not change (e.g., the relative timing pattern) as well as modifiable characteristics (e.g., force, speed, length). Thus, it is reasonable to assume that once athletes acquire a basic understanding of the fundamental movement pattern, they should begin practicing variations of that pattern. A quarterback who has developed a general motor program for throwing a football can begin varying his passes during practice by changing the speed of his arm movement, his release point, and his arm angle. In basketball, you might envision players practicing jump shots from different positions on the court to learn how they need to change the movement for different angles and distances.

A particular advantage of varied practice is that it strengthens both the relative timing pattern of the general motor program and athletes' capability to modify the pattern. In other words, they learn the rules for performing variations of the fundamental pattern, including new variations they might try to produce in a future competition. A quarterback who varies his passes during practice begins to understand the relationship between the speed of his arm movement and the accuracy of his passes or between his release point and the trajectory of the ball. By increasing the flexibility or adaptability of athletes' technical skills, varied practice allows them to transfer what they practice to other situations they might encounter in competition.

## Random Practice

Another way to enhance athletes' practice experiences is by randomizing their performance of different skills. In some respects, this practice structure is similar to varied practice. The main difference is that with **random practice,** athletes produce a different fundamental movement pattern (or general motor program) on each practice attempt instead of producing different variations of the same pattern. For example, instead of practicing variations of digging (varied practice), a volleyball player might practice a variety of movement patterns (e.g., digging, passing, blocking, and spiking) in a random order of 40 attempts. A random practice structure is certainly more challenging than a blocked structure that requires the player to dig 10 times, then pass 10 times, then block 10 times, and then spike 10 times. Although both random and blocked practice structures might contain the same number of repetitions of each technical skill, the random structure prevents athletes from repeating the same skill over and over.

A considerable amount of research in motor learning indicates that random practice produces superior learning and transfer to the competitive situation than does blocked practice, especially for athletes who must perform a number of different technical skills in their sport. Perhaps more important, athletes who practice under random conditions are better able to perform their skills in competition than are athletes who practice in a blocked format. That's because a random practice structure is more similar to the situations they encounter in competition.

Your athletes may not like a random practice structure, however, because they can't achieve the "rhythm" and gratifying results they do with blocked practice. For one thing, random practice doesn't allow athletes to quickly correct their mistakes (because they never perform the same pattern twice in a row). Therefore, you may need to remind them that a random practice structure will be frustrating at times, but

so will competition. The important thing is not how much athletes like practices but whether practices are preparing them—technically, tactically, and mentally—for the demands they can expect to face in competition. If your practices are achieving this purpose, then your athletes will have a lot of fun in competition.

## When to Use Different Practice Structures

For the most part, blocked practice works best during the first few minutes of a practice session as part of the general warm-up. It is also useful when athletes are practicing something new, such as a play, strategy, technique, or movement variation. However, once they seem to "get it," athletes should begin incorporating the newly learned behavior into more of a game-like practice structure. Here, keep in mind the principle of relevance: athletes who are required to produce a random array of actions during competition should practice those actions in a primarily random format. For example, offensive football players must be able to remember and execute a number of different plays and blocking maneuvers during a game. Therefore, they should practice their assignments in a primarily random fashion. Random practice is also beneficial for defensive players because during games they must adapt quickly to a random assortment of formations and movements of the opposing team. A varied practice format, on the other hand, is more relevant for athletes who must produce variations of the same general movement pattern. Tennis players need to be able to hit a variety of different serves to different locations in both the deuce and ad courts. Therefore, when practicing their serves in isolation, they should use a varied format, attempting different types of serves in a random order to a number of targets in both the deuce and ad courts.

## Developing Athletes' Anticipation

Another ingredient of effective practices is the development of athletes' anticipation. When they are able to practice their technical skills in competition-like settings, athletes develop a degree of certainty (or anticipation) that helps them know what to do when they are competing. A skilled gymnast knows how to focus her attention and manage her arousal when producing a series of technical skills during a floor exercise or balance beam routine. A skilled soccer player knows how and when to effectively deliver a particular type of pass to a teammate during an upfield rush. In sports such as football, basketball, and soccer, a clearly defined team strategy can also promote players' anticipation. When your players know in advance exactly what you expect each of them to do and practice their assignments on a regular basis, they will perform with confidence during competition. If they appear tentative when they're competing, you need to check their understanding of their responsibilities, clarify any misunderstandings, give them the opportunity to improve their anticipation during practice, and then praise them when they begin doing things correctly.

In addition to anticipating their own movements and correctly performing their individual assignments, athletes in some sports need to anticipate environmental events so they can prepare and respond to them more rapidly. Chapter 4 talked about how information processing takes time. However, with the games approach to practice, you can help your athletes speed up their decision making by recognizing regularities in environmental events. The most effective way of doing this is to emphasize situations or actions that occur on a consistent basis in competition.

## Developing Anticipation and Teamwork

Legendary former college football coach Robert Neyland of the University of Tennessee required all his offensive players to memorize their own position assignments as well as those of their teammates. Occasionally he would create practice situations where players changed positions in order to teach them an appreciation of their teammates' responsibilities. Neyland wanted to be certain his players knew what every athlete was doing on every play so they could effectively coordinate their actions during games. His players enjoyed many seasons of success because they developed a high level of anticipation of each other's movement patterns during practice sessions, giving real meaning to the word *team*.

Your athletes can develop anticipation of opponents' actions if you direct their attention to consistencies in opponents' mannerisms in certain situations. A defender in volleyball might watch the posture and hand action of an opposing setter to anticipate the direction of her set. Similarly, an outside hitter might pay attention to how opponents set up their block in order to determine which type of spike she should hit. Try using verbal cues to direct athletes' attention to relevant information for anticipation purposes. You might cue a defensive lineman in football to "focus on the hands of the center" or to "move when the football moves." By structuring practice sessions that allow your athletes to recognize and rehearse their responses to a variety of randomly presented environmental events, you will greatly enhance their anticipation of those events during competition. You'll know you are successful in doing this when

Athletes in some team sports need to have a clear understanding of what their teammates are doing.

your athletes seem to know in advance what is going to happen during competition.

## Games Approach to Practicing for Competition

The best practices prepare athletes technically, tactically, and mentally for the demands of competition. As mentioned earlier, keep in mind the principle of relevance when structuring your practices. In some cases, the most relevant practice structure might involve repetitions of the same movement (i.e., blocked practice). In the sport of track and field, high jumpers, long jumpers, discus throwers, shot-putters, pole-vaulters, and javelin throwers all perform repetitions of essentially the same movement when they are competing. Therefore, the most relevant practice structure for these individuals involves the repetition of their respective activities. However, during competition, these athletes also have to wait for various time periods between performance attempts. Thus, a relevant practice structure would involve waiting various amounts of time between trials so that athletes are forced to manage their energy, focus their attention, and adjust their arousal for each attempt.

In other sports, athletes must produce a wide variety of movements within the context of a dynamic environment. Basketball players must perform the skills of passing, catching, boxing out, rebounding, shooting, and defending in a random fashion throughout the course of a game. In addition, they must be able to adapt their skills to changing situations. Players must pass the ball in different ways, shoot the ball from various locations, grab rebounds that come off the backboard and rim in different fashions, and defend different types of opponents. For these sports, the most relevant practice structure requires athletes to experience a variety of gamelike situations and produce an assortment of technical skills in a random and varied fashion. For example, a high school basketball practice session might include the following segments:

1. A demonstration, with visual and verbal cues from the coach, of a reverse-turn defensive rebounding technique

2. A short one-on-one drill for players to practice the technique with a partner, with players alternately playing offense and defense

3. A 10-minute game, where teams are awarded one point for each basket and two points for every defensive rebound

4. A three-on-three game, with no points for baskets; teams get one point for every rebound (either offensive or defensive) and two points for every defensive rebound using the reverse-turn technique

5. A 5-minute wrap-up in which the coach gives feedback, obtains input from the players, and reemphasizes the main focus cues for executing the reverse-turn technique

However, certain situations within these sports represent a marked departure from the normal course of play. In basketball, the foul shot situation is entirely different from what players experience during the rest of the game. Here they must perform one specific skill in exactly the same way each time. Thus, a relevant practice structure for this skill might involve players shooting their foul shots in the following ways:

- At random moments
- In various states of fatigue
- One at a time, with at least several minutes between attempts
- With other players lined up along the foul lane
- With no other players along the foul lane (as is the case with technical foul shots)

Following are some other examples of relevant practice structure using the games approach:

- Lengthen the time between performance attempts for gymnasts and field athletes in track (i.e., throwers and jumpers) to simulate the typical wait these athletes experience between attempts in a meet.

- Have tennis and volleyball players practice their serves in a varied format, with brief periods of time between serves, as is the case in competitive matches. For example, form several lines of two or three players. The first player serves a particular serve to a particular target and then walks to the back of the line. The other players take their respective turns doing the same thing. On the next rotation, each player serves a different type of serve to a different location. Both the type of serve and location of the target continue to vary throughout the remaining rotations. Tennis players could also alternate serving to the deuce and ad courts.

- Expand batting practice to include pitchers pitching from the stretch position and other players practicing their base-stealing skills on a rotational basis. This practice setup gives batters and pitchers experience in situations involving a runner on first base and gives runners experience anticipating pitchers' movements to the plate.

- Insert special-teams plays at random intervals during a football practice instead of tacking them onto the end. This gives offensive and defensive players periodic breaks and keeps special-teams players more mentally involved throughout the practice session.

- Have soccer players who are not scrimmaging play two-on-two games in smaller areas adjacent to the main field. This gives them extra practice on their passing, dribbling, and tackling skills and allows them to refine their movements within the kind of random context they will experience during competition.

In chapter 9, you will learn how to plan your practices at various times during the course of a season so that your athletes can derive maximum benefit and develop the skills they need for competition success.

## Incorporating Mental Skills During Practices

Your athletes can also practice their mental skills using the games approach. Athletes who need to learn the correct sequence of actions or the fundamental pattern of relative timing for a technical skill can use the time between practice attempts to mentally rehearse the sequence or pattern. Then, when it's time to attempt the action again, they should have a slightly better idea of what to do. Athletes can use mental rehearsal of this type during competition as well, particularly for technical skills that are performed intermittently (e.g., hitting golf shots, kicking field goals) or when they must wait their turn to compete (e.g., offensive and defensive players who rotate into the game depending on the situation).

Once athletes have achieved an advanced level of technical skill, they can begin to mentally rehearse the look and feel of successful execution of the movement in a variety of situations. A football punter can create a mental image of a game situation and then see and feel himself confidently kicking the ball in a particular way to a particular target location. The beauty of mental imagery is that athletes can practice it any time and any place. Just like physical practice, mental rehearsal is more effective when it is attempted more frequently, in a random format, for brief periods of time (i.e., no more than a few minutes). Many of today's best athletes use imagery as a preperformance routine during competition (e.g., a softball batter preparing to hit or a gymnast preparing to perform on the parallel bars). These athletes believe that imagery prepares them mentally and emotionally for successful performance, and many say it is "like being there before I get there."

# SUMMARY

1. The games approach to practices emphasizes activities that are relevant to competition.

2. To maximize your teaching effectiveness, try to develop open, two-way communication with your athletes.

3. Always provide verbal instructions that are short, simple, and clearly worded.

4. Visual demonstrations of technical skills should always convey the essential features of the movement.

5. Both verbal instructions and visual demonstrations can be used to focus athletes' attention on the unique relative timing pattern of a technical skill.

6. When providing visual demonstrations, select a viewing perspective that best illustrates the essential features of the movement.

7. Use physical guidance procedures sparingly, and either withdraw them or intersperse them with unassisted practice as soon as athletes achieve a general idea of the desired movement.

8. Part practice and slow-motion practice of technical skills should preserve the fundamental relative timing pattern of the entire full-speed movement.

9. Blocked practice is sometimes beneficial during the early stages of learning when athletes are trying to acquire a basic idea of the fundamental movement pattern.

10. Varied practice helps athletes learn how to modify their technical skills for different situations.

11. In random practice, athletes produce a different fundamental movement pattern on each practice attempt. Compared with blocked practice, random practice promotes greater transfer of skills to competition.

12. You can improve your athletes' anticipation by directing their attention to consistent aspects of team strategy and the performance environment.

13. The best practices prepare athletes both physically and mentally for competition.

# KEY TERMS

assistive guidance

blocked practice

fractionization

games approach

knowledge of performance

knowledge of results

part practice

physical guidance

random practice

relevant practice

restrictive guidance

segmentation

simplification

slow-motion practice

two-way communication

unspoken communication

varied practice

verbal instructions

visual demonstrations

# REVIEW QUESTIONS

1. What are some things you might do to establish two-way communication with your athletes?
2. What are the primary functions of verbal instructions and visual demonstrations?
3. What is one advantage of physical guidance? What is one disadvantage?
4. When might part practice or slow-motion practice be necessary, and how might each be incorporated into a practice session?
5. How are varied practice and random practice similar? How are they different?
6. Why is it important for team sport athletes to develop anticipation about their opponents? Why is it important to develop anticipation about their teammates?
7. What principle do you need to keep in mind when using the games approach to prepare your athletes for competition?

# PRACTICAL ACTIVITIES

1. List three practice activities that would actively involve each of your athletes in some way and explain how each is relevant to competition.

    a.

    b.

    c.

2. For each of the previous activities, list one technical, tactical, and mental skill athletes would have the opportunity to practice.

    *Practice activity*                           *Skills practiced*

    a.                                            Technical skill:

                                                  Tactical skill:

                                                  Mental skill:

    b.                                            Technical skill:

                                                  Tactical skill:

                                                  Mental skill:

    c.                                            Technical skill:

                                                  Tactical skill:

                                                  Mental skill:

3. List three aspects of the environment in your sport that athletes need to anticipate in order to perform at their best. For each aspect, describe an activity you might use to help them develop their anticipation.

    *Environmental aspect*                        *Practice activity*

    a.

    b.

    c.

# 8

# Providing Feedback

When you finish reading this chapter, you should be able to explain

1. the difference between intrinsic and extrinsic feedback,
2. the relative advantages of verbal and visual feedback,
3. the difference between outcome feedback and performance feedback,
4. the difference between program feedback and parameter feedback,
5. the difference between descriptive feedback and prescriptive feedback,
6. when to provide feedback and when not to,
7. how much feedback to provide at one time,
8. how often to provide feedback, and
9. how detailed your feedback should be.

When athletes practice their skills, they occasionally require feedback about the kinds of adjustments they need to make to improve their performance. Studies indicate that feedback is one of the most powerful variables affecting skill learning. However, more recent research suggests that the quality of feedback provided is more important than the quantity. In other words, you should consider how and when to give feedback rather than assume that more is better. This chapter discusses various categories of feedback information you can give your athletes and suggests some factors you should keep in mind when doing so. First, though, you'll learn the difference between the feedback athletes can obtain for themselves, termed intrinsic feedback, and the feedback they will need from you, referred to as extrinsic feedback. Several categories of extrinsic feedback are discussed, including verbal and visual feedback, outcome and performance feedback, program and parameter feedback, and descriptive and prescriptive feedback.

The chapter concludes with a few additional considerations to keep in mind when providing feedback to your athletes. These include when to give feedback, how much feedback to give, how often to give it, and how detailed it should be. The key principle emphasized throughout this chapter is that the quality and timing of your feedback is more important than the amount or frequency of feedback.

## Intrinsic and Extrinsic Feedback

The traditional approach to practice places most of the responsibility for providing feedback on the coach. However, the games approach emphasizes the importance of helping athletes learn how to detect feedback for themselves and make corrections on their own. If you stop to think about it, this approach makes a lot more sense because athletes usually receive relatively little assistance from their coaches during competition.

The first thing you can do to help your athletes develop the capability to detect and correct their own errors is to encourage them to pay more attention to their own feedback. In motor learning literature, this type of feedback is labeled *intrinsic*. **Intrinsic feedback** is any sen-

Intrinsic feedback includes any sensory information that emerges naturally during sport performance, such as the sound and feel of the bat hitting the ball.

sory information that emerges from the outside environment or from within the athlete's own body. Examples of intrinsic feedback include the sight of a golf ball rolling to a stop in the fairway; the feel of the head, neck, and shoulders when heading a soccer ball; the sound of the bat making solid contact with the baseball; and the overall feeling of the gymnast's body during a back handspring.

If you want to help a tennis player attend more carefully to intrinsic feedback during the serve, you might instruct the player to notice the feel of his arm and shoulder at the point of contact with the ball. After the player completes the serve (let's say it failed to clear the net), you could ask him to discuss what he noticed and explain how that might have affected the outcome. Perhaps the player noticed that he didn't extend his arm very much, that the racket face was rather closed at impact, and that he contacted the ball a bit low and too far out in front of his body. Once he completes his analysis of intrinsic feedback, the player has several options for improving his next serve (e.g., tossing the ball higher, extending the arm and racket further, pointing the racket face toward the target at the moment of impact, and contacting the ball at a point more directly above his head). With repeated practice of this nature, the player will improve his serve performance and also develop the capability to detect and correct his mistakes when they occur. By designing practice experiences that encourage your athletes to evaluate their own intrinsic feedback, you help them learn how to make any necessary performance adjustments on their own during competition.

Athletes need to obtain feedback from an external source in addition to detecting it themselves. Feedback from an outside source that contains information athletes may not be able to pick up on their own is referred to as **extrinsic feedback**. Examples of extrinsic feedback include

## Practicing With Eyes Closed

Research on perception clearly indicates that vision dominates the other sensory systems. Although there is little question that visual cues are necessary for the successful performance of most technical skills, there are times when vision can prevent athletes from detecting other important sources of sensory information. For example, when practicing the golf swing, a player would notice the feel of the swing less if she practiced it with her eyes open than if she did so with her eyes closed. Thus, athletes can often benefit from keeping their eyes closed during technical skill practice, particularly when they need to devote more attention to the feel of the action. Closed-eyes practice might also help athletes detect errors in their movements that they would otherwise not notice. Finally, more advanced athletes might benefit from closed-eyes practice when they want to reconnect with the feeling associated with their movements.

verbal comments about an athlete's form, such as a golfer's pitch shot or a linebacker's tackle; a video replay showing a springboard diver's movements during a reverse pike; or a stopwatch displaying a runner's time in the 110-meter high hurdles. Chapter 6 discussed two types of goals athletes need to set: outcome goals and performance goals. In many cases, athletes are able to evaluate achievement of their outcome goals based on available statistics (e.g., batting average, field goal percentage). However, they will likely need your assistance when evaluating their achievement of some outcome goals and most performance goals. A gymnast might benefit from knowing the relative percentage of handsprings in a floor exercise that were timed correctly, undershot, and overshot. She would definitely need extrinsic feedback to evaluate her form during the routine.

To improve athletes' capability to detect their own errors, use extrinsic feedback to direct their attention to relevant intrinsic feedback. For example, if you coach softball and notice a batter hitting the ball on the handle of the bat, you might provide feedback that directs the player's attention to keeping her hands "inside the ball" (i.e., allowing for more frequent contact with the fat part of the bat rather than the handle).

Technically speaking, extrinsic feedback is a concrete means of providing performance evaluations. State feedback positively, reminding your athletes that what you say is primarily designed to help them move closer to their performance goals. That way, they will be more likely to interpret your feedback as beneficial rather than as threatening.

The extrinsic feedback you offer can take several forms and serve a number of purposes, sometimes simultaneously. Some of the categories of extrinsic feedback athletes can use to improve their technical skills include verbal and visual feedback, outcome and performance feedback, program and parameter feedback, and descriptive and prescriptive feedback.

## Verbal and Visual Feedback

Most of the extrinsic feedback you give your athletes will be presented verbally (i.e., spoken). You might tell a shortstop that she took her eyes off a ground ball that went through her legs or tell a high jumper that he arched his back too soon when attempting to clear the bar. As with any type of verbal communication, it is important to keep **verbal feedback** simple and direct to avoid overloading athletes with too much information (see figure 8.1). A good rule of thumb is to provide feedback for no more than one or two aspects of an athlete's performance at a time. To avoid miscommunication, ask athletes to explain what they heard you say or have them tell you what aspect of their performance they are going to try to correct during their next attempt.

If you have access to video technology, you can also provide athletes with **visual feedback** of their performance. Using portable video recorders and monitors, you can record athletes' movements from a variety of angles and then show them a replay for analysis purposes. Be sure that the viewing angle allows them to visually detect errors in their form or in the desired pattern of relative timing.

In some cases, you might be able to provide a split-screen display that shows athletes their performance alongside that of an experienced athlete. This is a good way to direct their attention to important differences between their movements and those of a more advanced performer.

When presenting visual feedback, be sure that athletes focus on the most important aspects of what they see. This is often a problem for inexperienced athletes who like to see themselves performing on video but aren't sure what to focus on. As with verbal feedback, point out only one or two elements at a time to avoid overloading athletes with too much information. For example, you might tell a beginning soccer player to focus solely on the placement of his plant foot just before the kick rather than on the complex mechanics of the hip and leg.

## Outcome and Performance Feedback

As mentioned previously, feedback can pertain to either the outcome of athletes' performance (e.g., movement time) or the quality of their movements (i.e., movement form). Since most athletes set both outcome goals and performance goals, you should provide extrinsic feedback that is relevant to both. For a basketball player who has an outcome goal of increasing his free throw percentage from 50 to 60 percent, you might display outcome feedback on a chart showing his daily percentage of successful free throws over a two-week period. If the player also has a

**FIGURE 8.1**   Extrinsic feedback is of little use if it overloads athletes with too much information.

Reprinted, by permission, from R.A. Schmidt and C.A. Wrisberg, 2004, *Motor learning and performance*, 3rd ed. (Champaign, IL: Human Kinetics), 296.

## Watching Video Replay

When athletes watch themselves on video, they tend to see some aspects of their movements better than others. One piece of information athletes should be able to pick up is the spatial relationship between various body parts. On video, a gymnast can see when and by how much her hips are elevated above her shoulders at a particular point in an uneven bar exercise. In a similar fashion, a football punter can see the relationship of his kicking foot to his knee at the moment of impact with the ball. Another piece of visual information athletes can pick up is the relative timing pattern of the movement. A soccer player, for example, should be able to see the relationship between the speed of the wrist, forearm, and upper arm during a throw-in.

Two things inexperienced athletes have difficulty detecting when they watch themselves on video are the feel of the movement and the forces they use to produce the action. A rookie pitcher watching a replay of one of his pitches might have difficulty recalling the feel of his total body action or the forces he used. Thus, when using video replay, direct athletes' attention primarily to the spatial characteristics and relative timing pattern of their movements if you want to achieve the greatest effect.

feedback. A golfer may not be aware that she has reached the green in regulation for seven of the first nine holes of a round or unable to see where her ball stopped after a chip shot to an elevated green. In situations such as these, outcome feedback can be helpful. However, in many sport situations, athletes are able to detect outcome feedback for themselves and don't require any additional information. A softball pitcher can see that a pitch was too low or that it landed in the dirt and eluded the catcher.

Because athletes are unable to observe the quality of their own movements while they are performing them, the type of extrinsic feedback they need most from you is **performance feedback.** You must be their "eyes," providing them with the form feedback they need in order to correct their mechanics. Video replay is a good way to show athletes their form and help them decide which aspects need to be targeted for correction or refinement.

## Program and Parameter Feedback

Chapter 3 discussed the concept of general motor programs. These programs, stored in an athlete's mind, contain the fundamental plans of action and relative timing patterns for different categories of movements (e.g., throwing, kicking, striking, jumping). An important aspect of general motor programs is a flexible feature called a parameter. Most programs contain several parameters that performers adjust to meet the demands of different situations. For example, a volleyball player using a general program for passing would adjust the parameters of force and arm angle to vary the speed and direction of her passes.

Two subcategories of performance feedback are program feedback and parameter feedback. As you might expect, **program feedback** directs athletes' attention to the relative timing pattern of their movements. In other words, it is designed to adjust the motor program. You might tell a soccer player who needs to move her lower leg faster than her upper leg (to achieve more velocity on her kicks) to "speed up the lower leg." By making this correction, the player

performance goal of improving the quality and consistency of his shooting form (e.g., balance before the shot, arm and leg extension during the shooting motion, wrist flexion during the follow-through), you could also display performance feedback by rating (on a scale of 1 to 3 for the three form components) the quality of his shooting form during the same two-week period.

**Outcome feedback** is important for athletes who are unaware of their results or unable to obtain them from available sources of intrinsic changes the relative timing pattern of the kick so that the lower leg moves faster than it did before, while the upper leg continues to move at the same speed. On the other hand, **parameter feedback** is what you give athletes who need to adjust an overall component of their actions (e.g., force, velocity, point of contact). For a baseball batter who needs to speed up his entire bat swing in a uniform way, you might provide feedback about the speed of his swings (using a radar gun) during batting practice.

Generally speaking, program feedback is more important during the early stage of technical skill learning when athletes are trying to get an idea of the correct relative timing pattern, or rhythm, of the action. However, it can also be beneficial for athletes who are trying to achieve greater efficiency by altering an existing relative timing pattern (e.g., a golfer trying to change her swing mechanics). Parameter feedback tends to be more helpful for athletes who are trying to adjust a general component of their overall movements in order to meet changing environmental demands (e.g., a quarterback increasing the speed of a pass to a wide receiver to prevent a defensive back from breaking up the play or decreasing the speed of a pass to a running back coming out of the backfield so as not to overpower him).

## Descriptive and Prescriptive Feedback

When giving athletes extrinsic feedback about their technical skills, you can either tell them what you saw (**descriptive feedback**) or tell them what you think they need to do based on what you saw (**prescriptive feedback**). For example, if you observe a basketball player not following through on her jump shot, you might say, "You didn't follow through." Although this type of descriptive feedback is satisfactory for experienced players who know what a correct follow-through is like, it may not be sufficient for inexperienced players who aren't sure how to make the necessary correction. Therefore, when you want to alert athletes to the types of corrections they must make to improve some aspect of their performance, you should provide them with prescriptive feedback. You might tell an

inexperienced basketball player to flex her wrist more forcefully as she releases the ball. That way she would have an idea of what she needs to do to improve the follow-through on her jump shot. In essence, prescriptive feedback represents another example of attention-focusing instructions (discussed in chapter 7). To provide helpful prescriptive feedback, you must be able to both detect errors in athletes' performance (e.g., see an incomplete follow-through at the end of a jump shot) and offer possible solutions for the problem (e.g., flex the wrist more forcefully at the point of release).

## Practical Considerations for Giving Feedback

You might find some practical considerations helpful when providing extrinsic feedback. These include when to give feedback, how much feedback to give, how often to give it, and how detailed to make it.

### When to Give Feedback

As long as athletes are attending to relevant sources of intrinsic feedback, they don't need (or usually don't want) additional information from you. Therefore, a good rule to keep in mind when considering when to give feedback is "When in doubt, be quiet." Recent research indicates that people profit more from feedback when they ask for it than when someone else (e.g., instructor, coach) decides they need it. Interestingly, these studies also show that learners are able to improve their skills with relatively little extrinsic feedback. In one study, participants who were instructed to ask for extrinsic feedback whenever they wanted it asked for it less than 10 percent of the time. Moreover, most of their feedback requests occurred during their first few learning sessions. These findings suggest that you should resist the temptation to provide assistance more frequently and instead allow athletes to practice their skills on their own. Of course, the more difficult the technical skill, the more likely they will want your feedback.

Least helpful for athletes is extrinsic feedback that is virtually identical to their intrinsic feedback. A gymnast who stumbles forward at

## "Sandwiching" Feedback

When athletes make mistakes, they need corrective feedback. However, correcting mistakes can be difficult if athletes are resistant to your feedback. To avoid resistance, convey corrective feedback in a way that is as nonthreatening as possible. A good way to do this is by using a "sandwich" approach (figure 8.2). A **feedback sandwich** consists of a sequence of statements that begins with a compliment followed by prescriptive feedback followed by some encouragement. Its effectiveness is based on an important principle of communication: *How* something is said is just as important as *what* is said.

Start by complimenting the athlete for something she did correctly or for a good effort. You might compliment a basketball player for hustling to get in position for an open jump shot. Once the player hears this compliment, she will feel less apprehensive and be more open to receiving corrective feedback. Next, give the athlete a prescriptive feedback statement: "Take just a little more time to square up for your shot." Finally, offer a word of encouragement: "If you keep working hard to get open but take a little more time to square up for your shot, you're going to like the result."

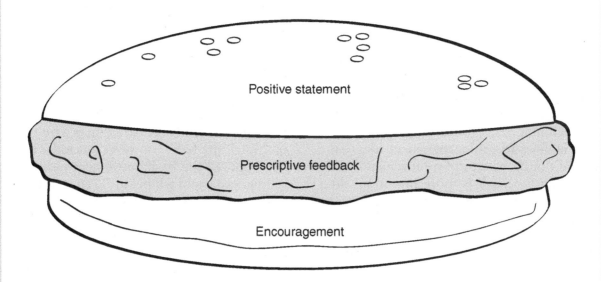

FIGURE 8.2 Coaches can use the "feedback sandwich" technique to enhance their communication with athletes.

the end of a dismount doesn't want to hear the coach say, "You overrotated on your dismount." Therefore, your goal should always be to provide feedback only when athletes are unable to pick it up on their own. If the gymnast asks why she keeps overrotating, this indicates that she does not know the reason and needs extrinsic feedback. If you have established good communication with your athletes (chapter 7), you should be able to discern when they need feedback and when they don't. Moreover, if your athletes enjoy open communication with you, they are more likely to request extrinsic feedback when they need it.

Since all learning involves some sort of problem solving, the most helpful feedback you can provide points athletes toward relevant sources of intrinsic feedback. For a softball batter, that feedback might be to focus on the feel of a level swing or on the relationship between the

Athletes are more likely to hear and use extrinsic feedback when they don't feel threatened.

position of the hands and the direction of the batted ball. Once athletes are able to identify relevant intrinsic feedback on their own, they will need even less extrinsic feedback from you. Program feedback is more important during the beginning stage of technical skill practice when athletes are getting the general idea of the relative timing pattern of a movement, while parameter feedback is more important after athletes demonstrate that they can produce the fundamental pattern on a consistent basis.

The games approach to practice suggests that athletes need to be given the opportunity to develop their skills in an independent fashion and engage in their own problem solving. Only when they appear to be at a dead end in their search for solutions or when they stop practicing and ask for your assistance should you offer feedback. The powerful aspect of this approach is that it allows you to capitalize on those teachable moments when athletes are motivated to hear what you have to say and more likely to incorporate it after they do.

## How Much Feedback to Give

The most important principle to remember when it comes to deciding how much feedback to give is "Keep it simple." *Simple*, however, does not mean simplistic. On the contrary, your feedback should provide athletes with the most

helpful information possible. Keeping extrinsic feedback simple means giving athletes the type of feedback that is most relevant at a particular moment. In other words, quality is more important than quantity. That way you will direct athletes' attention to the most important information without overloading them. For example, a beginning soccer player may need performance feedback about the rhythm of his leg swing during the kicking action rather than feedback about the various ways to change the speed and direction of his kicks.

The amount of feedback that is just right also depends on the experience level of the athlete. Extrinsic feedback for a beginning volleyball player should be restricted to one or two specific aspects of performance. If the player is learning how to set the ball, you might tell her to "keep your hands more relaxed" or "bend your knees a bit more" or "watch the ball." However, once the player has acquired the basic movement pattern for setting, you could tell her to "keep it softer and smoother" because the player would then know that "softer and smoother" means relaxing the hands, positioning the body, and anticipating contact with the ball.

Since athletes usually have more difficulty making program adjustments than parameter adjustments, be sure to make your program feedback simpler than your parameter feedback. A football quarterback might need to be told simply to "flick the wrist a bit more" (program feedback) to help him acquire the fundamental relative timing pattern for the forward pass. However, once he demonstrates a more consistent throwing pattern, the player could handle a more complex parameter feedback statement such as "Use more force and release the ball earlier," which would help him throw the ball farther.

Another way to increase the amount of feedback you provide without overloading athletes with too much information is to use summary feedback or average feedback after a practice session. **Summary feedback** tells athletes how they performed on each of several practice attempts, while **average feedback** highlights general tendencies in their performance. For a long jumper's last five jumps, summary feedback might be that his plant foot landed beyond the takeoff board on his first, third, fourth, and fifth jumps and on the takeoff board during his second jump. Average feedback for the athlete might be that his plant foot landed slightly beyond the takeoff board for the five attempts. An important issue to consider when giving summary feedback or average feedback is the number of performance attempts to include in the feedback statement. Generally speaking, the more complex the technical skill or the less experienced the athlete, the fewer attempts you should include in the feedback.

## How Often to Give Feedback

Recent research suggests that more frequent feedback is not necessarily better when it comes to promoting skill development. In fact, many studies have shown that practicing without extrinsic feedback can actually be more beneficial than practicing with it. Possible reasons for performance improvements in the absence of extrinsic feedback are that learners are forced to do more of their own problem solving and they devote more of their attention to available intrinsic feedback. For example, a baseball outfielder practicing his throws to different bases begins to notice the flight path of the ball, see how close to the target it comes, and feel the sensation of the throwing action. He also begins to recognize errors in his performance and think about ways to adjust his throws. The outfielder might also learn that, tactically speaking, throws need to be directed to the cutoff player so they can be caught and thrown to another base if necessary.

Another problem that arises when feedback is presented too frequently is that athletes become dependent on it. Let's say, for example, that the outfielder hears feedback after each of 10 throws to different targets. If the feedback is "Keep the ball lower," what do you think the player will try to do on his next throw? Keep the ball lower. If he hears "Follow through better," he will attempt to follow through better on

Athletes are able to develop their problem-solving skills better when extrinsic feedback is provided less frequently.

the next throw. In other words, each time the player receives extrinsic feedback, he immediately tries to incorporate the feedback on the next throw. The problem is that by making these moment-to-moment corrections, the player is unable to achieve much stability in his performance. As a result, he doesn't learn as much about the relationship between what he is doing and the result that he is getting. Although the outfielder's performance may appear to be improving with more frequent extrinsic feedback, he is probably not learning why this is the case. When he ceases to get extrinsic feedback, the player's performance is likely to regress to its previous level.

In light of the pitfalls of too frequent feedback, you need to decide how often to provide it in order to facilitate rather than impair your athletes' skill development. One way to do this is to reduce the frequency of extrinsic feedback whenever you see your athletes becoming more proficient. For simple skills and tactics, you should be able to do this rather early in practice. However, for more complex skills, you will probably need to wait until your athletes demonstrate an acceptable level of consistency. At that point, begin diminishing the frequency of your feedback. If an athlete's performance begins to drop off, you can increase feedback frequency until it improves. As mentioned before, your goal is to provide athletes with the type, amount, and frequency of extrinsic feedback that forces them to attend to the intrinsic feedback—the feedback they sense themselves—that is relevant for successful performance. The more they do this, the better they will be able to perform in competition without your assistance.

The games approach and the available research on the optimal frequency of extrinsic feedback are in agreement that less is better. Therefore, a general rule is to provide feedback to your athletes more frequently during initial learning and progressively less frequently as skill levels improve. Since the quality of your feedback is more important than the quantity, you should always consider both the content and the timing of your feedback messages in order to provide the most helpful assistance for your athletes.

Delaying feedback also has some benefits. A primary aim of the games approach is the development of athletes who are capable of functioning independently. One way to help your athletes achieve this goal is to encourage them to evaluate their own intrinsic feedback before offering feedback yourself. You should give athletes sufficient time to think about what they did and what the result was. The more complex the technical or tactical skill, the more time athletes will need to evaluate their performance. This means you may need to tolerate silence for a longer period of time when you are asking them to evaluate something relatively complex. By challenging athletes to evaluate their own errors and come up with possible solutions before giving them feedback, you facilitate both their skill development and their capability of detecting and correcting their own mistakes.

## How Detailed the Feedback Should Be

A final consideration when providing extrinsic feedback is how precise or detailed to make it. For example, you might tell a swimmer that his turns were "a bit faster" during a particular drill or that they averaged 0.5 seconds. Similarly, you might inform a volleyball player that her

### Importance of Follow-Up Extrinsic Feedback

When athletes receive extrinsic feedback, they typically use it to make the corrections called for. A soccer player who receives feedback about the quality of her footwork while dribbling the ball will probably devote most of her attention to her footwork when she resumes practicing. Similarly, a swimmer who gets feedback about a tactical move she needs to include in her races will focus on adding that move the next time she competes. In each case, the athlete needs to get follow-up feedback that informs her of subsequent improvements in the targeted behavior. You might tell the soccer player that her footwork was much better during today's practice, and you might congratulate the swimmer for including the tactical move in her next race and encourage her to execute it even earlier in future races. Until the athlete receives that information, any other extrinsic feedback—even that which is relevant to performance (e.g., proper form when the soccer player heads the ball or the quality of the swimmer's turns)—is not going to be very helpful. Thus, it is important to provide follow-up feedback whenever you instruct athletes to target a particular behavior for improvement. If you don't, they may wonder how important the behavior really is and lose their motivation to keep trying to improve or change it.

sets seemed to be achieving better trajectory during the previous game or that her outside sets were consistently achieving a peak height of 15 feet.

The research on feedback precision suggests that extrinsic feedback does not need to be extremely precise to be effective. This is particularly true during early learning, when athletes are just trying to get a general idea of the correct relative timing pattern. At that point, all they need to know is general information about the relative amount and direction of their errors. You might tell a beginning high jumper that her takeoff was a bit too early. However, once she achieves a higher level of technical skill, the athlete would benefit from more precise feedback that helps her fine-tune her movements (e.g., the duration in milliseconds of her final two steps).

One way to promote technical skill development while increasing feedback precision is through **bandwidth feedback**. To do this, establish a performance bandwidth—the amount of error you will tolerate before providing extrinsic feedback. As long as an athlete's performance remains within the tolerance zone, there's no need to give feedback. Normally you'll want to allow a wider bandwidth and provide more general feedback for athletes who are learning a new skill than for performers whose skill level is more advanced. The bandwidth for a beginning softball pitcher, for example, would allow any movements that conform to the basic relative timing pattern. If they don't, a general feedback statement might be "Slow down the stride leg, and speed up the arm action." As the pitcher's skill level improves, the bandwidth would be narrowed so that feedback is given to correct even small performance deviations. If her stride length was a bit too short, you might tell her to increase it by an inch or two. Since bandwidth feedback allows you to give feedback less often, athletes derive the same benefits as they do any time you reduce feedback frequency (as discussed previously). What you need to do is determine a performance bandwidth for athletes that allows them to improve their technical skills as much as possible without your assistance.

# SUMMARY

1. Intrinsic feedback is information that normally arises from either the external environment or from the performer's body during performance.

2. Extrinsic feedback is information that comes from an outside source (e.g., the coach, video replay) and that informs athletes about aspects of their performance they may not be able to pick up on their own.

3. An important function of extrinsic feedback is to make athletes more aware of the relevant sources of intrinsic feedback needed for skill improvement.

4. The most effective verbal and visual feedback is simple, is clear, and addresses no more than one or two features of the athlete's performance at a time.

5. Visual feedback is particularly useful for conveying information about the spatial patterning or relative timing characteristics of technical skills.

6. When using video replay with beginners, you may need to direct the athlete's attention to the most important sources of visual information contained in the display.

7. Program feedback is helpful for athletes early in skill learning when they are trying to acquire the fundamental movement pattern and relative timing characteristics of the action.

8. Parameter feedback is useful for athletes after they have acquired the general motor program for producing a movement and are trying to learn how to modify the program (e.g., using more or less force, moving at different speeds, and so on) in order to meet varying environmental demands.

9. Prescriptive feedback is more helpful than descriptive feedback for inexperienced athletes who are less likely to know how to correct their errors.

10. Athletes should be allowed the opportunity to evaluate their own performance before being given extrinsic feedback.

11. Extrinsic feedback is more effective when athletes request it than when they don't.

12. When the frequency of extrinsic feedback is reduced, athletes are forced to engage in problem-solving activity, attend to intrinsic sources of feedback, and learn how to detect and correct performance errors on their own.

13. Summary feedback, average feedback, and bandwidth feedback are effective ways of reducing feedback frequency while providing athletes with helpful information about their performance.

14. Beginners require less precise feedback than do advanced performers.

# KEY TERMS

average feedback

bandwidth feedback

descriptive feedback

extrinsic feedback

feedback sandwich

intrinsic feedback

outcome feedback

parameter feedback

performance feedback

prescriptive feedback

program feedback

summary feedback

verbal feedback

visual feedback

# REVIEW QUESTIONS

1. How would you know whether or not to provide extrinsic feedback to an athlete?

2. How would you determine the optimal viewing angle to use when presenting video feedback to an athlete?

3. Why is performance feedback usually more helpful than outcome feedback? What are some examples of outcome feedback that might be necessary in order for athletes to improve their performance?

4. What are some examples of program feedback and parameter feedback you might give a baseball or softball pitcher?

5. What's the difference between descriptive feedback and prescriptive feedback? What might be an example of each type of feedback given after the same performance?

6. What are two reasons for reducing the amount and frequency of extrinsic feedback you give your athletes?

7. What are two ways you might reduce the frequency of your extrinsic feedback yet still help athletes improve their skills?

# PRACTICAL ACTIVITIES

**1.** Describe a practice activity in your sport and list two ways you would determine when your athletes need your feedback and encourage them to do their own problem solving.

**2.** Describe a situation in your sport where video feedback of an athlete's performance might be beneficial. Then explain (a) how you would determine the most appropriate viewing angle for recording the performance, (b) how often you would provide video feedback to the athlete, and (c) how you would involve the athlete in the video review process.

# 9

# Combining the Practice of Technical, Tactical, and Mental Skills

*When you finish reading this chapter, you should be able to*

1. plan effective practices;
2. design practice activities that include technical, tactical, and mental skill development; and
3. evaluate the effectiveness of practice activities.

This book presents a number of issues and concepts to keep in mind when providing instruction for athletes. In chapter 2, you learned about important individual differences that will influence how you teach skills to your team. These include athletes' abilities and capabilities, age, previous experience, stage of learning, goals, and motivation. Chapters 3, 4, and 5 discussed the three main categories of skills your athletes need to learn in order to perform at their best on a consistent basis in competition: technical skills, tactical skills, and mental skills. Chapter 6 explained some ways to analyze the skills of your sport and determine which skills to emphasize with your athletes. Several instructional techniques for teaching sport skills were provided in chapter 7, along with some ways to structure practices to maximize your athletes' learning. Chapter 8 described some factors to keep in mind when providing feedback to your athletes as they refine their skills and prepare for competition. In this final chapter, you will learn how to plan effective practices; combine the rehearsal of technical, tactical, and mental skills in your practices; and evaluate the quality of your practices.

You know your instruction is effective when your athletes effectively employ their technical, tactical, and mental skills in competition.

It has been said that people don't plan to fail, but they sometimes fail to plan. For a coach, there are few things more frustrating than seeing your athletes struggle during competition and realizing that the situation could have been prevented with proper planning. Perhaps the best indicator of your success as a teacher is the performance of your athletes in competition. Do they execute their technical skills in an effective and efficient manner? Do they make the correct tactical decisions in the heat of battle? Do they remain focused and under control when confronted with the prospects of winning and losing? To achieve these objectives, athletes need to experience practice sessions that help them learn these skills so they will be able to perform them under competition-like circumstances. That's exactly what the **games approach** discussed throughout this book is designed

to accomplish. Famous Princeton basketball coach Pete Carril once said, "We will not do one single thing in practice that doesn't show up in a game." Carril's point, of course, was that if a practice activity isn't going to be useful in some form during competition, it has no business being included in a practice session.

As you proceed through this chapter, think about your own athletes and sport. Ask yourself whether the activities you have devised for your practices conform to coach Carril's principle. If not, and if you're unable to come up with a good reason for including a particular activity in a practice session, you might want to consider eliminating it.

## Planning Effective Practices

You should consider a number of factors when planning your team's practices. These include your athletes' readiness to learn (based on their capabilities, age, and experience level); the **technical**, **tactical**, and **mental demands** of your sport; and the degree of similarity between the practice experience and the competition experience. To sustain your athletes' motivation during practices, you also need to give them opportunities to experience success and have some fun.

To develop the most effective practice plans, follow these steps:

1. Identify the skills your athletes need to learn.
2. Determine your athletes' capabilities.
3. Assess your situation.
4. Establish your priorities.
5. Determine the best methods for teaching.
6. Create a practice plan.

You can find a more complete discussion of these steps in chapter 12 of Rainer Marten's *Successful Coaching,* and you will recognize some of these steps from earlier in this book. In those chapters, you learned about the first five steps. This chapter concentrates on the last one: creating practice plans.

Depending on the nature of your sport, you may find when planning practice activities that there are some skills all your athletes will need to learn and some that are necessary for only certain athletes. You also need to consider situational factors when planning your practices, such as the amount of practice time available each day, the number of practice days before and during the season, the number of support staff you have, and the availability of equipment and facilities. Which skills you emphasize and which teaching methods you use will depend on your athletes' present capabilities and the time and resources available to prepare them for competition.

Whether you coach a team sport or an individual sport, the best way to maximize the practice experience of all your athletes is to ensure that each is being challenged to improve his or her technical, tactical, and mental skills in some way. In chapter 6, you learned how to identify the technical, tactical, and mental skills of your sport and determine which are essential for all your athletes to learn. More advanced skills should be reserved for those athletes who demonstrate consistent proficiency in the essential skills. As you plan your practices, think about which athletes might benefit from extra repetitions of essential skills and which ones might be ready for more advanced skill practice.

Also, think of ways to keep all your athletes actively involved physically and mentally throughout practice so that there is minimal "standing around." One way to do this is to have different athletes working on different skills at the same time. Baseball or softball players who need extra fielding practice might have balls hit to them by an assistant coach or an experienced player during the usual delays in batting practice (e.g., when changing batters or when gathering the balls that have been hit). At the same time, more experienced infielders might be practicing a variety of run-down plays in an adjacent area. Players who aren't batting or fielding could serve as baserunners in order to create different gamelike situations that would enable batters and fielders to work on their tactical skills.

Always remember to keep the following questions in mind when developing practice plans and activities using a games approach:

- Is the activity relevant to some aspect of competition?
- Is the activity helping athletes develop the technical, tactical, and mental skills they need?
- Is the activity challenging (not boring or overwhelming)?

In chapter 5, the principle of limited attention capacity was discussed. From an instructional perspective, this principle suggests that you must consider how much information your athletes can attend to at any one time when designing practice activities. In some cases, athletes may need to practice a technical skill in isolation before they can handle any additional tactical or mental skills. The best way to determine when to include tactical or mental skills during a technical skill session is to evaluate the consistency of athletes' skill execution. When you see them performing a technical skill on a fairly consistent basis, you can begin adding the tactical and mental skills that are relevant to the performance of that skill. A volleyball player who demonstrates a consistent passing or hitting technique might begin practicing passing or hitting balls to different targets. The player might also begin developing a mental routine to use before each point—a relaxation breath; a single self-reminder, such as the play signaled by the coach, who she should be trying to pass the ball to, or where a good target for a spike might be; and a focus cue, such as "seams," in order to be sure to watch the ball.

By considering the various skill demands and **competitive circumstances** of your sport, you will be in a good position to determine which elements to emphasize during your practices. For example, one of the circumstantial aspects of placekicking and punting in football is the long period of time between kicks. The placekicker's outcome goal is to always kick the ball between the uprights, while the punter's goal is to vary his kicks depending on the field location. For pooch kicks (i.e., those attempted inside the opponent's 40-yard line), the punter tries to achieve greater altitude and less distance with the ball than for open field kicks (i.e., those attempted at a location between the opponent's 40-yard line and the kicker's 10-yard line). If he is kicking out of his own end zone, the punter must perform at a more rapid tempo than he does for a pooch kick or an open field kick. To help the placekicker and the punter prepare for competition, practice repetitions could be spaced out randomly over the course of a practice session, with each repetition coming from a different location on the field. Both kickers could also practice against a variety of defensive formations (e.g., different kick-block and kick-return schemes) and simulated game conditions (e.g., leading by 2 points with 30 seconds left in the first half, score tied late in the 4th quarter). This would force the punter to adjust his kicks according to the different formations and game conditions he will confront in competition (tactical skill) and would give both kickers the opportunity to practice focusing their attention and adjusting their arousal in order to achieve their most effective kicks under all types of competitive circumstances (mental skills).

When planning practice activities for some team sports, keep in mind that the technical, tactical, and mental skills needed on offense are often different from those needed on defense. When executing a half-court offense, basketball players need to be attentive to their teammates' actions, make quick and intelligent decisions (e.g., when to flash to the ball, move to a vacated spot, or make a backdoor cut), and take high-percentage shots. However, when playing defense, athletes need to be more attentive to their opponents' actions in order to improve their anticipation of the opponents' tendencies and prevent them from doing what they like to do. From an execution standpoint, defense is more about effort and aggressiveness, whereas offense depends more on poise, control, and concentration. Therefore, when designing practice activities that require players to switch back and forth from offense to defense, remind your athletes of the different tactical and mental demands of both, make sure they focus on the most appropriate cues when playing each, and alert them to the importance of adjusting their arousal level to accommodate the different emotional requirements of offensive (i.e., relaxed, fluid, smooth) and defensive (i.e., intense, aggressive) skills.

## Creating Practice Activities

Whenever possible, try to create practice activities that combine the **technical, tactical,** and **mental skills** important for successful performance (figure 9.1). For example, one practice activity from the sport of tennis that might achieve this goal is to have players play a certain number of points (e.g., 10, 15, 20) while focusing on the different skills. Before each "game," players could be instructed to focus on *one* of the following skills from *each* category:

### Technical skills

Hitting forehand and backhand groundstrokes crosscourt and down the line

Hitting serves down the "T," into the body, and out wide to both deuce and ad courts

### Tactical skills

Mixing up pace, depth, and target location to create open spaces on the opposing player's court

Demonstrating patience by hitting 10 balls before attempting a winner

### Mental skills

Creating a mental plan for each point

Focusing attention on the seams of the approaching ball

Using relaxation breaths or taking more time between points when the score gets close or arousal level is too high

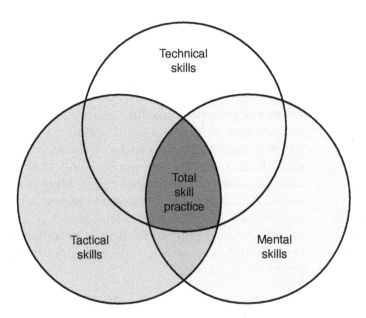

FIGURE 9.1    "Total skill practice" involves the simultaneous rehearsal of technical, tactical, and mental elements.

Afterward, the players could be asked to briefly discuss how well they think they achieved the instructed focus and how it affected their respective performance. In some cases, they might decide to continue to focus on a particular skill during the next game, or to emphasize a different one.

The primary goal of such activities is to heighten athletes' awareness of the importance of all three types of skills for achieving success. In addition, discussions emanating from your players' experiences can improve two-way communication and enable you to provide more helpful assistance.

You can take a similar approach when designing practice activities for large-squad team sports. Offensive and defensive football players might be instructed to focus on different mental skills before a drill, and soccer players might be told to focus on different tactical skills when playing offense and defense. After the drill or perhaps at the end of practice, players could be invited to discuss what they learned and how the skills they tried to focus on influenced their performance. In some cases, you (or perhaps an assistant coach) might need to conduct one-on-one debriefing sessions with more reserved athletes who are reluctant to speak up in a group setting.

However, most teams have at least a few players who have no qualms about speaking up or providing feedback to the coach. As long as open, two-way communication is maintained, postactivity discussion sessions such as these can be extremely beneficial for both coaches and athletes.

Whether you use a games approach or a more traditional approach for a particular practice activity, make sure to give your athletes the kinds of experiences that will benefit them the most during competition. Although technical skills

The best practices equip athletes with all the skills they need for competition.

should usually be emphasized first, tactical and mental skills should be introduced as soon as possible. You could encourage a volleyball player learning the jump serve (technical skill) to hit the serve to different targets (tactical skill) and develop a pre-serve routine (mental skill) as soon as she shows some general proficiency with the serving technique.

## Encouraging a Process Focus

One of the most challenging aspects of coaching is keeping athletes focused on the process of performing rather than on the outcome. Since sport outcomes tend to carry a large amount of emotional significance, it is often difficult for athletes to resist the tendency to think about them. Although winning is the desired outcome of any competition, the only things athletes have control over are their choices: what they are going to pay attention to, how they handle their emotions, and how they respond to adversity or misfortune during the course of a competition. The question then becomes, how should you coach your athletes to make the correct choices? The answer is to coach them to focus only on the

things that will give them the chance to perform at their best. If you use the games approach, you will advocate a focus on the relevant technical, tactical, and mental skills they need to execute rather than on the outcomes (figure 9.2). Creating practice activities like the ones suggested in the previous section is a good way to do this. By encouraging a **process focus** on the relevant skills, both in practice and during competition, and reminding athletes of those skills when you see their attention straying toward less relevant aspects of the competitive environment (e.g., spectator noise, poor officiating, trash-talking opponents), you will greatly enhance their prospects of success.

## Involving Athletes in the Planning of Practices

The games approach to skill instruction emphasizes the development of athletes' awareness of the various demands of their sport. Involving your athletes in the process of practice planning tells them you think their input is valuable. Athletes who contribute to practice planning are usually more motivated to practice and see more

FIGURE 9.2    Emphasize a process focus both in practice and in competition.

relevance in what they are doing compared with athletes who have no say. Some ways to involve your athletes in the planning process include asking them to

- discuss the technical, tactical, and mental demands of their sport;

- suggest some ways technical, tactical, and mental skills might be combined in practice activities;

- identify the focus and feeling they would like to have during technical skill performance; and

- suggest competition-like activities they think would foster the development of technical, tactical, and mental skills.

After all, it's the athletes who will be wearing the uniforms and doing the competing. By involving them in their own preparation, you are helping them identify the skills they need to develop to be successful in competition. As they improve their skills their confidence increases, and eventually they reach the point where they don't have to hope they're ready to compete—they will know they're ready.

Following are some practice plans for springboard diving, distance running, and soccer that show how the teaching of technical, tactical, and mental skills can be combined in a games approach. Notice that the practices have a lot of variety and competition-like activities, which increase athletes' enjoyment and skill development.

## Sample Springboard Diving Practice Session

The practice activity of one high school springboard diver illustrates how the technical, tactical, and mental skills of a sport can be practiced simultaneously in preparation for competition. This diver begins by identifying the focus cues and arousal levels she needs for each of her one-meter dives. The diver knows that if she focuses on the relevant cues and achieves the appropriate arousal levels (on a scale from 1, signifying "completely relaxed," to 10, signifying "completely charged"), she will optimize her chances of hitting each of her dives. Therefore, during practices, the diver prepares for each dive by focusing on the appropriate cues and adjusting her arousal level up or down as necessary. She also spaces out her dives by the amount of time she anticipates having to wait between dives during competition. As is the case in competition, she never attempts the same dive twice in a row during practice.

| Dive | Focus cues | Arousal level |
|---|---|---|
| Front 1 1/2 pike | Foot under, Close late | 5-6 |
| Reverse pike | Watch hands touch, Come out the side | 5-6 |
| Back pike | Watch hands touch, Come out the side | 5-6 |
| Back flip, 1 1/2 twist | Straight jump, Tight twists | 5-6 |
| Inward pike | Up and over the board, Close late | 5 |
| Front double pike | Throw out, Tight pike, Snap out | 7-8 |
| Front 2 1/2 tuck | Throw out, Tight tuck | 7-8 |
| Reverse 1 1/2 tuck | Head in, Tight tuck | 5-6 |
| Back 1 1/2 tuck | Head in, Tight tuck | 5-6 |
| Inward 1 1/2 pike | Arms all the way up, Relax | 7-8 |
| Front 1 1/2 full twist | Snap hard, Tight twist | 5-6 |

# Games Approach to Practicing Distance Running

Although distance running isn't a game, practicing distance running using the games approach can produce impressive results during competition. A race plan for a cross country race usually includes getting off the start line quickly, establishing tempo, maintaining that tempo throughout the first half to two thirds of the race, relaxing when pain sets in, and expending all remaining energy in the finishing kick. Technical components of the plan might include maintaining good posture, opening up the stride when running downhill, and using the arms to help the legs when fatigue sets in. Tactical components might include timely bouts of relaxed acceleration (e.g., when beginning the finishing kick or easing past another runner) or drafting behind other runners. Mental components might include focus cues such as "Stay tall," "Floppy face," and "Move the arms," as well as energy management activities such as relaxed breathing.

When runners are practicing, they could be encouraged to focus on different technical, tactical, and mental components of their race plans. For example, during a long road workout, they could practice opening the stride whenever they are running downhill and using their arms more when running uphill or when feeling fatigued (technical). At the same time, they could practice attacking the top of an approaching hill and accelerating over it, anticipating a turn in the road and leaning into it, or increasing speed when a teammate tries to pass (tactical). Finally, they could practice focusing attention on their breathing or the tempo they are trying to achieve, or relaxing the face, shoulders, and hands when pain begins to set in (mental). By practicing the relevant technical, tactical, and mental components of their race plans, runners become accustomed to staying focused on the process of performing. As a result, they will perform better in competition because they know they just need to do the same things they do every day in practice.

# Practice Plans for a Large-Squad Team Sport

When using the games approach in planning the practices of large-squad teams (e.g., football, soccer, volleyball), you still need to remember the following three questions listed earlier in this chapter: Is each activity (1) relevant to competition; (2) developing the essential technical, tactical, and mental skills; and (3) challenging? Notice how the following sample practice plan for a soccer team conforms to those criteria while also encouraging the input of players in order to determine the effectiveness of each activity and identify possible ways of making the practice more gamelike.

**Date:** August 25, hot and humid

**Level:** Varsity (high school)

**Point in season:** Fall preseason

**Practice start time:** 3:00 p.m.

**Length of practice:** 150 minutes

**Practice objectives:** (1) Improving conditioning, speed, and endurance; (2) developing the following passing skills: passing with a purpose (tactical skill); maintaining possession of the ball (technical skill); improving awareness off the ball (tactical skill); passing under pressure (mental skill); (3) developing the following tackling skills: tackling with the foot farthest from the ball (technical skill); anticipating the opponent's move (mental skill); going for the ball and not the opponent (tactical skill)

**Equipment:** One ball per player; goals or flags; cones and disc cones; scrimmage vests (at least two colors)

*(continued)*

## PRACTICE ACTIVITIES

| Time | Name of activity | Description | Key technical, tactical, and mental teaching points |
|---|---|---|---|
| 3:00-3:05 | Warm-up | Players begin with easy jogging. | Begin mental adjustment from everyday activities to soccer. |
| 3:05-3:15 | Warm-up | Players perform dynamic stretching and imagery. | Emphasize full range of motion.<br>Practice imagery of passing and tackling skills using first-person perspective. |
| 3:15-3:30 | Slalom drill | Stagger cones far apart for 180-degree turns; players run as fast as possible while dribbling around cones. | Keep ball close, emphasizing touching and moving faster through the cones.<br>Imagine cones are opposing defenders. |
| 3:30-3:45 | Heads-up drill | Players dribble randomly in the penalty area and call out number of fingers coach is holding up. | Keep head up.<br>Imagine teammates are oncoming defenders. |
| 3:45-4:00 | Wind sprints | Players run sprints of various gamelike lengths to cones situated at different locations from one end of the field to the other. Coach starts and stops each sprint with whistle, and assistant records slowest and fastest times. Players jog back to start in 60 seconds or less (a 3-to-1 ratio for their active recovery time to sprint time). | Attempt to improve both fastest and slowest total times compared with the previous practice or with previous best times.<br>Make sure recovery is active. |
| 4:00-4:05 | Fluid break and feedback | Everyone drinks 6 to 8 oz of sports drink or water. | Obtain player input and feedback as to how to make conditioning drills more gamelike. |
| 4:05-4:20 | 2v2 scrimmages: passing and tackling | Play 2v2: Set up multiple 15- × 20-yard grids. All players play at the same time in separate areas. Focus on passing, moving without the ball, and a combination of both. Three consecutive passes earn 1 point. Once the ball goes across the line, the opposing team takes possession and attempts to advance the ball toward opposite end line.<br>Play 2 minutes and then have teams switch grids to compete against other pairs. Allow 1 minute of rest between scrimmages. | Emphasize keys to successful passing:<br>• Make sure passes have good pace.<br>• Pass into space with accuracy.<br>• Focus on timing the pass and the run.<br>Freeze play when players aren't providing passing options or accurately reading each other. Reemphasize focus cues for passing.<br>Emphasize keys for tackling:<br>• Tackle with foot farthest from ball.<br>• Anticipate passer's movements.<br>• Go for the ball! |
| 4:20-4:35 | 4v4 scrimmages: passing and tackling | Play 4v4: Set up multiple 25- × 30-yard or 35- × 40-yard grids. All players play at the same time in separate areas. Incorporate passing and tackling. Tackles in which the ball is taken directly from a player earn 2 points. Three consecutive successful passes earns 1 point. When ball is advanced across the end line, opposing team takes possession and attempts to advance the ball toward opposite end line. | Emphasize positioning for tackling:<br>• Maintain balance.<br>• Anticipate the opponent's move.<br>• Focus on the ball.<br>• Slightly bend the knees.<br>• Lead with nontackling leg.<br>• Go for the ball! |
| 4:35-4:40 | Fluid break and discussion | Everyone drinks 6 to 8 oz of sports drink or water. | Obtain player feedback on 2v2 and 4v4 scrimmages; reemphasize key technical and tactical focus cues. |

*(continued)*

Adapted, by permission, from ASEP, 2004, *Coaching principles instructor guide*, 3rd ed. (Champaign, IL: Human Kinetics), 219-220. The soccer practice plan and its outcome (evaluation) were developed in collaboration with Bill Schranz, head women's soccer coach, Concordia University, Seward, NE.

**PRACTICE ACTIVITIES** (continued)

| Time | Name of activity | Description | Key technical, tactical, and mental teaching points |
|------|------------------|-------------|-----------------------------------------------------|
| 4:40-5:05 | 8v8 game | Play game in real time, but still with modified scoring: Tackles resulting in gain of possession and successful passes earn 3 points. Combinations of 5 passes earn 1 point. Goals earn 2 points.<br>*Variation:* To emphasize passing, combinations of 5 passes earn 3 points, and tackles in which possession is gained and successful pass is made earn 1 point.<br>If time allows, permit players to scrimmage in gamelike fashion without restrictions. | Offensive: Focus on combination passing.<br>Defensive: Focus on positioning for tackling, anticipating opponent's move, going for the ball, and maintaining possession after the tackle. |
| 5:05-5:15 | Cool-down | Players perform easy jogging while dribbling.<br>Players stretch, ice, and massage any tight muscles. | Practice imagery of passing and tackling skills from first-person perspective. |
| 5:15-5:30 | Fluid intake and discussion | Everyone drinks 6 to 8 oz of sports drink or water. Hold end-of-practice discussion and review. | Obtain general comments from players; review keys to effective passing and tackling; identify positives and areas in need of further improvement; obtain player feedback as to how to make scrimmages more gamelike while focusing on skill development; make any necessary announcements. |

## Evaluating the Effectiveness of Practice Activities

Arguably the best indicator of the effectiveness of your practices is the way your athletes perform in competition. If they execute their technical, tactical, and mental skills the same way they practiced them, both you and they should be pleased with their performance, regardless of the final outcome. However, if your athletes don't execute their skills the way they practiced them (which is unlikely if they practice diligently) or they do but the outcome is unsatisfactory, then some changes may need to be made.

Within a few days of the competition, you should spend some time talking with your athletes about aspects of their practices they believe were beneficial as well as aspects they think did not adequately prepare them for competition.

Practice elements that are judged to be beneficial should be retained and reinforced during subsequent practices. However, those that are not beneficial may need to be revised, eliminated, or replaced with other activities that when practiced will enhance the prospects of goal achievement in future competitions.

As mentioned previously, it is also a good idea to take some time at the end of each practice to obtain feedback from athletes about the relative benefits of various activities. During these debriefings, team members can discuss the strengths and weaknesses of the practice, determine which activities were more beneficial and why, and provide feedback as to which activities may need to be adjusted (and if so, how) or eliminated. In some cases, it might be helpful to use an evaluation form such as the one shown in figure 6.3 in chapter 6 (page

90) to determine the extent to which the various technical, tactical, and mental target behaviors of an activity are being executed correctly. Because it will probably be more difficult to observe your athletes' tactical and mental behaviors than their technical behaviors, it's a good idea to ask them to rate themselves on each behavior. You could also invite their suggestions as to how to improve the form or how you might help them improve the evaluation form. Regardless of how you do it, keep in mind that the evaluation process is primarily designed to achieve one objective: the most accurate assessment of the effectiveness of practice activities for helping your athletes develop the essential technical, tactical, and mental skills they need for competition.

The ultimate reward of effective coaching is seeing your athletes confident in their preparation and enjoying the challenge of competition.

## A Final Comment

As long as you remain a member of the coaching profession, you will face the challenge of designing the most beneficial practice experiences for your athletes. By identifying the technical, tactical, and mental demands of your sport; creating practice activities that include the technical, tactical, and mental skills athletes need in competition; and evaluating and refining your approach on an ongoing basis, you will be doing all you can to give your athletes the opportunity to perform at their best every time they compete. In doing so, you will experience the ultimate reward of coaching—seeing your athletes confident in the knowledge that they are totally prepared for competition and enjoying the challenge.

# SUMMARY

1. The most effective practices allow athletes to develop the technical, tactical, and mental skills they need for competition.

2. Effective planning is the key to effective practices.

3. The skills you emphasize in practice and the teaching methods you use will depend on your athletes' present capabilities and the time and resources available to prepare them for competition.

4. Situational factors to keep in mind when planning practices include the amount of practice time available each day, the number of practice days before and during the season, the number of support staff you have, and the availability of equipment and facilities.

5. You should consider three questions when deciding whether or not to include a particular activity in a practice session: Is the activity relevant to competition? Is it going to promote the development of essential technical, tactical, and mental skills? Is it challenging?

6. The technical, tactical, and mental demands of a sport can differ for different athletes and for the same athlete in different situations.

7. To promote the greatest transfer between practice and competition, practice activities should be performed under circumstances that simulate those of competition as much as possible.

8. The technical skills should be introduced and practiced first, and tactical and mental skills should be added as soon as possible.

9. The games approach to practice emphasizes a focus on the process of developing the technical, tactical, and mental skills that are essential for success.

10. Athletes who are taught to focus on the process of performing rather than the outcome during practices are more likely to focus on the process of performing rather than the outcome during competition.

11. Allowing athletes to provide input during practice planning increases their motivation to practice and helps them see the relevance of what they are doing.

12. Practice evaluation and skill refinement is an ongoing process.

13. The best indicator of the effectiveness of practice activities is the performance of athletes in competition.

14. Evaluation of the effectiveness of practice activities and competition performance should include the perceptions of the athletes themselves.

# KEY TERMS

competitive circumstances          process focus
games approach                     tactical demands
mental demands                     technical demands

# REVIEW QUESTIONS

1. What principle did former Princeton basketball coach Pete Carril use when determining which activities to include in his team's practices?

2. Why is it important to make practices as competition-like as possible?

3. What's the difference between a process focus and an outcome focus? Why is a process focus more effective than an outcome focus in the heat of competition?

4. What are some reasons for including your athletes in the planning and evaluation of practice activities?

5. How would you determine whether a practice activity benefited your athletes in competition?

# PRACTICAL ACTIVITIES

**1.** Create a practice plan for 30 minutes of a practice session. List two technical skills, tactical skills, and mental skills that athletes would have the opportunity to develop during that time period. For each skill, list one focus cue (word or phrase) that would facilitate practice of the skill.

**2.** Evaluate the previous practice plan with respect to the following criteria:

  **a.** Relevance to competition

  **b.** Active participation by all team members

  **c.** Challenges presented

  **d.** Enjoyment experienced

  **e.** Opportunity provided for athlete input and feedback

# APPENDIX A

# *Answers to Review Questions*

## Chapter 1

1. Learning is an internal state that changes with practice and can be estimated by observing athletes performing their skills on repeated occasions. To produce effective learning, coaches need to plan practices that promote the performance of correct behaviors.

2. Intentional learning is that which athletes are able to recognize as they improve their skills. Implicit learning is that which athletes are unaware of, yet it is reflected in improved performance. An example of intentional learning and implicit learning from the sport of soccer is the improved accuracy of a player's passes and an increased consistency of the placement of the plant foot, respectively.

3. The three basic ingredients of sport skill instruction are the athlete, the task or skill, and the environment. To provide the best instructional assistance, coaches must know the capabilities of the athletes they are working with, the complexity of the task or skill they are teaching, and the demands of the performance environment.

4. The three categories of skill elements that make up most sport skills are sensory-perceptual elements, decision-making elements, and motor control elements. When hitting ground strokes in tennis, a player must watch the approaching ball in order to perceive its speed and direction (sensory-perceptual element), decide what type of shot to hit, assuming the ball lands within the boundaries on the player's side of the court (decision-making element), and produce an effective swing that achieves the desired outcome (motor control element).

5. Sometimes athletes need time to experience the task without assistance to gain a sense of what works, what doesn't, and what happens when they try different things. Aspects of dribbling a soccer ball while being defended that players could discover or improve on their own include shielding the ball from the defender, dribbling with both the inside and outside of the foot, and visually scanning the field while dribbling.

## Chapter 2

1. An understanding of the concept of individual differences can help a coach design practices, create challenges, and provide the types of instructional assistance that meet the needs of all participants.

2. Capabilities that can be improved with practice include strength, flexibility, and stamina.

3. Athletes' dominant abilities might be determined by observing them performing a variety of skills on several occasions and noting their strengths and weaknesses.

4. Athletes of the same age can demonstrate considerable differences in performance depending on their respective types of previous experience, exposure to or familiarity with the skills of the sport (i.e., stage of learning), and personal goals.

5. Athletes in the mental stage of learning will appear more hesitant, and their movements will lack smoothness. Those in the practice stage will demonstrate consistently acceptable performance of the basic movements and some capacity to adapt their movements to meet changing environmental demands. Athletes in the automatic stage will appear nearly effortless in the way they move and show an ability to deal with various types of environmental information with little disruption in performance.

6. Knowing something about each athlete's motivation can help a coach design the type of practices that will be enjoyable, encourage athletes to try their best, and make them want to come back for more.

7. Athletes who are motivated to achieve success can be expected to set goals that involve some aspect of desired personal achievement (e.g., winning a batting title, improving free throw percentage from 60 to 70 percent, defeating a particular opponent).

8. It's not a good idea to try to predict the future success of a young athlete because various elements can change between the present and the future (e.g., physical maturation, motivation, the abilities important for beginning performance and advanced performance).

# Chapter 3

1. A football coach observing a highly skilled linebacker would see that the player consistently reads the play correctly, anticipates the ball carrier's movements, uses his hands to keep blockers away from his body, and executes tackles in a variety of ways but always with the correct form. A lesser skilled linebacker would be able to execute some tackles in a technically correct fashion but would be less adept at anticipating the opponent's actions and adapting his responses accordingly.

2. Tactical skills are the decisions athletes make and the strategies they employ to gain a competitive advantage over an opponent. A tactical skill in the sport of volleyball is to occasionally dink over an opponent that likes to block the hitter's spikes.

   Mental skills are the routines or procedures athletes use to remain focused and maintain their composure in the heat of competition. One mental skill for a volleyball player would be a pre-serve routine that includes a focus on the intended target and a relaxation breath.

3. Athletes performing technical skills in an open environment must be able to adapt their movements to environmental conditions much more rapidly than athletes performing in a closed environment. For example, a basketball player defending against a two-on-one fast break must be able to read the opposing players' actions, quickly decide whether to go for a steal or take a charge, and then execute the chosen action . . . all within 1 or 2 seconds. However, a player shooting a free throw performs essentially the same skill each time—focus on the rim and shoot the ball—and has up to 10 seconds to do so.

4. Some skills in the sport of soccer that athletes might control using a motor program are passing, shooting, heading, and performing a throw-in.

5. When performing a closed skill such as a tennis serve, a player could attempt to adapt the serving program by adjusting the speed of the swing, the angle of the racket face at impact, and the amount of spin imparted to the ball. When performing an open skill such as a three-on-two fast break in basketball, an offensive player would read the defense and then quickly decide on the type of pass to make (e.g., a bounce pass). The player would then adjust the details of the passing program (e.g., force, release point, passing hand) in order to execute the pass.

6. Some skills from the sport of gymnastics that have a speed–accuracy trade-off include routines on the balance beam, the parallel bars, and the pommel horse.

7. For all the skills identified in the previous question, a gymnast might eventually emphasize speed rather than accuracy when practicing the dismount.

# Chapter 4

1. Tactical skills concern the strategies athletes use to gain a competitive edge. From an information processing standpoint, a tactical decision involves the processing of environmental information (e.g., observing the opponent's tendencies, preferences, strengths, and weaknesses), deciding on a strategy that would be effective against the opponent (e.g., playing his own strength against the opponent's strength, playing to the opponent's weakness, doing something the opponent is not expecting), and executing a response that gains the intended advantage (e.g., producing a movement that catches the opponent off guard, forces the opponent to do something she doesn't do well, gains psychological momentum).

2. The three categories of information athletes need to process in order to perform effectively are relevant information in the environment (e.g., the speed of an approaching ball, the movements of an opponent, the intended target), information necessary for making an appropriate decision (e.g., the score, the athlete's own strengths and weaknesses, the cost of making a mistake), and information regarding how to produce the desired response (e.g., keeping the wrist firm on a topspin tennis ground stroke, staying relaxed and following through when shooting a free throw, wrapping the arms around a running back's legs when tackling).

3. A less experienced soccer player is likely to process environmental information that is not relevant (e.g., the facial expression of an opponent), make decisions that are predictable (e.g., passing to a teammate that is clearly open), produce responses that are ineffective (e.g., emphasizing accuracy to the extent that the pass lacks sufficient speed), and take a considerable amount of time deciding what to do and following through (e.g., passing, shooting, or dribbling). A more experienced player is likely to process environmental information that is relevant (e.g., the relative positioning of teammates and opposing players), make decisions that are creative (e.g., faking a pass and exploding past the opposing defender), produce responses that are effective (e.g., taking a shot on goal that either goes in or creates a scoring opportunity for a teammate), and take very little time deciding what to do and following through (e.g., deftly sending a touch pass to a teammate breaking away from a defender).

4. Athletes should have answers for the following three questions in order to make the most effective tactical decisions:

   a. What should I be looking for?

   b. What are my best options here?

   c. How do I need to feel and be focused?

5. A special-teams player in football who knows how close he can legally come to an opposing player fielding a punt, who understands his team's strategy of putting pressure on the opposing team, and who is aware that the opposing player receiving the punt is inexperienced might make the tactical decision to come as close to the player as possible and be alert to a possible fumble.

6. A basketball player realizes that her strengths are rebounding and defense; her weakness is shooting; and her role on the team is to create scoring opportunities by blocking shots, setting screens, and making the quick outlet pass. When confronted with a situation calling for a game-winning shot, the player would focus on screening a defender guarding one of the team's better shooters and positioning for a possible offensive rebound and put-back.

7. The games approach to practice is the best way to develop tactical skills because it places athletes in the kinds of situations they will be encountering during actual competitions. This will allow them to practice the various tactical decisions they will need to make when they compete.

# Chapter 5

1. Generally speaking, increases in arousal tend to increase the quality of athletes' performance. However, different skills are performed better at different arousal levels (e.g., golf is performed better at lower arousal levels than is wrestling), so more arousal is not always better.

2. As arousal increases, attention becomes more focused. This sharpening of focus helps athletes up to a point, but beyond that point, increasing arousal even further eventually produces a "deer in the headlights" focus that is so narrow it can diminish performance.

3. Trait anxiety is related to arousal in that athletes who tend to have higher levels of trait anxiety (i.e., the tendency to interpret situations as threatening) tend to be more highly aroused than athletes with lower levels of trait anxiety.

4. The principle of limited attention capacity indicates that people can attend to only a few things at any one time. Therefore, it is important for coaches to help athletes identify the sources of information that are important for successful performance (e.g., the location of the catcher's glove would be relevant for a pitcher to focus on before delivering the pitch) and instruct them to focus only on that information.

5. An internal focus is one that is directed toward the athlete's thoughts or feelings, while an external focus is one that is directed toward information in the environment. An internal focus is beneficial for a gymnast before attempting a high bar routine. The gymnast uses the focus to imagine the execution of various elements in his routine and to adjust his arousal so that he feels the way he wants to before beginning the routine. The gymnast shifts to an external focus when performing his routine by visually locating the position of the bar before grasping it each time and by locating the position on the mat where he wants to stick his dismount.

6. Relevant environmental information is that which is important for successful performance, while irrelevant environmental information contributes nothing to performance. In a pressure situation, where attention can be devoted to only one or two things at a time, it is extremely important for athletes to be focused *only* on the most relevant environmental information. For example, a tennis player serving for match point to win a tournament needs to focus on the targets she intends to hit rather than on spectators, officials, or the body language of her opponent.

7. Working memory is like a temporary workspace that athletes use to hold the information they will need during a particular performance. Long-term memory is a vast storage area in the brain that contains all an athlete's memories of previous events and people. Before a match against a familiar opponent, a wrestler would retrieve from long-term memory everything he remembers about that opponent from previous matches (e.g., the opponent's strengths and weaknesses, the moves the opponent likes to use in different situations, and so on) and move it to working memory. This allows the wrestler to anticipate and prepare responses for the opponent's moves and plan his own attack.

8. An athlete using an internal imagery perspective would see and feel things the same way she would if she were physically performing her skills. An athlete using an external imagery perspective would see and feel things the same way she would if she were viewing a video replay of her performance. A gymnast imagining a balance beam routine from an internal perspective would see and feel the event the same way she would if she were performing it. However, if she imagined the same routine from an external perspective, the gymnast would see it from the perspective of the judges, which would give her a better idea of what her form might look

like. Her feeling of the movements using an external perspective would depend on how closely she connected what she "observed" in her form to what that might feel like.

## Chapter 6

1. The four principles of effective goal setting emphasize the following characteristics: challenging, attainable, realistic, and specific. These characteristics are essential because challenging goals are motivating, attainable goals take into consideration the possible constraints to goal achievement (e.g., time available to practice), realistic goals are defined relative to the athlete's current level of performance (i.e., targets for improvement are based on past performance), and specific goals allow athletes to measure their improvements in tangible ways (e.g., an increase in free throw percentage from 65 to 70 percent).

2. Performance goals are more effective than outcome goals because athletes have more control over their performance (e.g., achieving solid contact during each at-bat in today's baseball game) than they do over the outcomes (e.g., going two for four in today's game).

3. The relative timing pattern and coordination pattern of the football punt could be described in the following way. The supporting leg moves forward, the arms are extended, and the ball is released. The kicking leg then flexes at the knee and begins to move forward at the thigh. The lower leg trails the thigh until a 90-degree angle is formed. At that point the thigh begins to slow down while the lower leg and kicking foot accelerate forward and upward and the foot, moving at a high velocity, makes contact with the ball (adapted from Carr, 2004).

4. The perceptual elements of technical skills pertain to the information athletes pick up from the environment (e.g., the speed of an approaching ball, the weight of a softball bat, the movements of an opposing ball carrier), while the conceptual elements pertain to the relevant knowledge or strategies of the sport (e.g., advancing a baserunner from second to third with no outs when batting in softball, timing a pass that avoids an offside in soccer or ice hockey). Both elements are essential for the successful execution of most technical skills.

5. Target behaviors are the technical, tactical, and mental skills or skill elements a particular athlete might focus on to achieve performance success. For example, a volleyball coach might instruct a beginning backline player to focus on the following target behaviors when preparing to receive an opponent's serve: (a) Watch the seams of the ball from the moment it leaves the server's hand (perceptual element of the technical skills of passing or digging and the mental skill of attention focusing), and (b) extend the arms and relax the hands (movement elements of the technical skills of passing or digging and the mental skill of adjusting arousal). However, the coach might instruct a more advanced backline player to focus on the following target behaviors in the same situation: (a) Locate the opposing team's weakest backline player (tactical skill and mental skill of attention focusing), and (b) pass the ball to the setter in such a way as to enable her to set the team's best hitter (movement element of the technical skill of passing).

## Chapter 7

1. Some things a coach can do to establish two-way communication with athletes include maintaining eye contact when athletes are speaking; letting them finish speaking before responding; asking them to repeat what they heard in order to be sure they understood it; using a positive tone of voice and avoiding sarcasm; encouraging them to provide input during practices or in preparation for competition; discussing ideas with them before making decisions; and obtaining feedback from them after practices and competitions to determine what helped, what didn't, and what might be added, changed, or deleted.

2. The primary functions of verbal instructions and visual demonstrations are to direct athletes' attention to the rules of the sport; the key elements of technical, tactical, and mental skills (e.g., relative timing patterns, strategies, emotional control); and the types of feelings they can expect to experience when practicing and competing.

3. An advantage of physical guidance is that it can give athletes a general idea of the desired pattern of a movement they are learning until they are able to produce the movement on their own. A disadvantage of assistive guidance, one type of physical guidance, is that the feel of the guided movement is different from the feel of the movement when performed without assistance.

4. Part practice or slow-motion practice might be necessary when a technical skill is so complex that athletes have difficulty identifying or focusing on the relevant features. A volleyball player might use part practice to rehearse the run, jump, and toss when learning the jump serve. Once she has automated those parts, the player could add the hitting action. A group of offensive linemen might use slow-motion practice to initially rehearse their respective blocking assignments for a running play they are trying to learn.

5. Varied practice and random practice are similar in that both challenge athletes to produce different movements from one attempt to the next. They are different in that in varied practice, athletes perform different variations of the same general movement pattern (e.g., a softball pitcher throwing a rise ball, a drop ball, a curveball, and a changeup is practicing variations of the same general throwing pattern), while in random practice, athletes perform different movement patterns (e.g., a volleyball player attempting a pass and then a block and then a spike is practicing three different general movement patterns).

6. Team sport athletes need to develop anticipation about their opponents because it will help them recognize and, if necessary, respond more rapidly to what their opponents might do during competition (e.g., a volleyball team that knows what types of attacks to expect from an opponent can set up blocks more quickly). Team sport athletes need to develop anticipation about their teammates because if they know what they can expect from each other, they can devote more attention to their own performance and also coordinate their respective movements more effectively (e.g., a tennis doubles team attempting to break their opponents' serve, offensive linemen executing their respective blocking assignments during a running play, soccer players executing an offensive attack).

7. When using the games approach to prepare athletes for competition, coaches need to keep in mind the principle of relevance. In other words, how the coach organizes practice and how he or she creates opportunities for athletes to practice their skills should be as similar as possible to what athletes will need to deal with and execute during actual competition.

# Chapter 8

1. Before providing extrinsic feedback, coaches need to first be sure that athletes don't have access to the intrinsic information needed to evaluate their own performance or outcome; are not attending to the relevant sources of intrinsic information or feedback (e.g., the feel of a mechanically correct swing and the speed of the approaching ball when batting in baseball or softball); and are not able to interpret that information or feedback (e.g., batters must be able to feel an incorrect swing or know that they missed the pitch because they misread the speed of the approaching ball). If any of the previous conditions apply, then the coach needs to provide extrinsic feedback.

2. To determine the optimal viewing angle to use when presenting video feedback to athletes, a coach must decide which visual information is the most important for performance improvements to occur and which angle provides the best view of the correct relative timing pattern of the movement.

3. Performance feedback is usually more helpful than outcome feedback because in many cases athletes are able to obtain outcome feedback on their own (e.g., whether they made the tackle, won the point, made the shot, or got the hit). However, in sports where outcomes are measured in units of time (e.g., running events in track) or distance (e.g., field events in track) or determined by a judge's rating (e.g., gymnastics, figure skating, springboard diving), athletes need outcome feedback to evaluate their performance.

4. An example of program feedback for a softball pitcher is a verbal statement such as "Slow down your throwing shoulder, and speed up your wrist action" or a video replay showing the need for that kind of adjustment in the relative timing pattern. An example of parameter feedback is "Slow down your arm action" or a video replay illustrating that the pitcher's control is being sacrificed because her overall arm speed is too fast.

5. Descriptive feedback contains information about an athlete's performance, while prescriptive feedback includes suggestions for improving the performance. An example of descriptive feedback for a wide receiver after an incomplete pass is "You didn't separate yourself from the defensive back." An example of prescriptive feedback after the same play is "Next time try making your cuts a little sharper to get more separation between you and the defensive back."

6. Coaches should try to reduce the amount and frequency of extrinsic feedback they give to athletes because doing so forces athletes to evaluate their performance on their own, encourages athletes to do more problem solving and not depend so much on the coach, and gives athletes the confidence they need to make the correct adjustments during competition when they don't have the time or luxury to stop and ask for the coach's assistance.

7. Some ways a softball coach might reduce the frequency of extrinsic feedback yet still help infielders improve their defensive skills might be to conduct a defensive drill without feedback and then, after the drill, ask the players to first provide their evaluations of what they thought they did well and not so well, both individually and as a group, and then suggest some things they need to focus on next time to improve their performance.

## Chapter 9

1. The principle former Princeton basketball coach Pete Carril used when designing his team's practices was to include only those activities that would be useful in some form during competition.

2. It's important to make practices as competition-like as possible to produce the greatest transfer of technical, tactical, and mental skills to the competition setting. When athletes practice the way they need to play in competition, they are more likely to play that way when they get to the competition.

3. A process focus emphasizes the things athletes need to do to perform at their best, while an outcome focus emphasizes winning and losing. A process focus is more effective than an outcome focus in the heat of competition because it emphasizes elements that are under the athlete's control (e.g., watching the ball, following through on the kick, staying smooth during the race, and so on).

4. Athletes who are involved in planning practices are usually more motivated to practice than athletes who are not because they appreciate that their opinion is valued and see the relevance in what they are doing (i.e., how practices are preparing them for competition).

5. The best indicator of the effectiveness of practice activities is athletes' performance in competition. However, it's a good idea to occasionally seek athletes' input to determine which practice activities they feel are preparing them for competition and which ones are not.

# APPENDIX B

# *Answers to Practical Activities*

## Chapter 1

1. A practice activity from the sport of softball that illustrates the principle of specificity of training is to have outfielders practice their throws to bases under gamelike conditions (e.g., runners on first and third, tie score, one out, second inning). A coach hits the ball in the air, on a line, or on the ground into the outfield, and the fielder has to decide where to throw the ball and then attempt to produce an accurate throw. The game situation can be changed from throw to throw by allowing baserunners to advance as they normally would in a game or by substituting other runners and notifying outfielders of a new situation. By practicing this way, outfielders develop both their judgment and the accuracy of their throws in much the same way they are required to do so in competition.

2. Five processes necessary for successful performance of the throwing task described in the previous answer would be: determining the correct base to throw to (thought), correctly orienting the body for the throw (behavior), keeping the arm relaxed (feeling), focusing on the target (behavior), and producing a mechanically-correct overhand throwing motion and ball release (behavior).

3. Three questions the softball coach should consider when teaching outfielders the throwing task described in the answer to the first activity are: What factors should players consider when deciding which base to throw to? How relaxed should the throwing arm be in order to produce the most effective throws? What should the release point be in order to achieve the most accurate throws?

## Chapter 2

1. A basketball coach might describe a point guard as a player who needs to handle the ball well, make accurate passes, have a good understanding of the various offensive sets, make good decisions under pressure, and be a floor leader. The coach might list the following perceptual and motor abilities from figure 2.1 as being necessary for success at the point guard position:
   - Aiming (for making accurate passes)
   - Control precision (for dribbling and making accurate passes)
   - Explosive strength (for elevating on jump shots)
   - Gross body coordination (for performing multiple tasks)
   - Manual dexterity (for dribbling)

2. The following dominant abilities might be observed in two different players:

## Player A

### Stronger abilities

Multilimb coordination
Speed of limb movement
Reaction time

### Weaker abilities

Static strength
Stamina

## Player B

### Stronger abilities

Manual dexterity
Dynamic flexibility
Stamina

### Weaker abilities

Aiming
Control precision

3. Player A appears to be better suited ability-wise for success, based on the demands of the point guard position and the stronger and weaker abilities observed in each player. Player A's stronger abilities combine the general traits of coordination and speed, which are essential for point guards. Player A's weaker abilities are both improvable through standard strength and conditioning activities. Player B has good manual dexterity but is weaker in the areas of aiming and control precision. Therefore, player B would benefit from practice experiences that enable her to improve the accuracy and control of her passes. Two such activities are presented in the following full-court fast break drills:

a. Three-player parallel lane passing: In this drill, players remain in their respective lanes (left side, middle, right side) while sprinting up the court, making chest passes without dribbling, and one player making a final bounce pass to a teammate on the wing, who shoots a bank jump shot.

b. Three-player weave: In this drill, players pass and then go behind the player they passed to, exchange various types of passes without dribbling, and make a final bounce pass to a teammate on the wing, who shoots a bank jump shot (adapted from Wissel, 2004).

# Chapter 3

1. A softball pitcher would illustrate effective technical, tactical, and mental skill execution by throwing a mechanically correct off-speed pitch (technical), throwing the pitch to a batter who is expecting a fastball (tactical), and taking a relaxation breath and focusing on the catcher's glove before the pitch (mental).

2. Following are three examples of practice activities that illustrate a basketball coach's knowledge of the relative importance of mental activity, skill structure, environmental predictability, and the type of control needed:

a. A brief imagery session during a water break that helps reinforce in players' minds their respective assignments for a new inbounds play (illustrates the importance of mental rehearsal in movement planning)

b. An offensive set that requires players to execute a series of discrete movements (pass, screen, catch, shoot) against a one-on-one defense (illustrates how a specific sequence of discrete skills can be performed in an open environment)

c. A one-on-one dribble and defend drill that requires players to advance the ball the length of the court under defensive pressure (illustrates the use of both open-loop and closed-loop control in the execution of the dribbling and defending actions, respectively)

3. The speed–accuracy trade-off is an important consideration in the following sport situations:

   a. A linebacker achieving the correct pursuit angle on a sweep play

   b. A pole-vaulter approaching the box

   c. A volleyball player passing the ball

   A coach's knowledge of the principle of speed–accuracy trade-off could result in the following instructions to help athletes improve their performance:

   a. The linebacker could be instructed to match his speed to that of the ball carrier so he doesn't overrun the play should the runner choose to cut back.

   b. The pole-vaulter could be given a lighter pole that is easier to control so the vaulter would not have to sacrifice running speed to plant the pole accurately in the box.

   c. The volleyball player could be instructed to focus on achieving an accurate passing platform (i.e., arm angle) and let the speed of the approaching ball dictate the speed of the pass.

## Chapter 4

1. In the sport of volleyball, a setter must constantly set the ball to teammates in ways that enhance their chances of hitting a winner. To do this, the setter must be aware of her hitters' capabilities, the location of stronger and weaker players on the opposing team, the kinds of defensive sets the opposing team likes to use, and the type of set that will maximize her team's chances of winning the point. To help a setter understand what to look for, what to do, and how to do it, a volleyball coach might create a gamelike situation where the opposing players are instructed to call out the location of the set (left, center, right) as soon as they recognize it. The setter's task is to delay their response by anticipating their movements, disguising the type of set she is going to hit as effectively as possible, and then accurately executing the set she selects. To prevent the opposing team from anticipating the set, the setter might also be instructed to look for opportunities to occasionally dink the ball instead of setting it.

2. A tactical blueprint for a quarterback facing a blitz situation in football might be as follows:

   | Relevant knowledge | Options available |
   |---|---|
   | Down and distance | Run the play |
   | Play called in huddle | Roll outside of hash marks and throw pass out of |
   | Skill and experience of offensive line | bounds |
   | Possible audibles | Audible to another play |
   | Receiving skills of blocking back | Let defenders penetrate and throw swing pass to |
   | Time-outs left | blocking back |
   | Time on play clock | Call time-out |
   | Score | Take a sack |

## Chapter 5

1. Three performance situations that occur regularly in the sport of volleyball are serving, passing, and blocking. The primary demand of serving is to hit the ball to the intended target in a way that makes it difficult for the opposing team to create an effective attack. The demands of passing include a level of accuracy and timing that produces an efficient and rhythmic ball exchange. The demands of blocking include anticipating the opposing hitter's actions, as well as timing the block so as to disrupt the attack and ideally win the point. Table A illustrates the feelings and focus that might produce effective performance in each of these situations (adapted from Kus, 2004).

TABLE A

## Feel and Focus That Produce Effective Performance in Volleyball Skills

| Situation | Feel | Focus |
|---|---|---|
| Serving | Relaxed | Type of serve, target, and solid contact with ball |
| Passing | Relaxed, hands loose, arms out front | Seams of approaching ball, target for the pass, positioning of the body, good platform |
| Blocking | Relaxed, aggressive, hands at shoulder level | Attacker's movements, timing of hitter's jump, area above net, hitter's attacking arm |

2. Practice activities that might help players improve their mental skills for serving, passing, and blocking follow:

   a. Serving—practicing all serves with a pre-serve routine that includes a visual focus on the target, a relaxation breath, and a simple focus cue (such as "Smooth and solid")

   b. Passing—a two- or three-player passing drill that emphasizes a focus on the seams of the ball and a relaxed posture with hands loose and arms out front

   c. Blocking—a blocking drill that emphasizes a relaxed and aggressive posture, a visual focus on the hitter's movements and attacking arm, and a takeoff timed to occur just *after* the hitter takes off

3. A brief imagery script a player could use for imagining a volleyball serve might include the following statements:

   *It's late in the final game of the match, the score is tied, and it's my turn to serve. I take the ball from the official, look to the coach for the type of serve to hit, and take my position behind the service line. I feel the weight of the ball in my off hand as I focus on the target. I take a nice relaxation breath and remind myself to stay smooth and solid through the movement. I slowly accelerate toward the service line, toss the ball, and focus on the seams. I feel my body leave the floor, coiling and then uncoiling, as my hand makes solid contact with the ball. As I look across the net, I see the ball traveling straight to the target. Then I feel myself moving into position to defend any possible return.*

# Chapter 6

1. Following are some of the key elements of the technical skill of the tennis volley (adapted from Brown, 2004):

   a. Movement elements: use tight grip, take short backswing, bend knees to keep eyes at ball level, swing from shoulder, make contact well in front of body

   b. Perceptual elements: watch speed, spin, and flight path of ball; watch preparatory movements of opponent

   c. Conceptual elements: hit volleys deep, hit to open areas of court, make opponent move, hit to opponent's weaker side

2. Possible target behaviors for a defensive back making a tackle in American football can be found in the checklist on page 153.

3. Three target behaviors an inexperienced defensive back might be instructed to focus on would be the technical skill elements of focusing on the hips of the ball carrier and tightly wrapping the arms and the mental skill of matching the ball carrier's intensity. A more advanced player might be instructed to focus on the tactical skills of taking on blockers, clogging up the play, and forcing the ball carrier toward other tacklers or, in the case of a particularly elusive running back, the

# Checklist for Target Behaviors

Technical skill: _Making a tackle_

## Technical skill elements

### MOVEMENT ELEMENTS

*Preparation phase*
__1. _Weight balanced on balls of feet_
__2. _Knees slightly bent_
__3. _Elbows flexed and hands relaxed_

*Execution phase*
__1. _Extend from waist_
__2. _Use the legs_
__3. _Shoulder to target_

*Follow-through phase*
__1. _Wrap arms tight_
__2. _Maintain forward momentum_
__3. _____

### PERCEPTUAL ELEMENTS

*Preparation phase*
__1. _Watch hips of ball carrier_
__2. _Judge speed of ball carrier_
__3. _Anticipate point of contact_

*Execution phase*
__1. _Focus on target_
__2. _Feel thrust of body forward_
__3. _____

*Follow-through phase*
__1. _Feel tight arms_
__2. _Listen for whistle_
__3. _____

### CONCEPTUAL ELEMENTS

*Preparation phase*
__1. _Bring body under control_
__2. _____
__3. _____

*Execution phase*
__1. _Use shoulder not arms_
__2. _Drive through the target_
__3. _____

*Follow-through phase*
__1. _Keep arms wrapped until whistle blows_
__2. _____
__3. _____

## Tactical skills

__1. _Force ball carrier toward other tacklers_
__2. _Take out blockers before ball carrier_
__3. _Clog up the play if unable to make tackle_
__4. _____
__5. _____

## Mental skills

__1. _Shift visual focus as needed_
__2. _Stay aggressive_
__3. _Increase arousal to match opponent's intensity_
__4. _____
__5. _____

technical element of watching the ball carrier's hips. The rationale for these instructions is that a beginning player needs to focus more on the technical and mental fundamentals of tackling than would a more advanced player who has automated the tackling movement and can devote more attention to tactical skills or perhaps a particular technical skill element.

# Chapter 7

1. The following three-on-three drills (adapted from Wissel, 2004) are three practice activities that actively involve each member of a 12-player basketball team and that are relevant to competition. Each drill could be practiced on the two available baskets at each end of the floor; players could rotate so they gain experience running the play and defending against it.

   a. Dribble Screen and Weave—Three offensive players set dribble screens for each other, while three defensive players execute the possible defenses against the maneuver (i.e., get in the path of the receiver to prevent the handoff, jump-switch into the path of the receiver, and trap the player receiving the ball with two defenders).

   b. Half-court Offense Versus Passive Defense—Players can practice a variety of offensive–defensive options. Having the defense play in a less aggressive manner allows offensive players to recognize each defense and react with an appropriate offensive option. It also allows defensive players to develop anticipation of each other's movements in each of the defensive options.

   c. Defensive Positioning—Offensive players practice a variety of maneuvers (e.g., dribbling, passing, screening, cutting) in a spontaneous fashion, while defensive players practice a variety of defensive responses both on and off the ball (e.g., strong-side wing denial, weak-side help). Players can switch back and forth between offense and defense at the end of each possession (i.e., basket scored, ball stolen, and so on) simulating the alternating offensive and defensive aspects of an actual game.

2. Players would have the opportunity to practice the following skills during each of the previously listed activities:

| Practice activity | Skills practiced |
|---|---|
| a. Dribble Screen and Weave | *Technical skills:* dribbling, screening, shooting, trapping, drawing a charge |
| | *Tactical skills:* offensive and defensive team coordination |
| | *Mental skills:* attention focusing, communicating, interpreting offensive and defensive moves, decision making |
| b. Half-court Offense Versus Passive Defense | *Technical skills:* dribbling, passing, screening, shooting, rebounding, defending, trapping |
| | *Tactical skills:* offensive and defensive strategies and team coordination |
| | *Mental skills:* attention focusing, interpreting offensive and defensive moves, decision making, anticipation |
| c. Defensive Positioning | *Technical skills:* dribbling, passing, screening, cutting, shooting, rebounding, trapping, drawing a charge |
| | *Tactical skills:* on- and off-ball defensive maneuvers |
| | *Mental skills:* attention focusing, communicating, interpreting offensive moves, decision making |

3. Players need to anticipate the following three aspects of the environment in the sport of basketball to perform at their best:

    a. How and when to move without the ball

    b. An opponent's dribbling strengths and weaknesses (e.g., prefers dribbling with right hand, doesn't dribble well from right to left)

    c. Actions of a defender while being guarded on the perimeter

    Activities (adapted from Wissel, 2004) a coach might use to help players develop anticipation for each of these situations include the following:

    a. Executing the V-cut and backdoor cut. These maneuvers can be practiced in any two-on-two or three-on-three drill. When the defender has a foot and hand in the passing lane, the player being guarded uses a V-cut to take the defender toward the basket and then sharply changes direction. When the defender has a foot and hand in the passing lane to deny a pass from the perimeter, the player cuts behind the defender toward the basket. This move also works any time the defender's head is turned away from the player and toward the ball.

    b. One-on-one dribbling drills with frequent rotation. By defending different teammates, players will have the opportunity to observe different dribbling styles and practice their responses to each.

    c. Drive-step drills involving watching the position of the defender's hands and then responding. For example, if the defender's hands are down, the player being guarded uses the drive step and then shoots the jump shot; if the defender's hand is up on the side of the drive step, the player uses the straight drive to the basket.

# Chapter 8

1. One American football practice activity is the "dime package" drill. Teams use this defensive alignment when facing an opponent with a strong passing attack or in third down and long yardage situations when the opponent inserts extra wide receivers. The package includes an extra defensive back (i.e., five rather than the usual four) and requires considerable coordination and discipline to ensure that no receiver is left uncovered.

    The most straightforward way for a coach to determine when to give players feedback during this activity is to make sure the players feel free to request it any time they have questions. For example, a defensive back might not know whether his pass coverage technique is correct or might wonder how much territory he is expected to cover in the dime package. If the player doesn't feel threatened to ask the coach for feedback he is more likely to do so. Other factors the coach should consider in deciding when to give players feedback include the players' stage of learning and whether the player is able to obtain the necessary information on his own. Generally speaking, the coach would need to provide more feedback for a beginning player than for an experienced player. However, any time the coach senses that a player's intrinsic feedback is inadequate he should give feedback. For example, if the coach senses that one of the defensive backs is misjudging the amount of territory he's supposed to cover, the coach could provide visual feedback by walking along the boundaries of the area while the player watches.

2. A situation in the sport of basketball that lends itself to the use of video feedback is the free throw situation, specifically the free throw shot. (a) A basketball coach determines the most appropriate viewing angle for recording free throw performance by observing the movement from a front view, side view, and rear view to determine which characteristics are best observed from the different angles. The coach then selects the angle that provides the most comprehensive view of the correct form. (b) Once the player begins practicing the free throw shot, the coach decides how often to provide feedback by observing the consistency of the player's movements.

Once the movements achieve an obvious consistency, the coach calculates shooting accuracy (e.g., number of shots made out of 10). If accuracy is relatively high (e.g., 65 to 70 percent), feedback is not necessary. However, if accuracy is low (e.g., <50 percent), the coach provides feedback to identify the movement component(s) requiring the player's attention. The player then resumes practice, focusing on improving that component. The coach again withholds video feedback until the player achieves a reasonable level of movement consistency. Once a sufficient level of consistency is achieved, the coach again calculates the player's shooting accuracy. If it has improved, additional feedback is not provided. If not, the process is repeated and another component targeted for improvement. (c) Throughout the video review process, the coach involves the player by asking him to indicate the keys to successful free throw shooting, which one(s) he appeared to perform correctly, which one(s) he appeared to perform incorrectly, and which one(s) he thinks he needs to focus on to improve his accuracy during the next round of practice attempts.

# Chapter 9

1. A practice plan for 30 minutes of a high school baseball practice follows.

**Objectives:** (1) improving coordination and communication during relay throws on extra-base hits; (2) developing the following defensive skills: throwing to the correct target (tactical skill); producing overhand throws that can be cut off (technical skill) and fielding the throws in position to make the tag or throw to the next target (technical skill); communicating with the thrower (mental skill); (3) developing the following baserunning skills: tagging the inside corner of the base (technical skill); anticipating the strength and direction of the throw (tactical skill); staying aggressive (mental skill); watching the coach (at base) and teammate (at home plate) for instructions (mental skill)

**Participants:** two players at each defensive position (one active, one mirroring); rotate players after each repetition; use pitchers as baserunners (no sliding)

| PRACTICE ACTIVITIES | | | |
|---|---|---|---|
| **Time** | **Situation** | **Defensive focus cues** | **Baserunning focus cues** |
| 3:00-3:10 | Bases empty | Outfielders<br>Find the cutoff (tactical) | Find the ball (mental)<br>Know the situation (tactical) |
| | | On a line (technical)<br>Over the top (technical)<br>Good ears (mental)<br><br>Infielders<br>Line it up (tactical)<br>Shout it out (mental)<br>Soft hands (technical)<br>Quick hands (technical)<br>Catch and throw (technical)<br>Strong tag (technical) | Inside corner (technical)<br>Accelerate through the base (technical)<br>Pick up the coach (mental)<br>Watch catcher's eyes (mental) |
| 3:10-3:13 | Feedback and discussion | | |

| Time | Situation | Defensive focus cues | Baserunning focus cues |
|------|-----------|----------------------|------------------------|
| 3:13-3:27 | Runner on first | Outfielders<br>Good ears (mental)<br>Find the cutoff (tactical)<br>Frozen rope (technical)<br>Hit the chest (technical)<br>Know the situation (tactical)<br><br>Infielders<br>Shout it out (mental)<br>Line it up (tactical)<br>Know the situation (tactical)<br>Good ears (mental)<br>Soft hands (technical)<br>Quick hands (technical)<br>Catch and throw (technical)<br>Strong tag (technical) | Look ahead (mental)<br>Know the situation (tactical)<br>Watch leading runner (tactical)<br>Inside corner (technical)<br>Accelerate through (technical)<br>Expect to score (mental)<br>Pick up coach (mental)<br>Pick up teammate at plate (mental)<br>Watch catcher's eyes (mental) |
| 3:27-3:30 | Feedback and discussion | | |

2. The practice plan can be evaluated as follows:

  a. Relevance to competition: two most common situations requiring relay throws; success requires coordination and communication; defense must know situation, runners' speed, and strength of outfielder's throwing arm

  b. Active participation by all team members: defensive players actively involved on each play, either throwing, catching, and baserunning or mirroring the movements of a teammate (e.g., mirroring shortstop would perform the same movements as partner shortstop but remain several steps behind); baserunners either running or recovering and observing signals of coach (at base) or teammate (at home) on each play

  c. Challenges presented: on defense, accurate throws, clear communication, smooth catches and tags (or subsequent throws), attention shifts, awareness of situation; for baserunners, aggressive running, clear communication, awareness of situation

  d. Enjoyment experienced: active physical involvement, tactical and mental challenges, gamelike situations, spirited competition with teammates

  e. Opportunity for athlete input: brief team discussion at conclusion of each baserunning drill

# GLOSSARY

**abilities**—Inherited and relatively stable traits that predispose people to excel in particular types of activities (e.g., large physical stature, good eye–hand coordination, and exceptional leg power might predispose one individual to excel in the sport of basketball; small physical stature, a high level of dynamic strength, and good total body coordination might predispose another person to excel in gymnastics).

**ambient vision**—The visual system that operates at a nonconscious level and helps athletes determine where they are in the environment and where they are in relation to other objects or people (e.g., a football wide receiver sensing the location of the sidelines and defenders while watching the approaching ball; a cross country runner sensing her position in the pack without actually looking at other runners); used for movement control.

**arousal**—The level of a person's central nervous system activation; varies from very low levels during relaxed states to very high levels during intense activity or excitement.

**assistive guidance**—Any apparatus or technique that conveys the desired movement pattern in a passive fashion (i.e., the athlete does not actively control the movement but passively experiences it in order to get some idea of the correct pattern). For example, a tennis coach might grasp the hand of a player and guide the player's hand and arm through the movement plane required to produce a topspin forehand ground stroke.

**attention**—The focusing of conscious mental activity; limited in capacity (i.e., athletes can attend to only a few things at any one time).

**automatic stage**—The final and most advanced stage of technical skill learning; characterized by near-effortless movement execution, attention directed to other aspects of the performance environment (e.g., a basketball point guard dribbling the ball upcourt while evaluating the defensive formation of the opposing team and calling out a play), and stylistic details (e.g., the emotion and expression of a skilled gymnast performing a floor exercise).

**average feedback**—Information about the general features observed in a series of movements (e.g., a punter generally making contact with the ball at waist height during a series of punts; a batter generally swinging too late during a round of batting practice; a swimmer beginning her flip turns too early during a series of turns).

**bandwidth feedback**—Information provided only when an athlete's performance fails to reach a particular level (e.g., a runner's time only if it is more than five seconds slower than the goal time).

**blocked practice**—A practice structure that involves several repetitions of the same skill (e.g., 20 pitch shots in golf, 10 free throw shots in basketball, 15 flat serves to the deuce court in tennis).

**broad focus**—Used by athletes when attending to a number of things at one time (e.g., a quarterback looking over the alignment of the opposing team's defense; a soccer goalie attending to the relative positions of several opposing players before a corner kick).

**capabilities**—Similar to abilities but modifiable with practice (e.g., limb flexibility can be improved with stretching exercises, arm and shoulder strength can be improved with weight training, and so on).

**CARS**—An acronym representing the four major principles of goal setting: challenging, attainable, realistic, specific.

**closed-loop control**—A type of control in which athletes use sensory information to adjust their movements (e.g., a running back using the vision of defenders to avoid being tackled; an outside hitter in volleyball using vision of the opposing team's block to determine the type of hit to execute; a distance runner adjusting her stride to avoid a collision with another runner).

**closed skills**—Skills performed in an environment that is generally predictable and allows athletes to prepare their movements in advance (e.g., hitting a tennis serve, shooting a free throw shot, throwing the discus, hitting a golf shot, performing a gymnastics routine).

**cognitive components**—The mental aspects of technical skills (e.g., an option quarterback must be able to read the defense to determine which of several choices has the best chance of succeeding; a gymnast must know how and when to adjust a floor exercise; a baseball pitcher with an opposing runner on first base must decide whether to deliver the pitch, step off the rubber, or throw to first).

**competitive circumstances**—Practice situations that include as many factors as possible that are present during an actual competition (e.g., practicing free throw shots the way they would occur during a basketball game: no more than two at a time, spaced out at random intervals, when players are fatigued as well as nonfatigued).

**conceptual elements**—One of the three elements of technical skills; the strategic and rule-bound aspects of a sport (e.g., balls hitting the line in tennis and volleyball are "good"; use of the hands in soccer is permitted only by the goalie and during throw-ins; the strike zone in baseball is defined by the width of the plate and the distance between the batter's chest and knees).

**continuous skills**—Technical skills consisting of repetitive and rhythmic movements, sometimes having no recognizable beginning and ending points (e.g., distance running, cycling, the freestyle stroke in swimming).

**coordination pattern**—The unique pattern of coordinated activity among several combinations of joints and muscles that characterizes every technical skill (e.g., the leg stride and arm swing elements of the tennis ground stroke; the repetitive and alternating arm and leg actions of freestyle swimming; the leg thrust and arm pull in rowing; and the running approach, foot plant, and arm extension in the javelin throw).

**cue utilization hypothesis**—The notion that errors in information processing are related to the performer's arousal level. When arousal level is low, athletes' minds tend to wander and they sometimes process a lot of irrelevant information (e.g., a basketball player

sitting on the bench watching spectators instead of attending to the moves of an opposing player). When arousal level is high, athletes' attention narrows and they tend to lock in on one or two things, and one may be less important than the other (e.g., a tennis player focusing on the opponent's body language rather than on a strategy for playing the next point).

**decision-making elements**—Those aspects of sport skills dealing with the choices athletes make to enhance their prospects of successful performance (e.g., a soccer player's decision to trap an approaching ball, deflect it, or pass it to a teammate).

**descriptive feedback**—Information about what an athlete appeared to do (e.g., released the ball too soon; lost form during the last 10 meters of the race).

**discrete skills**—Technical skills that are usually brief in duration and consist of well-defined beginning and ending points (e.g., a golf putt, a baseball swing, a tennis volley).

**external focus**—Used by athletes when attending to information in the environment (e.g., the location of an opponent or teammate; the speed and trajectory of an approaching ball).

**external imagery perspective**—A mental imagery perspective used by athletes who picture themselves performing from a third-person perspective, as if they were seeing themselves on television (e.g., a gymnast imagining herself executing a balance beam routine as it would appear from the judge's perspective).

**extrinsic feedback**—Information provided by an outside source (e.g., the coach, a video recording, a stopwatch) and in addition to the information athletes are able to obtain on their own (e.g., the sight of the ball after a missed putt; the feel of the legs during a long jump).

**feedback sandwich**—Corrective information provided between two positive comments (e.g., "I like your aggressiveness when there is a rebound opportunity. However, you should try to focus a bit more on getting in good rebounding position when the shot is taken. You'll establish better positioning, and you'll be a great help to this team.").

**focal vision**—The visual system that operates at a conscious level and helps athletes identify objects or people in the environment (e.g., a quarterback focusing on a particular wide receiver).

**focus**—Used by athletes when they need to devote their attention to a specific environmental or bodily cue (e.g., a runner focusing on relaxing his shoulders when experiencing fatigue or pain; a tennis player focusing on the seams of an approaching ball).

**fractionization**—A type of part practice involving the isolated rehearsal of one component of the movement (e.g., the plant component of the pole vault, the toss component of the volleyball jump serve, the leg kick component of the breaststroke in swimming).

**games approach**—Emphasizes practice activities that contain the technical, tactical, and mental skills athletes need to develop in order to be successful in their sport.

**goals**—The desired outcomes athletes hope to achieve as a result of their sport participation.

**goal setting**—The process by which an athlete identifies a standard of performance or result she aspires to achieve. A necessary component of most skill improvements.

**habituation**—A diminished response to the same situation with repeated exposure to that situation (e.g., the basketball player who becomes less disturbed by poor calls by officials; the athlete whose performance becomes less affected by the noise of opposing spectators).

**implicit learning**—Relatively permanent changes in performance that athletes may not notice (e.g., a baseball infielder's improved anticipation of the path of different types of ground balls; a football receiver running a pass route more precisely; a basketball point guard running the offense more smoothly).

**individual differences**—Differences that normally exist in the personal characteristics and life experiences of people (e.g., body type, physical abilities, sociocultural background, socioeconomic level, personality).

**information processing**—A sequence of mental events that begins with an interpretation of the environment, followed by a decision whether to respond (and what type of response is called for), followed by a plan for producing the chosen response (e.g., a soccer goalie perceives the speed and direction of a shot on goal, decides to deflect the ball over the top of the goal, and prepares to extend his hands upward with palms upturned in order to deflect the ball in an upward direction).

**intentional learning**—Relatively permanent changes in performance that athletes are aware of (e.g., a bat swing that feels smoother, a golf shot that is more accurate, a gymnastics routine that is more fluid).

**internal focus**—Used by athletes when attending to their thoughts or to information inside their bodies (e.g., a volleyball player deciding which type of serve she should hit; a sprinter focusing on his breathing before hearing the "set" command of the race official).

**internal imagery perspective**—A mental imagery perspective used by athletes who picture themselves performing from a first-person perspective, as they would see and feel things during an actual performance (e.g., a distance runner "seeing" and "feeling" himself running in a cross country competition as he would during an actual race).

**intrinsic feedback**—Information that accompanies movement performance and is readily available to the athlete (e.g., the location of the ball after a golf shot; the feel of the foot at the point of contact with the soccer ball).

**inverted-U principle**—One explanation for the relationship between arousal level and performance; specifically, as arousal increases from a low level to a moderate level, performance increases as well; however, further increases in arousal level are accompanied by diminished performance. The optimal arousal level for performance success is dependent on an athlete's trait anxiety, the demands of the technical skill being performed, and the athlete's interpretation of the situation.

**irrelevant environmental information**—Any information in the performance environment that is not important for achieving performance success (e.g., the style of the opposing team's uniforms, the score).

**knowledge of performance**—Information (usually provided by the coach) that indicates the quality of an athlete's movements (e.g., a basketball coach might tell a player to follow through a bit more when releasing the ball on her jump shot).

**knowledge of results**—Information that indicates the outcome produced by the athlete's movements (e.g., a track coach might tell a sprinter that his time in the 100-meter dash was 10.3 seconds).

**learning**—The relatively permanent change in performance that occurs with practice; an internal state that can be inferred only by repeated observations of athletes' actions.

**learning style**—The preferred way a person learns. The three most common learning styles are visual, auditory, and kinesthetic.

**long-term memory**—Contains all the information athletes have stored from previous life and sport experiences.

**mental demands**—Psychological aspects of performance that athletes must learn to control in order to be consistently successful in their sport (e.g., focusing attention, managing arousal, exercising patience).

**mental imagery**—A form of mental rehearsal in which the athlete imagines herself performing or competing, using either an external or internal perspective (e.g., a gymnast imagining herself executing a balance beam routine as it would appear from the judge's perspective; a distance runner seeing and feeling himself running in a cross country competition as he would during an actual race).

**mental skills**—Skills used to deal with the psychological demands of sport performance and competition (e.g., focusing attention, controlling emotions, adjusting arousal level).

**mental stage**—The initial stage of technical skill learning; characterized by considerable trial and error; goal is to achieve a general idea of how to perform the skill.

**motivation**—Concerns the reasons athletes choose to participate in a sport, why they perform with different levels of intensity from time to time, and why they continue to participate in a sport rather than drop out.

**motor components**—The mechanical aspects of technical skills (e.g., a smooth, level swing in softball; the three-step approach, contact, and follow-through of a placekicker in football).

**motor control elements**—Those aspects of sport skills dealing with the mechanics of the desired movement the athlete is trying to produce (e.g., an accelerated shoulder rotation and elbow extension when performing the volleyball spike).

**motor programs**—General plans of action that contain all the details of a movement; can be adapted to meet the demands of different situations (e.g., a pitcher might use a program for throwing a softball that can be modified to produce different types and speeds of pitches); particularly useful for the control of discrete skills or those requiring open-loop control.

**movement elements**—One of the three elements of technical skills; the unique pattern of coordinated muscular activity that characterizes a skill (e.g., the stride and swing phases of batting; the alternating arm action and flutter kick in the freestyle swimming stroke; the leg and arm extension and wrist flexion in the basketball jump shot).

**narrow focus**—Used by athletes when attending to no more than a few things at one time (e.g., a sprinter focused on the firing of the starter's gun; a soccer player focused on the seams of the ball when attempting a header).

**open-loop control**—A type of control used for rapid movements or when athletes don't have time to adjust a movement once they initiate it (e.g., a soccer goalie diving to stop a shot on goal; a tennis player hitting a crisp volley; a football center's snap for a punt or placekick).

**open skills**—Skills performed in an environment that is generally unpredictable or changing and that requires athletes to adjust their movements according to demands (e.g., playing a point in tennis or volleyball; defending an opponent in soccer or basketball; hitting a baseball; catching a football).

**outcome feedback**—Information about the results of an athlete's performance (e.g., the distance of a golf drive; the time in the 55-meter hurdles; the number of team rebounds in a basketball game).

**outcome goals**—Goals that emphasize the end result an athlete is trying to achieve in a particular event or over the course of a competitive season (e.g., a free throw percentage of 70 percent for the season; a time of 10 seconds in the 100-meter dash in the conference championship meet; a batting average of .300 for the season).

**parameter feedback**—Information about the general properties of an athlete's movements that may need to be adjusted to meet environmental demands (e.g., increasing the overall speed of the arm during a volleyball spike to increase kill percentage; decreasing the force used to throw a swing pass to a running back to make the ball easier to catch; extending the arms further during the butterfly stroke to achieve greater propulsion).

**part practice**—Any activity involving the practice of a technical skill in a simpler form; the three primary types of part practice are fractionization, segmentation, and simplification.

**perceptual elements**—One of the three elements of technical skills; the interpretation of environmental information essential for successful skill execution (e.g., a golfer reading the break and speed of a green before a putt; a soccer goalie estimating the speed of the approaching ball; a swimmer estimating the time to wall contact before a flip turn).

**performance feedback**—Information about the quality of an athlete's movements (e.g., follow-through of the arm and hand on the volleyball serve; coordination of the plant and pull action in the pole vault; timing of the baton handoff in the 400-meter relay).

**performance goals**—Goals that emphasize improvements in an individual athlete's skill execution (e.g., a basketball player improving his free throw percentage from 60 to 65 percent; a swimmer staying more relaxed during the final 25 meters in the 100-meter freestyle; a batter visually focusing on the pitcher's release point on every pitch).

**performing**—The observable act of technical skill execution (e.g., throwing a football, running the 110-

meter hurdles, hitting a baseball, setting a volleyball, heading a soccer ball).

**physical guidance**—Any technique that conveys the idea of the correct movement by having the athlete physically experience the movement in a modified form (e.g., a dismount in gymnastics using a safety harness).

**practice stage**—Second stage of technical skill learning; characterized by skill refinement, increased consistency of performance, incorporation of the skill into the sport environment, and the development of error detection capabilities; the stage where most athletes spend the majority of their time.

**prescriptive feedback**—Information about what an athlete might try to do on the next performance attempt (e.g., release the ball later in the pitching motion; stay relaxed and pump the arms during the last 10 meters of the race).

**principle of limited attention capacity**—The notion that people are able to attend to only a relatively small amount of information at any one time.

**principle of specificity of training**—The notion that the most effective training is that which emphasizes the same activities and experiences athletes need in order to achieve success in competition; similar to the games approach to coaching (Martens, 2004).

**principle of speed–accuracy trade-off**—For technical skills requiring both speed and spatial accuracy, increasing the speed of the movement (up to around 80 percent of maximal force) usually results in diminished accuracy, and vice versa (e.g., pitching a baseball, serving a volleyball, hitting a tennis ground stroke).

**process focus**—Emphasizes the technical, tactical, and mental elements of performance that athletes are in control of (e.g., relaxing the body, watching the ball, looking for the open teammate) rather than elements they have no control over (e.g., the score, officials' decisions, a past mistake).

**process-focused instructional approach**—An approach to coaching that emphasizes asking the right questions rather than anticipating the right answers; includes identifying the essential ingredients of skilled performance, knowing the strengths and weaknesses of athletes, emphasizing the systematic practice of behaviors essential for success, encouraging athletes to focus only on the things they are in control of, and providing timely assistance.

**program feedback**—Information about the relative timing pattern, or rhythm, observed in an athlete's movements (e.g., accelerating the hands throughout the bat swing; moving both hands down and up together during the tennis serve; maintaining a consistent stride frequency during the middle stage of a 1,500-meter run).

**random practice**—A practice structure that involves the performance of several different technical skills with few or no consecutive repetitions of any one skill (e.g., a baseball drill in which the shortstop fields a ground ball, throws to first base, receives a throw from the catcher, and throws to third base).

**relative timing pattern**—The time course, or rhythm, of muscular activity during the performance of a technical skill (e.g., the slower leg stride, more rapid hip and shoulder rotation, and still more rapid arm and hand action during a bat swing); the relative speed of contraction of the different muscles used to produce a skilled movement.

**relevant environmental information**—Any information in the performance environment that is important for achieving success (e.g., for a basketball player, the speed and trajectory of an approaching ball or the tendency of an opposing player to dribble to her right with her right hand).

**relevant practice**—Any practice activity that incorporates the same technical, tactical, and mental skills used in competition (e.g., a basketball drill in which defensive players practice switching defenses and offensive players practice recognizing and adapting to the switches).

**restrictive guidance**—Any apparatus or technique that allows the athlete to actively control a movement while gaining a better understanding of its correct execution (e.g., springboard divers or gymnasts using a safety harness when initially learning a difficult dive or element).

**segmentation**—A type of part practice involving the progressive rehearsal of multiple parts of a complex technical skill until the entire skill is learned. For example, a gymnast might practice the first part of a new high bar routine until he feels comfortable with it, then add the second part to the first until he masters the two together, then add the third part to the first two until the three are mastered, and so forth until he has learned the entire routine.

**sensory-perceptual elements**—Those aspects of sport skills dealing with athletes' interpretations of sensory information (e.g., a distance runner's perception that the pack is moving too slow; a defensive back's perception of the speed of a receiver he is covering).

**serial skills**—Technical skills consisting of a sequence of discrete skills, usually performed in a specific order (e.g., the hop, step, and jump in the triple jump in track and field; the catch, pivot, and throw during a double play in baseball).

**simplification**—A type of part practice involving the rehearsal of a simplified version of a technical skill (e.g., slow-motion rehearsal of the body rotation and release during the discus throw; the use of an oversized glove when learning to catch fly balls in baseball).

**skill**—The execution of a task or activity in a proficient manner (e.g., Peyton Manning's proficiency in passing a football; Annika Sorenstam's proficiency in hitting golf shots; Michael Jordan's proficiency in coming up with the right basketball shot with the game on the line).

**skill analysis**—The process used to determine the elements of a technical skill that are essential for successful performance; once the analysis is completed, those specific elements should be emphasized during instruction and in practice activities.

**slow-motion practice**—A type of simplification involving the practice of a technical skill at slower than normal speeds. This type of practice can be useful early in the learning process to help athletes acquire a general understanding of the fundamental coordination pattern.

**specificity hypothesis**—The notion that the abilities important for the performance of any given technical skill are specific to that skill and completely different from the abilities important for the performance of any other technical skill (e.g., the abilities important for shooting a basketball are unique to that skill and completely different from the abilities important for kicking a soccer ball).

**stages of learning**—The three phases of improvement that characterize the learning of most technical skills; specifically, the mental stage, the practice stage, and the automatic stage.

**summary feedback**—Information about the quality or outcome of several movements or movement bouts (e.g., the times for each of five consecutive 400-meter runs; video replay of the release point for each of five attempts at throwing the discus).

**tactical demands**—Strategic decisions athletes must be able to make to be consistently successful in their sport (e.g., adjusting a defensive strategy to minimize the effectiveness of an opponent; using more topspin on tennis ground strokes under windy conditions).

**tactical knowledge**—Consists of factors that influence the quality of decision making, such as a knowledge of the rules, of an effective game plan, of possible weather conditions, of one's own and one's opponents' strengths and weaknesses, and of strategic options for various situations.

**tactical skills**—Any skills that enable athletes to gain an advantage in competition, including decisions about what technical skills to use in certain situations, how to maximize the performance of a technical skill, and how to capitalize on the weaknesses of an opponent.

**target behaviors**—The observable aspects of athletes' performance that indicate correct skill execution (e.g., a quarterback leading the receiver with a pass so that the receiver is able to catch it in stride; a basketball player blocking out an opposing player in preparation for a rebound; a volleyball player penetrating the plane above the net when blocking).

**team strategy**—A plan devised by a coach to maximize his or her team's chances of success; the plan is based on the strengths and weaknesses of the coach's athletes as well as those of the opponent.

**technical demands**—The movement, perceptual, and conceptual demands of technical skills necessary for successful execution (e.g., the correct relative timing pattern of the movement, relevant vs. irrelevant environmental information, and the rules of the sport).

**technical skill elements**—Movement, perceptual, and conceptual elements of technical skills (e.g., producing the coordinated limb movements that effectively achieve the desired goal; visually focusing on appropriate cues; understanding the spatial characteristics of the competitive environment and the abilities of teammates).

**technical skills**—The fundamental movements found in every sport, including the relative speed of contraction of the different muscles used to produce the skill (e.g., the technical skill of free throw shooting begins with the player facing the goal with legs bent and hands grasping the ball at waist level, then proceeds to the execution of the following coordination pattern: an extension of the legs, arms, and hands and a flexion of the dominant wrist to propel the ball toward the basket).

**trait anxiety**—A person's general tendency to perceive events as threatening; varies from seldom to most of the time.

**two-way communication**—A type of communication that involves the sending and receiving of messages by both the coach and the athlete. Coaches can promote this type of communication by showing respect for the athlete's opinion, listening when the athlete speaks, and encouraging the athlete to provide input and feedback.

**unspoken communication**—A type of communication in which messages are conveyed by a person's body language (e.g., a coach smiling after an athlete gives a good effort during a demanding practice; an athlete sitting on the bench with slumped shoulders and a sad facial expression after being criticized by the coach for making a mental error in the game).

**varied practice**—A practice structure that involves the performance of several different versions of a single technical skill, with few or no consecutive repetitions of any one version (e.g., a baseball pitcher throwing a fastball, then a slider, then a curveball, then a changeup, then a drop ball; a basketball player shooting a jump shot from the head of the key, then from the baseline, then from the free throw line extended).

**verbal feedback**—Information presented in a spoken form (e.g., the coach's comments to a basketball player returning to the bench; a comment by a teammate to relax more when shooting a jump shot).

**verbal instructions**—An instructional technique in which the coach conveys information by telling athletes what they should try to do. For example, a tennis coach might instruct a player to "keep the ball deep" against a particular opponent.

**visual demonstrations**—An instructional technique in which the coach conveys information by showing athletes what they should try to do rather than telling them. For example, a track coach might demonstrate the correct technique for executing the baton exchange in a relay race.

**visual feedback**—Information presented in a visual form (e.g., video replay of a gymnastics routine).

**working memory**—A mental workspace athletes use to store a few important pieces of information they need to be aware of for a particular performance situation (e.g., a pitcher reminding himself that the batter he is about to face has a tendency to swing at the first pitch, particularly if it is a fastball).

# BIBLIOGRAPHY

Adams, J.A. (1971). A closed-loop theory of motor learning. *Journal of Motor Behavior, 3,* 111-150.

Allard, F., & Burnett, N. (1985). Skill in sport. *Canadian Journal of Psychology, 39,* 294-312.

Anshel, M.H. (1990). An information processing approach to teaching motor skills. *Journal of Physical Education, Recreation and Dance, 61*(5), 70-75.

Beals, R.P., Mayyasi, A.M., Templeton, A.E., & Johnston, W.L. (1971). The relationship between basketball-shooting performance and certain visual attributes. *American Journal of Optometry and Archives of American Academy of Optometry, 48,* 585-590.

Blandin, Y., Lhuisset, L., & Proteau, L. (1999). Cognitive processes underlying observational learning of motor skills. *Quarterly Journal of Experimental Psychology: Human Experimental Psychology, 52A,* 957-979.

Boschker, M.S.J., Bakker, F.C., & Michaels, C.F. (2002). Memory for the functional characteristics of climbing walls: Perceiving affordances. *Journal of Motor Behavior, 34,* 25-36.

Brown, J. (2004). *Tennis: Steps to success* (3rd ed.). Champaign, IL: Human Kinetics.

Carr, G. (1997). *Mechanics of sport.* Champaign, IL: Human Kinetics.

Carr, G. (2004). *Sport mechanics for coaches* (2nd ed.). Champaign, IL: Human Kinetics.

Carril, P., & White, D. (1997). *The smart take from the strong.* New York: Simon & Schuster.

Chelladurai, P., & Turner, B.A. (2006). Styles of decision making in coaching. In J.M. Williams (Ed.), *Applied sport psychology* (5th ed., pp. 140-154). New York: McGraw-Hill.

Christina, R.W., Barresi, J.V., & Shaffner, P. (1990). The development of response selection accuracy in a football linebacker using video training. *The Sport Psychologist, 4,* 11-17.

Christina, R.W., & Corcos, D.M. (1988). *Coaches guide to teaching sport skills.* Champaign, IL: Human Kinetics.

Del Rey, P., Whitehurst, M., & Wood, J.M. (1983). Effects of experience and contextual interference on learning and transfer by boys and girls. *Perceptual and Motor Skills, 56,* 581-582.

Easterbrook, J.A. (1959). The effect of emotion on cue utilization and the organization of behavior. *Psychological Review, 66,* 183-201.

Elliott, R. (1991). *The competitive edge.* Englewood Cliffs, NJ: Prentice-Hall.

Etnier, J., & Landers, D.M. (1996). The influence of procedural variables on the efficacy of mental practice. *The Sport Psychologist, 10,* 48-57.

Eys, M.A., Burke, S.M., Carron, A.V., & Dennis, P.W. (2006). The sport team as an effective group. In J.M. Williams (Ed.), *Applied sport psychology* (5th ed., pp. 157-173). New York: McGraw-Hill.

Flach, J.M., Lintern, G., & Larish, J.F. (1990). Perceptual motor skill: A theoretical framework. In R. Warren & A.H. Wertheim (Eds.), *The perception and control of self motion* (pp. 327-355). Hillsdale, NJ: Erlbaum.

Fleishman, E.A. (1964). *The structure and measurement of physical fitness.* Englewood Cliffs, NJ: Prentice-Hall.

Fleishman, E.A. (1965). The description and prediction of perceptual motor skill learning. In R. Glaser (Ed.), *Training research and education* (pp. 137-175). New York: Wiley.

Gabriele, T., Hall, C.R., & Lee, T.D. (1989). Cognition in motor learning: Imagery effects on contextual interference. *Human Movement Science, 8,* 227-245.

Gallimore, R., & Tharp, R. (2004). What a coach can teach a teacher, 1975-2004: Reflections and reanalysis of John Wooden's teaching practices. *The Sport Psychologist, 18,* 119-137.

Gentile, A.M. (1972). A working model of skill acquisition with application to teaching. *Quest,* Monograph XVII, 3-23.

Gibson, J.J. (1979). *The ecological approach to visual perception.* Boston: Houghton Mifflin.

Gould, D. (2006). Goal setting for peak performance. In J.M. Williams (Ed.), *Applied sport psychology* (5th ed., pp. 240-259). New York: McGraw-Hill.

Guadagnoli, M.A., Holcomb, W.R., & Weber, T.J. (1999). The relationship between contextual interference effects and performer expertise on the learning of a putting task. *Journal of Human Movement Studies, 37,* 19-36.

Hanin, Y.L. (1980). A study of anxiety in sports. In W.F. Straub (Ed.), *Sport psychology: An analysis of athlete behavior* (pp. 236-249). Ithaca, NY: Mouvement.

Haywood, K.M. (2005). *Life span motor development* (4th ed.). Champaign, IL: Human Kinetics.

Hebert, E.P., Landin, D., & Solomon, M.A. (1996). Practice schedule effects on the performance and learning of low- and high-skilled students: An applied study. *Research Quarterly for Exercise and Sport, 67,* 52-58.

Henry, F.M. (1968). Specificity vs. generality in learning motor skill. In R.C. Brown & G.S. Kenyon (Eds.), *Classical studies on physical activity* (pp. 331-340). Englewood Cliffs, NJ: Prentice-Hall. (Original work published 1958.)

Hick, W.E. (1952). On the rate of gain of information. *Quarterly Journal of Experimental Psychology, 4,* 11-26.

Hyman, R. (1953). Stimulus information as a determinant of reaction time. *Journal of Experimental Psychology, 45,* 188-196.

Janelle, C.M., Barba, D.A., Frehlich, S.G., Tennant, L.K., & Cauraugh, J.H. (1997). Maximizing performance feedback effectiveness through videotape replay and a self-controlled learning environment. *Research Quarterly for Exercise and Sport, 68,* 269-279.

Keele, S.W., & Hawkins, H.L. (1982). Explorations of individual differences relevant to high level skill. *Journal of Motor Behavior, 14,* 3-23.

Kernodle, M.W., & Carlton, L.G. (1992). Information feedback and the learning of multiple-degree-of-freedom activities. *Journal of Motor Behavior, 24,* 187-196.

Knudson, D.V., & Morrison, C.S. (1997). *Qualitative analysis of human movement.* Champaign, IL: Human Kinetics.

Komaki, J., & Barnett, F.T. (1977). A behavioral approach to coaching football: Improving the play execution of an offensive backfield on a youth football team. *Journal of Applied Behavior Analysis, 10,* 657-664.

Kus, S. (2004). *Coaching volleyball successfully.* Champaign, IL: Human Kinetics.

Lambert, S.M., Moore, D.W., & Dixon, R.S. (1999). Gymnasts in training: The differential effects of self- and coach-set goals as a function of locus of control. *Journal of Applied Sport Psychology, 11,* 72-82.

Landers, D.M., & Arent, S.M. (2006). Arousal-performance relationships. In J.M. Williams (Ed.), *Applied sport psychology* (5th ed., pp. 260-284). New York: McGraw-Hill.

Landin, D. (1994). The role of verbal cues in skill learning. *Quest, 46,* 299-313.

Landin, D., & Hebert, E.P. (1997). A comparison of three practice schedules along the contextual interference continuum. *Research Quarterly for Exercise and Sport, 68,* 357-361.

Leavitt, J.L. (1979). Cognitive demands of skating and stickhandling in ice hockey. *Canadian Journal of Applied Sport Sciences, 4,* 46-55.

Lee, T.D., Wulf, G., & Schmidt, R.A. (1992). Contextual interference in motor learning: Dissociated effects due to the nature of task variations. *Quarterly Journal of Experimental Psychology, 44A,* 627-644.

Magill, R.A., & Wood, C.A. (1986). Knowledge of results precision as a learning variable in motor skill acquisition. *Research Quarterly for Exercise and Sport, 57,* 170-173.

Martens, R. (2004). *Successful coaching* (3rd ed.). Champaign, IL: Human Kinetics.

Martin, G.L., & Hyrcaiko, D. (1983). *Behavior modification and coaching: Principles, procedures, and research.* Springfield, IL: Charles C. Thomas.

McBride, E., & Rothstein, A. (1979). Mental and physical practice and the learning and retention of open and closed skills. *Perceptual and Motor Skills, 49,* 359-365.

Miller, G.A. (1956). The magical number seven, plus or minus two: Some limits on our capacity for processing information. *Psychological Review, 63,* 81-97.

Murray, M.C., & Mann, B.L. (2006). Leadership effectiveness. In J.M. Williams (Ed.), *Applied sport psychology* (5th ed., pp. 109-139). New York: McGraw-Hill.

Newell, K.M., & McGinnis, P.M. (1985). Kinematic information feedback for skilled performance. *Human Learning, 4,* 39-56.

Nideffer, R.M., & Sagal, M. (2006). Concentration and attention control training. In J.M. Williams (Ed.), *Applied sport psychology* (5th ed., pp. 382-403). New York: McGraw-Hill.

Orlick, T. (1986). *Psyching for sport: Mental training for athletes.* Champaign, IL: Leisure Press.

Orlick, T. (2000). *In pursuit of excellence* (3rd ed.). Champaign, IL: Leisure Press.

Ota, D., & Vickers, J.M. (1999). The effects of variable practice on the retention and transfer of two volleyball skills in club-level athletes. *International Journal of Volleyball Research, 1*(1), 18-24.

Poon, P.P.L., & Rodgers, W.M. (2000). Learning and remembering strategies of novice and advanced jazz dancers for skill level appropriate routines. *Research Quarterly for Exercise and Sport, 71,* 135-144.

Prezuhy, A.M., & Etnier, J.L. (2001). Attentional patterns of horseshoe pitchers at two levels of task difficulty. *Research Quarterly for Exercise and Sport, 72,* 293-298.

Pronk, N., & Gorman, B. (1985). *Soccer everyone.* Winston-Salem, NC: Hunter Textbooks.

Radlo, S.J., Janelle, C.M., Barba, D.A., & Frehlich, S.G. (2001). Perceptual decision making for baseball pitch recognition: Using P300 latency and amplitude to index attentional processing. *Research Quarterly for Exercise and Sport, 72,* 22-31.

Ravizza, K., & Hanson, T. (1995). *Heads-up baseball.* Indianapolis: Masters Press.

Rosenbaum, D.A. (1980). Human movement initiation: Specification of arm, direction, and extent. *Journal of Experimental Psychology: General, 109,* 444-474.

Schmidt, R.A. (1975). A schema theory of discrete motor skill learning. *Psychological Review, 82,* 225-260.

Schmidt, R.A., Lange, C.A., & Young, D.E. (1990). Optimizing summary knowledge of results for skill learning. *Human Movement Science, 9,* 325-348.

Schmidt, R.A., & Sherwood, D.E. (1982). An inverted-U relation between spatial error and force requirements in rapid limb movements: Further evidence for the impulse-variability model. *Journal of Experimental Psychology: Human Perception and Performance, 8,* 158-170.

Schmidt, R.A., & Wrisberg, C.A. (2004). *Motor learning and performance* (3rd ed.). Champaign, IL: Human Kinetics.

Schmidt, R.A., Zelaznik, H.N., Hawkins, B., Frank, J.S., & Quinn, J.T. (1979). Motor-output variability: A theory for the accuracy of rapid motor acts. *Psychological Review, 86,* 415-451.

Schoenfelder-Zohdi, B.G. (1992). Investigating the informational nature of a modeled visual demonstration. Unpublished doctoral dissertation, Louisiana State University, Baton Rouge.

Seat, J.E., & Wrisberg, C.A. (1996). The visual instruction system. *Research Quarterly for Exercise and Sport, 67,* 106-108.

Shea, C.H., Kohl, R., & Indermill, C. (1990). Contextual interference: Contributions of practice. *Acta Psychologica, 73,* 145-157.

Shea, C.H., Wright, D.L., Wulf, G., & Whitacre, C. (2000). Physical and observational practice afford unique learning opportunities. *Journal of Motor Behavior, 32,* 27-36.

Sherwood, D.E., Schmidt, R.A., & Walter, C.B. (1988). The force/force-variability relationship under controlled temporal conditions. *Journal of Motor Behavior, 20,* 106-116.

Smith, P.J.K., Taylor, S.J., & Withers, K. (1997). Applying bandwidth feedback scheduling to a golf shot. *Research Quarterly for Exercise and Sport, 68,* 215-221.

Smith, R.E., & Smoll, F.L. (1991). Behavioral research and intervention in youth sports. *Behavior Therapy, 22,* 329-344.

Tubbs, M.E. (1986). Goal setting: A meta-analysis examination of the empirical evidence. *Journal of Applied Psychology, 71,* 474-483.

University of Illinois Extension. Helping children succeed in school: Learning styles. Retrieved May 19, 2006, from www.urbanext.uiuc.edu/succeed/04-learning-styles.html.

Vealey, R.S., & Greenleaf, C.A. (2006). Seeing is believing: Understanding and using imagery in sport. In J.M. Williams (Ed.), *Applied sport psychology* (5th ed., pp. 306-348). New York: McGraw-Hill.

Ward, P., Williams, A.M., & Bennett, S.J. (2002). Visual search and biological motion perception in tennis. *Research Quarterly for Exercise and Sport, 73,* 107-112.

Weeks, D.L., & Kordus, R.W. (1998). Relative frequency of knowledge of performance and motor skill learning. *Research Quarterly for Exercise and Sport, 69,* 224-230.

Whiting, H.T.A., & Vereijken, B. (1993). The acquisition of coordination in skill learning. *International Journal of Sport Psychology, 24,* 343-357.

Wightman, D.C., & Lintern, G. (1985). Part-task training strategies for tracking and manual control. *Human Factors, 27,* 267-283.

Williams, A.M., & Davids, K. (1998). Visual search strategy, selective attention, and expertise in soccer. *Research Quarterly for Exercise and Sport, 69,* 111-128.

Wilson, V.E., Peper, E., & Schmid, A. (2006). Strategies for training concentration. In J.M. Williams (Ed.), *Applied sport psychology* (5th ed., pp. 404-422). New York: McGraw-Hill.

Wissel, H. (2004). *Basketball: Steps to success* (2nd ed.). Champaign, IL: Human Kinetics.

Wrisberg, C.A. (1994). The arousal-performance relationship. *Quest, 46,* 60-77.

Wrisberg, C.A., & Liu, Z. (1991). The effect of contextual variety on the practice, retention, and transfer of an applied motor skill. *Research Quarterly for Exercise and Sport, 62,* 406-412.

Wrisberg, C.A., & Pein, R.L. (2002). Note on learners' control of the frequency of model presentation during skill acquisition. *Perceptual and Motor Skills, 94,* 792-794.

Wulf, G., Lauterbach, B., & Toole, T. (1999). The learning advantages of an external focus of attention in golf. *Research Quarterly for Exercise and Sport, 70,* 120-126.

Wulf, G., McConnel, N., Gärtner, M., & Schwarz, A. (2002). Enhancing the learning of sport skills through external-focus feedback. *Journal of Motor Behavior, 34,* 171-182.

Wulf, G., Shea, C.H., & Matschiner, S. (1998). Frequent feedback enhances complex motor skill learning. *Journal of Motor Behavior, 30,* 180-192.

Wulf, G., Shea, C.H., & Whitacre, C. (1998). Physical guidance benefits in learning a complex motor skill. *Journal of Motor Behavior, 30,* 367-380.

Wulf, G., & Toole, T. (1999). Physical assistive devices in complex motor skill learning: Benefits of a self-controlled practice schedule. *Research Quarterly for Exercise and Sport, 70,* 265-272.

Young, D.E., & Schmidt, R.A. (1992). Augmented kinematic feedback for motor learning. *Journal of Motor Behavior, 24,* 261-273.

Yukelson, D.P. (2006). Communicating effectively. In J.M. Williams (Ed.), *Applied sport psychology* (5th ed., pp. 174-191). New York: McGraw-Hill.

# INDEX

*Note:* The letters *f* and *t* after page numbers indicate figures and tables, respectively.

# ABOUT THE AUTHOR

**Craig A. Wrisberg, PhD,** is a professor of sport psychology in the department of exercise, sport, and leisure studies at the University of Tennessee at Knoxville, where he has taught since 1977. During the past 30 years he has published numerous research articles on the topics of anticipation and timing in performance, knowledge of results and motor learning, and the role of cognitive strategies in sport performance. He is also the coauthor (with Richard Schmidt) of the popular text *Motor Learning and Performance*, published by Human Kinetics. In 1982 he received the Brady Award for Excellence in Teaching and in 1994 the Chancellor's Award for Research and Creative Achievement.

A former president of the Association for Applied Sport Psychology (AASP) and the North American Society for the Psychology of Sport and Physical Activity, Dr. Wrisberg is a fellow of both AASP and the American Academy of Kinesiology and Physical Education.

In addition to teaching and conducting research, Dr. Wrisberg provides mental training services for student-athletes in the men's and women's athletics departments at Tennessee. In his work with athletes, he applies many of the important concepts and principles covered in *Sport Skill Instruction for Coaches.*

*You'll find other
outstanding sport skill
instruction resources at*

# www.HumanKinetics.com

*In the U.S. call*

## 1-800-747-4457

Australia.................................................08 8372 0999
Canada ................................................1-800-465-7301
Europe.........................................+44 (0) 113 255 5665
New Zealand...........................................0800 222 062

**HUMAN KINETICS**
*The Information Leader in Physical Activity & Health*
P.O. Box 5076 • Champaign, IL  61825-5076 USA